RUSSIA GETS THE BLUES

Music, Culture, and Community in Unsettled Times

MICHAEL URBAN
with the assistance of ANDREI EVDOKIMOV

Cornell University Press
Ithaca and London

Copyright © 2004 by Cornell University

First published 2004 by Cornell University Press
First printing, Cornell Paperbacks, 2004

Printed in the United States of America

Library of Congress Cataloging-in-Publication Data
Urban, Michael, 1947–
    Russia gets the blues : music, culture, and community in unsettled times / Michael Urban with the assistance of Andrei Evdokimov.
        p. cm. — (Culture and society after socialism)
Includes bibliographical references (p.   ) and index.
    ISBN 0-8014-4229-X (cloth : alk. paper) — ISBN 0-8014-8900-8 (pbk. : alk. paper)
    1. Blues (Music)—Russia (Federation)—History and criticism.   2. Popular music—Russia (Federation)—1991–2000—History and criticism.   I. Evdokimov, Andrei, 1962–
II. Title.   III. Series.
ML3521.U6 2004
781.643'0947—dc22

                                                                                2003022700

Cornell University Press strives to use environmentally responsible suppliers and materials to the fullest extent possible in the publishing of its books. Such materials include vegetable-based, low-VOC inks and acid-free papers that are recycled, totally chlorine-free, or partly composed of nonwood fibers. For further information, visit our website at www.cornellpress.cornell.edu.

Cloth printing   10 9 8 7 6 5 4 3 2 1
Paperback printing   10 9 8 7 6 5 4 3 2 1

781.6430947
Urb

Contents

Preface

It seems to have been jet lag that catalyzed the inception of this book. Anyway, that's how I experienced it. Having just returned from two months of teaching in St. Petersburg in the spring of 1998, I found myself inexplicably aroused from a deep sleep, proclaiming as I sat up in bed in the middle of the night: "the blues." I had been looking around for a new research topic during my Petersburg stay and had come home apparently empty-handed. Yet lodged in my head were a number of startling images of blues performances that I had taken in and endearing memories of blues performers and fans whom I had gotten to know there. Previously, I had heard blues played in a few Moscow nightclubs, but these occasions had counted merely as enjoyable diversions from the research that I was then conducting on politics. The sojourn in St. Petersburg altered my orientation. What got me out of that sleep were the very remembrances that I had been relating to my wife before falling into it: recollections of the intense and ebullient atmosphere that I had encountered at blues performances—people just throwing themselves into the music, as exemplified in one noteworthy instance by a young theater director, propelled from his seat at the rear of the club by a driving blues number, turning hand-springs from one end of the room to the other—and visages of shabby communal apartments, jammed with instruments and equipment, where the city's penurious bluesmen practiced and rehearsed their music amid the clutter of domestic life.

A visit to a scholarly conference the following October gave me the chance to contact some members of Moscow's blues community—of greatest importance as things developed, Andrei Evdokimov—and to begin formulating a specific plan for this study. The plan itself was neither sophisticated nor complex. It involved immersing myself as much as possible during the summers of 1999, 2000, and 2001 in the world of Russian blues, which meant listening to all the recordings that I could get my hands on, attending as many performances as possible (some forty in all), conversing informally with scores of performers, fans, nightclub managers, radio-show hosts, and critics, and conducting forty-four formal interviews with many of these same people.

The results of those efforts appear here as a sociomusical portrait of Russia's blues community—those performers, fans, and promoters who have adopted this particular foreign musical idiom and found in it a template for fashioning and making sense of their lives during a period of social convulsion and routinized uncertainty. Investigating this phenomenon engages directly the issue of new forms of sociability emerging in communism's wake. These forms are represented in this book not only by the ways in which Russians have appropriated blues music and its attendant cultural practices as ciphers for interpreting their world and their places within it, but also as media that initiates more or less consciously employ to express their lives. The converse holds true as well. Inquiries into the reception of this music encounter at every turn the persistence of longstanding cultural patterns which condition that reception itself, engendering foreign-domestic hybrids that lend to the country's blues community a palpably Russian character, just as blues music registers a change in the consciousness and practices of those Russians who have embraced it. Consequently, two analytic currents run through this book. One situates the blues idiom in the subject's position and examines its effects on Russians who have been drawn to the music. This current refers to cultural transmission, the flow of new information across borders both material and symbolic that makes some difference in the lives of those receiving it. The second current—cultural reception—reverses the arrangement of subject and object in order to investigate the influence that Russian cultural practices have had on the manner in which the blues idiom has been appropriated, interpreted, performed, and appreciated by members of this musical community.

With respect to the process of cultural transmission, attention turns to those elements of the blues form which generate meaning: its distinctive sound and the associations that it conjures; its capacity to convey both raw feelings and subtle emotional shadings; the attitude that it projects toward the world; and the stances that it provides to those in it. Certainly, whatever meanings that Russians might take from this music would be conditioned by their own culturally informed experience. Nonetheless, as a foreign idiom operating on their soil, blues presents to Russians a number of interpretative and expressive possibilities. The tack taken here is to consider them as elements of cultural transmission that expectedly will undergo modifications in the course of their reception. Along these lines, transmission includes far more than the simple introduction of a foreign cultural product. It involves the cultivation among recipients of a number of micropractices appropriate to the genre and its reproduction locally—

on an elementary level, everything from, say, musicians mastering the blues sound by learning the techniques of bending a note on guitar or harmonica to audience members participating in performances by acquiring the habit of clapping time on the second and fourth beats of the measure rather than on the first and third beats, to which they are accustomed. These aspects of the transmission process figure heavily in the account of the music's progress in Russia contained in chapters 2–5. There, the narrative forfeits a claim to neutrality or truck with relativism. Rather, by applying the standards of the genre as known by my collaborator Andrei Evdokimov and myself, we describe and assess the extent to which Russian performers have progressed in the African American blues idiom, rendering judgments about the authenticity and quality of their playing along the way. This approach is sanctioned by an interest in transmission: What kind of blues do Russians play and how proficiently do they perform it? However, it also stems from our own attachment to blues music and our unconcealed hope that it flourishes in Russia. These chapters are therefore organized diachronically, reporting on the progress of the blues idiom in Russia over time.

The remaining chapters provide a more synchronic treatment of the subject, focusing in particular on Russians' reception of the blues. In the same way that this foreign import includes within itself a set of finite possibilities for generating meaning, so the receiving culture exercises certain constraints in this respect, seizing on some features of the music while neglecting or screening out others. These constraints, of course, only operate through the medium of actual people, people who make choices about what to play or what to listen to. Although these choices appear to be conditioned by affinities obtaining between the receiving culture and the transmitted musical form, learning—which expands the range of receptivity—can also occur. Learning and choice operate at the vortex of the currents of cultural transmission and reception. They act and react on the received materials and the prevailing cultural context, propelling forward the process of cultural change, represented in this study of a new musical community by the very words "Russian blues."

What do Russian listeners hear in blues music? How do they connect the music to their own lives? These questions are seminal to the investigation of cultural change in this book. They are framed by the fact that the collapse of an entire social order in Russia has been coextensive with the advent of blues music and the formation of the country's blues community. Emerging in unsettled and uncertain times, this community has found in the music a set of coded responses to its turbulent surroundings, amounting to a stance that puts a distance between itself and an inhospitable world. But "distance," here, implies neither escape nor retreat.

Rather—and in correspondence with the blues aesthetic itself—it involves a surmounting of trouble's immediacy by playing back experiences in song, thereby summoning the will and confidence to endure, refusing to relinquish hope even while recognizing there are no grounds for optimism.

It is in the particular space made available by this distancing that Russia's blues community has formed. Equally, it is here that aspects of the receiving culture couple with those of the blues idiom, producing a particular foreign-domestic hybrid that exhibits a number of apparent anomalies. For instance, although blues has its origins in the "low" culture of the African American South, it has been transformed in Russia into an object of "high" culture. The deepest renditions of this music—what aficionados would call "gut-bucket blues"—are precisely the forms that one is likely to encounter in the country's most refined and sophisticated nightspots. Moreover, blues as a popular idiom has relied on direct and earthy language to reach its audience, articulating those truths that resonate in the everyday consciousness of everyman; yet in Russia it is sung almost exclusively in English, which both performers and their audiences rarely understand. These seemingly incongruent juxtapositions can be traced to the cultural practices associated with the principal social group that has adopted blues, namely, members of the country's intelligentsia. As bearers of intelligentsia culture, Russian bluesmen regard themselves as commissioned to both create and to enlighten. Accordingly, they see their purpose as faithfully reproducing what is now an international music—a part of "world culture" as they often say—and introducing their compatriots to the cultural treasure that they have discovered. The normative valence of their efforts is thus thought to increase in proportion to its proximity to original blues roots—accounting for the association between the gut-bucket variety and the posh venues—just as singing in English, regardless of intelligibility, is regarded by most as essential to preserving the music's authenticity.

The question of musical authenticity occupies a central place in the consciousness of Russia's bluesmen and therefore receives extensive consideration in this book. As they apprehend the matter, authenticity includes two dimensions: replicating the sound and style of blues in accord with standards particular to the genre; and performing the music in such a way as to directly convey real feelings. In this respect, we are reminded of the fact that the arrival of blues in Russia has been concomitant with an invasion of commercial culture. The country's bluesmen take an exceptionally dim view of that commercial invasion and position themselves against it, emphasizing in contrast to the superficiality of mass-marketed pop the authentic qualities of the music that they perform. Consequently, the reader will often encounter in these pages recurring oppositions that delineate the boundaries of Russia's blues community: commerce versus culture, money versus art, authentic blues versus shallow and formulaic pop. These oppositions issue from the clash of old and new, appearing in this instance as the contradiction obtaining between, on one hand, the traditional norms of the Russian intelligentsia—borne by the country's bluesmen—which valorize creativity and free expression, and, on the other, the introduction of market-based social relations making the physical survival of performers contingent on some measure of commercial success, thus subjecting their art to a constant threat of profanation. Rather than fixed and finely drawn, these normative boundaries reflect the flux of the larger society as well as the influx of new musical information; they are therefore continually assessed and contested by community members. The scrupulous attention that members devote to boundary maintenance tends to reflect both their expressed desire to prevent the corrupting influence of pop from contaminating their music—and thus degrading their community—and the strategies of individual members for raising their respective stocks of cultural capital amid what are fundamentally new commercial circumstances.

The distinction between culture and commerce is sharpened by the fact that membership in Russia's blues community is, at bottom, the result of personal choice. Particularly for performers, it involves a decision to master a foreign musical idiom not broadly represented on the country's soundscape, which enjoys no obvious advantage over competing genres with respect to the musical possibilities that it provides, and which holds out very slender prospects for achieving any measure of commercial success. Choosing blues, then, commits the performer not only to a particular music. In a personal sense, there seems to be more at stake, as suggested by the Russian term *bliuzmen* (bluesman) which connotes someone who has imbibed and now displays the blues ethos. The pronounced cognitive component of this choice is further enlarged by the fact that this idiom has been relatively unknown and must be digested intellectually, as well as emotionally, if it is to be performed in accordance with the standards of the genre. This cognitive component is, however, simultaneously both integral to the formation of community and a source of divisions within it. Outwardly, at least, all performers appear to attach great import to the notion of playing genuine blues, yet they often fall into dispute as to what this might actually mean in a given instance. Moreover, those who have developed repertoires that include a few crowd-pleasing rock or pop songs often experience the censure of others in the community who regard their efforts as a vulgarization of musical standards. These instances readily reflect the oppositions between culture and commerce that establish community boundaries.

In addition, however, they instantiate the contradictory role of the bluesman as it has been scripted in Russia. In one respect, the bluesman plays blues; his vocation is to render faithfully the music of this genre valorized by the community. In another—and in consonance with the norms of the country's intelligentsia—his work is regarded as socially significant inasmuch as it involves enlightening others about this esteemed musical form. Strategies that seek to accomplish this second objective by playing to audiences some familiar material in order to draw them into the performance thus not only run afoul of the first imperative, but are widely regarded as indicative of base motives on the part of the performers themselves (the desire to make money or become a star). Accordingly, these efforts are perceived by others in the community as violations of the norm of authenticity, as disturbances of community boundaries and as depletions of the common store of cultural capital. Regardless of their actual results, flirtations with musical genres that are, indeed, popular are assessed negatively, as retarding rather then pushing forward the enlightenment project. In this respect another distancing—that between the country's intelligentsia and the larger society—is evident in the microcosm of the blues community. In the role of enlighteners, Russia's bluesmen claim both valuable cultural knowledge for themselves and determination to bring this knowledge to others. Whether these others actually respond positively to their efforts is not directly at issue. Rather, posture seems to trump practice. Simply the profession of special knowledge and the readiness to share it serve to distinguish bluesmen on the cultural field as worthy exponents of intelligentsia norms and to set them invidiously apart from the unenlightened. Yet, practically speaking, these two orientations basic to the bluesman's identity—reproducing authentic blues and endeavoring to widen its public appeal—are at loggerheads. The discourse associated with each of them provides the terms in which rivalries and conflicts among performers are often expressed. In the same way that popularizers are rebuked for diminishing the music's authenticity and thus "discrediting" it, so purists are taken to task for "snobbism" by neglecting to promote its public appeal. These divisions, in turn, appear to be reinforced by the pattern of social relations within the community.

The modal units of organization within Russia's blues community—individual blues bands evincing strong affective ties among their members—tend both to sustain the community itself and to amplify the normative division within it. Bands are usually formed, either consciously or unconsciously, along the lines of the Soviet *kollektiv* (collective), under-

stood in this context as a synthesis of players with different styles and ca-
pabilities all working creatively toward a common objective and bearing
personal responsibility to one another for the results of their efforts. The
bonding among musicians that usually occurs within their respective
bands thus reciprocally reinforces the commitment of individual members
to the common project of performing blues music. Given the dispiriting
conditions and perpetual poverty that most blues players endure in Russia, it would be difficult to overestimate the importance of this organizational pattern for keeping blues alive on Russian soil. At the same time,
however, the close bonding within these groups seems to contribute to the
intensity of conflicts among them. This is perhaps most apparent with respect to gaining access to the means of performance, venues in which to
play, owing to the fact that a number of leading blues performers function
as booking agents for nightclubs. Their tendency is to exchange dates
among themselves, leading to an arrangement in which certain bands regularly play within the circuits controlled by their leaders who do the booking while other bands encounter serious difficulties in lining up jobs. The
excluded bands tend to expand their resentment of the favored groups
into a normative critique of their style, proficiency, and commitment to the
blues idiom, often insisting that the popular success enjoyed by certain of
their rivals is itself indication of the fact that they have caved in to commercial pressures and no longer even attempt to play "real blues."

To some extent, the very novelty of the music in Russia invites disputes
about which performers are playing authentic blues. Because the community is based on an imported genre that requires conscious interpretation, differences of this type are all but prescripted. Interpretations can
vary and reinterpretations are always possible, especially because the volume of information about blues has been expanding exponentially since
the end of communism. The introduction of a commercial basis for performance only complicates the matter. For instance, some Russian players
adopt sartorial trappings modeled on the images of foreign bluesmen, images usually drawn from contemporary films. Many of them regard this
practice as an effective way to enlarge the audience for blues, arguing that
by visually catching the attention of those unfamiliar with the music, they
stand a much better chance of involving them in the overall performance.
As instrumentally rational as this approach appears to be, other bluesmen
deride it. They complain that dressing up in this way profanes the whole
enterprise, especially by canceling the sense of individuality—an authenticity of the self—that they find central to the blues aesthetic.

However, divisions in the blues community are one side of the story. The
other is represented by a common set of practices issuing from the manner in which Russians have appropriated blues in ways that position them

favorably against the surrounding society. That is, on one hand, blues as a Western import distinguishes its exponents from the discredited Soviet past. It therefore appears as an avenue to an imagined modernity, a window onto Western culture. On the other hand, the blues tradition has nothing in common with the vulgar materialism practiced by Russia's nouveaux riches, the explicit manifestation of Westernization in contemporary Russian society. Identification with the country's blues community thus situates its members at invidious remove from both a feckless past and a deplorable present. Likewise, it validates their sense of moral worth by sharply distinguishing them from, say, yesterday's Young Communist who has gone over wholeheartedly to making money or today's young entrepreneur getting rich in the netherworld of corrupt business practices. It would be in part for this reason that the norm of authenticity assumes such importance within the community. Deviations from the genre's standards in the direction of pop are immediately associated with commercial culture and, therefore, with those whom community members tend to regard as unprincipled, uncultured, and worse. A sociology of signs—cultural practices read as signifying affiliation with one or another social group—would thus be integral to an account of why the blues idiom has come to mean so much for those Russians who have embraced it.

The presentation of my research material raised some problems with respect to balancing description and analysis. Imagining that Western readers—or, for that matter, the overwhelming majority of Russian ones—have had no exposure to blues played in Russia, I wrestled with the issue of how and where to introduce the story of the music's development there. Quite simply, without that descriptive background, without knowing something about the performers, their music, and the venues where they play it, what sense could the reader make of my analysis of this musical community? In the end, I decided to include it as a sequence of chapters (2–5) following an overall introduction to the subject in chapter 1 that establishes the setting, inquires into the circumstances and factors that have conditioned the reception of the music, and sketches the significance that it holds for its Russian exponents. The descriptive accounts in chapters 2 to 5 introduce the reader to the history of this musical form in Russia, focusing on the performers and their music, emphasizing the "backward" direction of the music's progress in the country which began in mimicry of the style in which blues initially arrived—British blues-rock of the 1960s and 1970s—and then turned back toward the African American roots of the blues genre. Some indications of the development of a specifically "Russian blues" appearing at the beginning of the new century are also discussed. Chapter 6 focuses on the principal components of Russia's blues community, its forms of organization, normative structures, and relationships across community boundaries. From the perspective of politics, chapter 7 synthesizes key features of the materials thus far presented and frames the blues community within its larger environment, showing that those who have adopted the blues idiom have found in it both a particular way of situating themselves in the world and a set of responses to it.

Three technical points require clarification. The first concerns the authorial use of the first person pronoun. My intention has been to use the singular form in all instances in which the observations, assessments, and so forth belong to me alone. However, in those sections of the book produced in collaboration with Andrei Evdokimov, the plural ("we") replaces the singular. The second consideration refers to translation. Some Russian bands carry English-language names, others, Russian ones; sometimes nightclubs have been christened with the native tongue while in other cases English has been employed. The rule that I have followed has been to use English in those instances in which Russians have used it, and transliterated Russian—marked by italics in its first appearance—in those cases in which names appear in that language, followed by parenthetical English translations.

Acknowledgments

I would first like to thank my collaborator, Andrei Evdokimov, without whose assistance this book would not have been possible. When it comes to the blues in Russia, he is simply *the* most knowledgeable individual: he has broadcast a national radio program in Russia on blues music for over fifteen years; he has participated in the organization of blues festivals in the country; he has written articles on blues music for Russian publications; and, he directs the principal Internet website devoted to blues in Russia: www.blues.ru. He knows everybody in Moscow's blues scene and has close contacts with a dozen or so blues bands performing elsewhere in the country. His knowledge has been brought to bear in chapters 2–4 and in the third segment of chapter 5, the first drafts of which we jointly composed in his apartment, largely on the basis of his answers to my questions. I have subsequently reworked those drafts by blending in other materials, but his ideas, interpretations, and thick descriptions fill these portions of this book.

My gratitude also goes to a group of individuals too numerous to mention here (although many of their names appear in these pages)—those members of Russia's blues community who made time for me and my questions, who invited me into their homes and to their performances, who, with a disarming generosity of spirit, treated me as one of their own. I can only hope that my accounts do some justice to the lives of these extraordinary individuals who pursue their passion for blues in the face of daunting material conditions. If, as is often said, Russia is indeed looking for her heroes today, then the search might well begin with them.

A number of individuals have read all or part of this book at various stages of its gestation, contributing ideas, suggestions, and criticisms that have improved its content immensely. I wish to thank in that respect: Eliot Borenstein, Donald Brenneis, G. William Domhoff, Eugene Huskey, Richard Jennings, Alexei Kuzmin, Vladimir Padunov, Mark Slobin, Vadim Volkov, and Alexei Yurchak. The editors of this series—Bruce Grant and Nancy Ries—provided detailed reflections on the penultimate draft. Not only were their penetrating comments a great help to me in producing the final version of the text, but the supportive, collegial tone that suffused even their most pointed revelations of my shortcomings did a lot to enable me to overcome at least some of them. I was fortunate to have Zachary Bowden as a research assistant for a few months during the course of this project. His reconnaissance in the library as well as his informed comments on the work helped me to rethink profitably certain aspects of my argument.

I am grateful to the National Endowment for the Humanities, the International Research and Exchanges Board, and the Division of Social Sciences of the University of California, Santa Cruz for their financial support. My thanks also go to *The Russian Review* for permission to reprint parts of my article, "Getting By on the Blues: Music, Culture and Community in a Transitional Russia," 61 (July 2002), pp. 409–35.

Reserving pride of place for last, my deepest gratitude goes to my wife, Veronica, whose sympathy, understanding, hard work (she did all of the word processing), and creative ideas contributed in innumerable ways to this project. I am dead lucky to have married a woman who, in addition to all of her other qualities, does not seem to mind spending a summer or two in Russian blues joints. This book is dedicated to her.

RUSSIA GETS THE BLUES

CHAPTER ONE

Why Blues?

Blues in Russia is a postcommunist phenomenon. In part, its relatively late appearance in the country had been due to the communist state's policies of cultural repression and censorship that severely restricted contact with the outside world. Of even greater import in this regard, however, would be the Western music for which the Iron Curtain proved no match: rock. Curiously, rock 'n' roll has accounted both for the delayed emergence of blues and for its initial development on Russian soil. Throughout the communist epoch, popular tastes had never singled out blues for special attention. Moreover, during the late Soviet period when rock had become the rage, the listening public drew no particular distinction between these two music styles. Accordingly, the handful of Russian musicians who had managed to acquire some recordings from which they learned to play blues were generally regarded as rock musicians, a judgment reinforced by the British style of blues-rock that most of them performed. Only in communism's aftermath did blues precipitate out of the country's rock movement as an identifiable musical form—played by particular bands at particular venues—with its own following.

Moscow was the principal site for these developments. By the mid-1990s, some forty blues bands were active in the capital, generating the sensation that a Russian blues boom was indeed under way. Dozens of clubs featuring blues had sprung up, from fashionable nightspots that seemed almost directly plucked from, say, New York or Paris to low-end joints with a rough-and-tumble atmosphere. Most of these blues clubs were thriving, and so were the performers. At a time when average monthly wages hovered around the two hundred dollar mark in the capital, many bluesmen were making one hundred dollars per night and more, some playing as many as twenty-five dates per month.[1] However, the financial crash of August 1998—in which the ruble lost two-thirds of its value in three weeks—swiftly undermined Moscow's nightclub economy and, along with it, the city's blues scene.[2] Within a few months, almost half of the restaurants in town had shut down.[3] Many blues clubs closed, too, and, among those that managed to remain open, diminished revenues were often unable to support live performances. Nationwide, monthly incomes declined precipitously, from an average of 170 dollars in May 1998 to only sixty dollars in May of the following year.[4] Yet, although the steep drop in disposable income sharply pruned Moscow's burgeoning blues scene, it by no means eradicated it. Moreover, in other parts of Russia where the blues had put down roots, things continued much as they had before the crash. New bands formed and new clubs opened.

By century's end, the novelty and faddishness that had surrounded the Russian blues scene in the mid-1990s had largely disappeared. But blues still retains a not inconsiderable number of devotees. Relying on the estimates of knowledgeable informants, I would conservatively conjecture that some twenty thousand Russians are closely connected to this music as performers, promoters, or fans. Some multiple of that number—perhaps by a factor of ten or more—would approximate the extended audience for blues, taking into account those who might not place it at the top of their list of musical preferences but whose listening habits would nonetheless include this type of music. How and why have these Russians become involved with blues?

This chapter takes a crack at that question in full expectation that the answers will be provisional, awaiting more complete development as this book progresses. This is, after all, a big question in which a number of separate yet related issues are lodged. Here, I focus on some of them, beginning with the matter of social conditions. Do those historical circumstances surrounding the creation and development of blues music in the United States evince any meaningful similarities with conditions prevailing in postcommunist Russia? In other words, do aspects of each setting help to account for the reception of this music by African Americans at the beginning of the twentieth century and by Russians at century's end? Turning to the music itself, I inquire into those aspects of blues that appear to hold a particular attraction for Russian performers and audiences. At issue here are both musical content and listener receptivity. Therefore, the discussion concerns the appeal that the music holds for its Russian aficionados, and those aspects of Russian culture that appear to resonate with the blues idiom. Thereafter, attention is focused on the process of cultural transmission, that is, on the ways in which cultural objects, on crossing frontiers, register some change in the lives of those adopting them, while they are themselves modified in the course of adoption. Finally, this chapter broaches a question to which the discussion often returns in subsequent ones: What light is shed on the larger society by means of an investigation of that group of people—"the blues community"—connected to one another through their participation in this music?[5]

The Setting: Parallels with the U.S. Experience?

The blues was born in the rural South of the United States amid the so-cioeconomic dislocations following the abolition of slavery and, later, the end of Reconstruction.[6] Former slaves were set free to make their way in a new world in which the direct dominion of the masters had been su-perceded by other forms of economic exploitation which—along with the socio-political constraints and indignities attendant on segregation and overt racial oppression—consigned them to the miserable bottom of a rigid social hierarchy. Under these circumstances, skin color alone served as a constant, visible reminder of their status in a world in which the idea, much less the actual condition, of social equality held no practical signif-icance, even as a remote prospect. In the post-slavery South, the dream of freedom had been eclipsed by a crushing sense of disappointment with that long-awaited liberation on which hopes and expectations had been pinned, coupled with a host of new problems ushered in by liberation it-self: the need to make autonomous economic and sexual choices and to struggle with a new set of constraints—above all, finding and maintain-ing gainful employment—impinging on the individual.[7] Blues represented a reaction to those conditions. It indexed that "trouble" facing everyman and found ways to surmount it in song. Confronted by ubiquitous and de-grading inequalities, it resolutely asserted the dignity of the individual. In the face of hopelessness, it mustered both lament and laughter to affirm the individual's capacity to resist and to endure. Dreadful circumstances notwithstanding, blues never stopped talking about freedom and about what the individual might make of it.

On the surface, at least, some obvious historical parallels can be drawn between these conditions in the United States and those prevailing in Rus-sia. As Peter Kolchin has noted, by the eighteenth century Russian serf-dom had become in key respects a version of the chattel slavery practiced in the American colonies and, later, in the United States.[8] Accordingly, con-ditions of bondage generated a culture of personal dependencies in which the ethic of submission would supplant any notion of social equality.[9] Al-though the communist epoch altered the face of the country in innumer-able ways, it also sustained this culture of personal dependencies and thus retarded the development of equality in the social consciousness.[10] As Katherine Verdery has argued, the authority structures of communist sys-tems scripted citizens in the role of supplicants, and officials in that of par-ents or teachers. Abuses and indignities suffered by the former might give rise to a narrative of "rights"—"They don't have the right to do this to me" or "I have a right to . . ."—but "right" in this context should not be con-fused with a general statement about social relations among formally equal individuals. Rather, "right" would function purely as an expression of individual lament or accusation.[11]

The comparability of these social orders—U.S. slavery and Russian serfdom—has been employed by some scholars to frame another comparability in their modes of social expression: whether in the folklore of slaves and serfs in an earlier period or in *belles lettres* of more recent times.[12] Moreover, the fact that blues took root in Russia only after the collapse of communism invites us to underscore the significance of these parallels. In the same way that blues appeared in the postemancipation period and wrestled with the new problems besetting those liberated from slavery, so blues music only became an identifiable form on the Russian soundscape in the aftermath of the country's liberation from communism, where dashed hopes for a better life kept close company with a myriad of new problems for the individual. Should we then push the comparison further and entertain the idea that roughly the same set of circumstances that conditioned the appearance of blues music in the United States was also present among Russians in the postcommunist period, thus helping to account for its reception there?

A number of those interviewed for this study would respond in the positive. Aleksei Agranovskii, both a biologist at Moscow State University and leader of the blues band, *Chernyi khleb* (Black Bread), himself raised the question:

> Why has blues music come to Russia? Well, what we've got in Russia now is just the same thing that existed in the United States when blues first appeared. A big element here is frustration. There are a lot of Russians who feel that they've actually become different people now that the Soviet Union no longer exists. They feel they've become Negroes. Yesterday they were slaves and our forebears were slaves, too, for many years. People actually feel this. Now what have we got? Well, our freedom, you might say, along with a mass of other problems in which money always seems to figure. Blues is a way to surmount the hang-ups and complexes associated with all that. It is a music that expresses instability and expresses ways in which one can deal with it.[13]

Vitalii Andreev, vocalist and leader of St. Petersburg's Big Blues Revival, remarked on the U.S.-Russian comparison thusly:

> I think that the problems are quite the same . . . It's not very important whether we are in America a century ago or in Russia today. Take the example of Vladimir Vysotskii, the great Russian poet . . . In one of his songs you will find the following question: "Today they were given freedom. And

what will they do with it?" That is, you have so many young people entering a totally new economic situation, namely, some kind of market economy, one in which every man is for himself. Totally different, totally new economic relations. And, of course, as a people we are completely unprepared for this. Our experience has been one of being an employee working for the state. And now employment is greatly reduced and people are thrown out onto the street.[14]

Similarly, Iaroslav Sukhov, a Petersburg artist and blues-lover, noted that:

blues music began to be socially more appreciated after our revolution, after liberation from communism, because we learned that the machine is different but the oppression remains. Simply different levers are used, now more economic levers as opposed to the physical ones in the past. And it happens that you find much more resonance in the blues to this kind of life . . . It makes things much more transparent. I find it very attractive because you are chopped down by the crowd in the kind of protest associated with rock 'n' roll [during communism's final years]. But in blues you remain yourself.[15]

These remarks are broadly representative of the views expressed by a number of individuals in our sample, suggesting an awareness in the blues community of a parallel that obtains between the conditions in which they find themselves and those that they envisage in the American South a century earlier. However, in the face of these perceptions, some aspects of the comparison raise doubts about its validity. For instance, whereas blues had become a genuinely popular music among blacks in the South, it occupies only a small segment on Russia's musical map. Moreover, the blues emerged as an indigenous response to the particular situation confronting blacks in the American South, whereas in the Russian context it appeared as an import to which are attached certain claims to cultural distinction, as detailed below. Consequently, the parallel itself can be regarded as, at best, partial. Nonetheless, from the point of view of many of our subjects, it informs their sense of place in the world. By drawing attention to it, they give voice to one of the myths bolstering the identity of Russia's blues community which traces a relationship between social context and cultural expression, enabling at least some Russian bluesmen to see themselves in a role not unlike that played by their musical heroes in the United States. Moreover, the parallel seems to speak directly to *their* experiences in the postcommunist milieu. They make the connection in their own lives between new, unsettled, and inhospitable social conditions, and the blues idiom as a way of making sense of them.

The desire to make sense of one's position amid the dislocation and chaos attending Russia's postcommunist transformation has already summoned into existence armies of bunco artists and crackpot cults, making fortunes large and small.[16] In Moscow alone, "healers" and assorted purveyors of the black arts have come to number around fifty thousand by the end of the 1990s.[17] The text of a handbill advertising a blues performance in St. Petersburg, provides a glimpse of how those in the blues community position themselves within this jumbled social context:

5 March 1999
INTERNATIONAL CENTER FOR BUSINESS COLLABORATION
Club "BLUES ON THE CORNER"
Esteemed ladies and gentlemen!
St. Petersburg's best blues group
"BELINOV BLUES BAND"
is happy to congratulate you and to share
your company on the eve of International Women's Day
Concert begins at 19:00
Admission is free
Address: Square of the Proletarian Dictatorship, number 6
Second floor (opposite Smolnyi Cathedral)

The entire text of the original handbill is in Russian with the exception of two key signifiers which appear in English—the name of the club ("Blues on the Corner") and the name of the band ("Belinov Blues Band"). One reading of this use of English would be that it signals the presence of valorized cultural products associated with the West: the club, the band, the blues. Another would understand the use of English as a code indicating to the reader just what type of people—"cultured ones"—would be welcomed at this event.[18] However, a third reading of this text—in no way opposed to the other two—might see in it a defocusing of the Russian context which teems with confusion. The physical location is a large new building, the International Center for Business Collaboration (a name that provides an official representation of the marketizing economy but one that most Russians would likely interpret as the place where large-scale swindles occur), that is located on the Square of the Proletarian Dictatorship, itself standing opposite a grand religious edifice, Smolnyi Cathedral, whose adjoining buildings for some seven decades had housed the city's Communist Party headquarters and, later, the office of the city's mayor (more swindles there). Moreover, the text employs a stilted prose— "Esteemed ladies and gentlemen! . . . is happy to congratulate you and to share your company"—to invite would-be patrons. These are rather stock expressions in Russia today, but they are rooted in the past. Above all, that past most immediately signifies "Soviet," as the particular holiday being marked, International Women's Day, would readily connote.

In the context of this collection of discordant signifiers, "blues" appears as a sign distancing—as the English language in the handbill would suggest—the subject from his or her surroundings. This distancing function of the music itself would be represented textually here as an accessible enclave ("on the corner") situated at one remove from layers of the past and present that are referenced as matters of fact in the handbill.[19] Accordingly, the signifiers at play here neither deny nor negate the surroundings; they instead place the individual squarely within them while simultaneously providing a certain distance from them. It would be in the space thus created that community can form and identity can be constructed.

Interview respondents expressed themselves in various ways on this issue of blues as a personal compass for charting one's direction amid unsettled and uncertain surroundings. Mikhail Mishuris—vocalist and leader of Moscow's hottest new blues band in 2001, Mishuris and His Swinging Orchestra—referenced the characteristic of "cool" in the bluesman's demeanor.

> In blues, you need to be cool. All kinds of trouble may have found you, but you need to be cool. And this is the same in Russia. When all the idols [from the communist era] were broken, young people needed to find something that will help them to live. Some fundamentals. Some personal ideology . . . You need to start from somewhere to find yourself. And blues ideology, blues mythology, is a good start.[20]

Aleksei Kalachev, narrator of a popular weekly blues program on national radio, emphasized the importance of storytelling in this respect.

> I use all my talent and experience in order to put on a show that does more than simply play records, but actually involves telling tales, adding commentary, and producing entertainment. Our surveys show that a number of people are attracted to the program because they like to hear these stories and my commentary. You see, irrespective of skin color, bluesmen in the United States have been living through problems that are exactly the same as the ones that people in Russia have to endure. Therefore, when I tell tales about [their experiences in the United States] there is a receptive listening audience.[21]

Kolia Gruzdev, a young guitarist with St. Petersburg's Soul Power Band, indexed the social turbulence surrounding performers—and the creative impulses that it occasions—in his remarks that:

Watching, say, a Muddy Waters video shows me that although there are real differences, the idea of this music is very close to what we are doing here . . . I think that when black people play blues, they feel the same way. They have nothing to lose . . . And that's what the Russian soul is like. In the old times, Pushkin created in a bad political situation. The Decembrists and the Silver Age poets were always in a bad situation. Now is really a strong period for us. Nobody knows what is going to happen and it's a real good time to create things. And you've got a certain freedom because you don't know what is going to happen. And we have to adapt. And when you do that all the time, you stop thinking about difficulties. Your "immune system" helps you to react to these difficulties, helps you not to pay attention to them. Musicians are very special people in this respect. [We can't earn a decent living and] so we are not satisfied with our roles, [but] there's no way to stop. Like in [rushing] water, you're being dragged along by it.[22]

With respect to new challenges which many Russians have been ill-prepared to meet, blues guitarist Valerii Belinov related the following story:

We had this group, Rhythm and Bluesy, and we recorded a tape of our original music in August 1991, just before the putsch in Moscow. We sent out the tape to about seventy different companies and we got no favorable replies. So this was very depressing because a person like myself who plays music certainly wants to see the end result of his labors. The end result is mainly the appreciation of other people and that door was closed to me at this point, so it was depressing. But this experience helped me to surmount some of my naiveté. Like all other Soviet people, we didn't have any idea about how to construct a real business, so what we did was actually funny. And it is even funnier when you think about it. Here we were, Soviet people with a real desire to enter the world stage of music, but with no idea whatsoever as to how this is done . . . What buttons to push? What makes this big entertainment industry go? We simply had this naive desire to be a part of it, but no idea about how to go about doing that.[23]

A final parallel attending the context in which blues music was introduced both in America's urban north and in Russia concerns the fact that the music seemed to have made a successful journey thanks to the fact that in each case it had brought an appreciative audience in tow. When American blues migrated from primarily rural settings to urban centers such as Chicago and Oakland during and after World War II, its raw, abrasive sound was not immediately well received by local residents for whom "blues" had meant something far more polished and jazzy. It was African American migrants from the South who supplied the audience for blues in the Northern cities, filling the jukes to listen to that music in whose traditions they were already rooted.[24] Likewise, in postcommunist Russia, much of the initial audience for blues music arrived in the form of young foreigners from the West (primarily from the United States) who, as part of a U.S. blues revival during the late 1980s and early 1990s, had developed a taste for this music while at college. Rather like their black counterparts a couple of generations earlier, they had come for jobs (and adventure) and would frequent the blues joints popping up all over Moscow to spend some money, hear some blues and, often enough, introduce their Russian friends to this music.

The Attraction of the Music

Although outwardly a simple music, blues consists of a rich synthesis of African and European musical forms that has married the rhythmic structures of the former to the latter's tonal harmonies, altering these in the process as well through the introduction of "blue" notes (the flattened third and seventh).[25] The music's proximate sources are also multiple and varied, from field hollers and work-gang chants to gospel music, minstrelsy, ragtime, and marching bands.[26] It is perhaps the inner complexity of this synthesis that has contributed to the impact of blues on the musical mainstream, enabling it to revolutionize popular music, first in the United States and later around the world. In the words of Susan McClary, "a music scholar of a future time might well look back on the musical landscape of the 1900s and label us all 'blues people': those who inhabited a period dominated by blues and its countless progeny."[27]

Long before blues had taken its place on the country's soundscape, Russians had become rather well acquainted with one of its derivatives: rock 'n' roll. What was it about blues itself that attracted a cohort of musicians and fans to rock's progenitor in the postcommunist period? On the face of things, blues music would represent a questionable choice for any Russian musician intent on expanding his stocks of either commercial or cultural capital. Nearly all songs in the blues idiom seem to be musically very limited, employing the standard twelve bars in a three-chord progression.[28] Blues would appear to enjoy no commercial advantage owing to its danceability, due to the fact that it finds itself in competition with other musical genres—rock, reggae, ska, Latin, and so forth—that are, if not more rhythmic, equally danceable. Because blues in Russia is almost invariably sung in English, meanings conveyed by the lyrics are unavailable to most of the audience. Moreover, most Russian blues singers themselves speak very little if any English and their attempts to mimic the lyrics of songs from recorded versions are apt to produce both a large number of mondegreens as well as an ample measure of unintelligible utterances. Compounding this difficulty is the problem attending the rich idiomatic content of blues lyrics whose references and seminal figures would, again, be almost entirely lost on audience and performers alike. Lastly, there is the problem of pronunciation. Imagine hearing in place of a blues phrase such as "I'm sho' boun' tah git me one" that same line sung straight as "I am sure bound to get me one" intoned with a heavy Russian accent.

In the presence of these sonic barriers, what accounts for the appeal of blues among Russians? Here, I stick to the sonorous side of the matter, discussing cultural aspects in the following section and returning to them in chapters 6 and 7 once the remaining pieces of the puzzle have been ferreted out of the particular structure and dynamics of the country's blues community. The first thing to underscore in this respect would be the connection between sound and the social. As Richard Leppert reminds us, "whereas sight distances, music envelopes."[29] This enveloping, as Jacques Attali has stressed, is thoroughly social; music, from state anthems to protest songs, mediates our collective existence, reinforcing the sense that "society is possible."[30] Blues represents a premier example of the sociability conjured in musical performances, calling forth collective emotions, engendering common feelings.[31] Here, the discussion of the music's capacity to engage the listener in a socially relevant way is organized around four elements which together make up the blues sound: rhythmic groove, texture, stylistics, and lyrical intonation. These can be depicted as layers in a vertical structure.

The bottom layer is occupied by the music's African rhythmic base which produces an effect variously known as "groove," "vital drive," or "forward-propelling directionality."[32] As these terms suggest, the rhythm drives the music forward and draws the listener along with it into a sensation of movement. Charles Kiel and Steven Feld have theorized this effect as "groove," which is created by the beat pulling against the steady pulse of the rhythm which the listener himself supplies. In this respect, the beat is slightly "out of time," a characteristic of blues music that is usually supplied by the bass playing a little ahead of the pulse while the drums lag a little behind it.[33] The groove, then, leaves a space at the center of the beat. That space is filled by the listener's experience of the music's pulse, thus engaging him or her directly in producing the sensation of the rhythm, an activity often manifested outwardly by the tapping of feet or the bobbing of heads.

This aspect of blues has exercised a powerful attraction among Russian performers and listeners, dozens of whom raised the issue of the music's rhythmic energy during interviews and conversations. Aleksandr Bratetskii—a young medical student and harmonica ace who has moonlighted with Moscow's Blues Rhythm Section and, later, Blues Spinners—remarked that:

> When I first heard blues music, it just grabbed me. All of those people that I was listening to, Muddy Waters and others, have a certain kind of energy, a kind of primordial energy. It's not the energy of the wild animal but something deeper. And in this primordial energy you can hear the social context, [things] for which we don't really have words in the end.[34]

Nikolai Arutiunov, veteran vocalist and leader of Moscow's *Liga bliuza* (Blues League) put it this way:

> I love rhythm and blues because to me it has that energy. We have this kind of slang expression, it's called *ugar* [the slang is derived from one of the word's literal meanings that refers to carbon monoxide poisoning]. So *ugar* means that you hear the music and you are filled, overfilled, with energy. Immediately. I love music that . . . carries that kind of energy . . . I love hard rock. That is really energetic music, but it depends on loudness to reach you. Blues is able to reach you just the same and does not depend on that kind of loudness at all. It creates the same effect but does not involve any earsplitting in the process.[35]

Layered atop the music's drive or groove would be a number of instrumental and vocal techniques derived from African musical traditions that distort in one way or another the clarity of melodic notes. This distortion—accomplished by bending or blurring notes on, say, a guitar, or by means of vocal techniques ranging from gospel-inspired melisma to the calculated stutter or repeated broken phrase (with all manner of growl or falsetto in between)—provides the particular texture of blues music.[36] The texture amounts to more than simple color or adornment. Distorted melodic notes have the effect of both filling the groove and playing against it, thus accentuating the music's drive and articulating in various ways its rhythmic pulse. Take, for instance, the high-pitched guitar note played at the tonic by bending the flattened seventh a whole step. This note might be struck twice at the beginning of a phrase, on the upbeat and the downbeat, and then sustained for a measure or more. In so doing, the guitar seems to arrest the beat momentarily while simultaneously carrying it forward toward a musical resolution of the tension created by the sustained note, dissolving it in a glissando that completes the phrase. Playing off of and against the music's drive in this way, lead instruments such as guitars and harmonicas further accentuate the music's rhythmic thrust, while involving listeners directly in the music's emotively suggestive texture.

The texture of the blues sound is central to the music's ability to signify.

Whether through the medium of instruments or voices, it "suggests something beyond the capacity of the words to articulate."[37] With respect to vocal effects, St. Petersburg guitarist, Sasha Suvorov (who speaks no English), notes that, "when a blues singer sings, he is singing emotions. The words are just vehicles to carry that emotion and it is the emotion that I can hear."[38] Similarly, fellow St. Petersburg singer-guitarist Edik Tsekhanovskii points out that "if you listen to the voices of bluesmen—for example, Muddy Waters or, even better, John Lee Hooker—you hear a certain timbre in their voices. That's a kind of message, a kind of indication of what they've lived through. That's blues."[39] In regard to instrumental voicings, singer-guitarist Aleksei Baryshev, leader of the Blackmailers Blues Band of Vladimir, maintains that "the emotional element in blues is conveyed by the sound, and it is important to be able to produce a dirty, cirrhotic sound in order to anchor a lot of those emotions."[40] Contrapuntally, singer-guitarist Giia Dzagnidze, who leads Moscow's Modern Blues Band, draws attention to the way in which a distorted guitar sound can be used to frame and to amplify the impact of clean notes, making them "sound a little cleaner, a little more precise. And, if you think about it, each note must express life. Or, if not life as a whole, each note must express that certain moment in your soul as you play."[41]

The listener's involvement is further engaged at a third layer in the structure of blues music: stylistics. Variations on the call-and-response pattern—whose sources lie in field hollers, work songs, and gospel music—constitute the core of this musical style. Call-and-response in its most direct variant takes the form of questions posed by the singer to the audience. As he intones a lyric of, say, unrequited love, the singer might deliver a spoken aside to the listeners, along the lines of: "Does somebody know what I'm talking about?" The audience's shout of "yeah" thus completes the call-and-response. This stylistic pattern is also apparent in the interchange between voices and instruments, whereby a sung phrase (call) is followed by a riff on guitar or harmonica (response). Although the audience is less actively involved with this version of the call-and-response exchange, the same dialogic technique is evident.[42] Call-and-response forms of involvement are also readily apparent in hand clapping—especially when the band goes largely silent and the leader turns to the audience with an implicit request to clap time with him as if to revive the whole effort—and in dancing in which the response is not sonorous but kinetic and kinesthetic.[43] Due to the fact that call-and-response techniques are integral to blues stylistics—exemplified by, say, guitar voicings that follow sung phrases or by band members echoing the refrain intoned by the singer in songs such as "Got My Mojo Workin'"—Russian performers practice them to varying degrees. Yet they do so unconsciously. Only one person in the interview sample raised the subject: Mikhail Mishuris, who learned these techniques while attending Chicago's Old Town School of Folk Music in the late 1990s. When call-and-response methods were mentioned to other blues musicians in conversation, the response was generally simple appreciation for the background knowledge on blues stylistics thereby provided.

The next layer of elements in blues music inducing audience involvement consists of the lyrics. With some exceptions, the surface content of blues lyrics would scarcely seem to fire the imagination. Indeed, to the uninitiated the repetition of laments pertaining to personal predicaments ("My baby left me." "I'm so broke and disgusted.") or to exultant emotions ("I've been drinkin' gin like never before. I feel so good, I just want you to know.") can seem trite. Naturally, since most Russian blues performers do not speak English, the semantic content of the lyrics usually holds no particular import for them.

Vocalists who have translated that content and are thus aware of its meaning in English often display small regard for it. Mikhail Sokolov— a veteran Moscow player whose vocals and harmonica front Blues Hammer Band—would be speaking for many of his colleagues when he remarks that "blues is a rather primitive music with a banal content. Really banal, like 'You don't love me, so I'm gonna get drunk,' or 'I really cried a lot when you threw me out.' This is banal and pretty much all the texts are alike, am I not right?"[44] However, the meaning and impact of blues lyrics lie a step or so removed from their surface content. Rather like the intricacies of blues rhythms and textures that seem at first altogether simple and undemanding, blues lyrics constitute a critical element in a musical language that is "refined, extremely subtle, and ingeniously systematic."[45] With neither a command of the language nor familiarity with the cultural associations encoded in the lyrics, Russian performers and audiences are not much attuned to the references, nuances, and suggestive tropes vocalized in blues songs. But the nonlinear narratives commonly employed in this idiom that spit out terse statements and powerful, compact images "close to instinctual sources" can engage them in another level of understanding.[46] As is the case with related musical genres such as rock 'n' roll, blues does not so much convey a cognitive content to its audiences as it demands from them a response.[47] It is the directness of the lyrics, coupled with the first-person expressions of the vocalist with whom the audience—drawn in by the rhythmic, instrumental, and stylistic devices discussed previously—is encouraged to identify, that gives blues its particular impact on listeners. As American bluesman Charlie Musselwhite has remarked, apropos contemporary conditions:

In today's world, the blues is kind of like an antidote to all the computers and things all around us that lack a human quality. It doesn't matter where you live or what kind of background you come from: when you hear the blues, it reminds you that you are human and it hooks you forever.[48]

His comments are echoed in the reminiscences of a young St. Petersburg guitarist, Volodia Rusinov, who recalled his initial exposure to the music.

At first, I bought an anthology of Eric Clapton's stuff. When I heard his work with the Blues Breakers and Cream, it just knocked me out. It was like this huge amount of musical information that I now had to process. I had to listen to it over and over again [because] I had never really heard music like this before. One of the things that impressed me about this music was that it was so direct. It's not jazz; you don't need all that stuff. Direct and simple emotions are what blues features.[49]

Blues speaks both with and beyond its lyrical content. That is, the typical blues situation—one that ostensibly motivates vocalized expression and is thematized in that expression itself—is one that is in some way or other unright. Blues lyrics usually content themselves with naming that situation. Descriptions tend to be thin and analyses even thinner or absent entirely. Rather, the lyrics conspire to subvert that situation in another way, relying on startling images ("I feel like slappin' a pistol in your face") or pointed ironies rather than on linear narratives to undo the already devalued present. Whether enlisting humor to defy hardship or overblown statements ("I'm gonna murder my baby") to redress the moral outrages that have been suffered, blues lyrics combine protest with affirmation through a reassertion of the primacy of desire, insisting that the individual has not and will not succumb to misfortune.[50] Moreover, the vocal techniques already noted—the growls, wails, and screams—carry the communicative enterprise beyond the lyrics, indicting the words themselves, their inadequacies or even euphemistic qualities, as somehow complicit in the unright situation.

These aspects of blues singing point beyond the situation that they describe and beyond the words used to describe it. They conduce to a release of repressed feelings, to catharsis. This cathartic effect is the product of all of the elements discussed hitherto—the groove, the texture, the call-and-response style, as well as the lyrics—that are brought together in performance.[51] In this respect, blues music accomplishes a transition reminiscent of Walter Benjamin's reworking of the Freudian categories, melancholy and mourning.[52] As with the blues itself, both of these states of mind reflect an unright situation. Yet Benjamin draws a deep distinction between them. On one hand, melancholy connotes an introverted condition of grief in which actions are deprived of value, and knowledge-seeking contemplation intended to change the world leads instead to the cul-de-sac of depression and insanity. On the other, mourning implies a certain "loyalty to the world of things" and a resolve to occupy one's ostensible place within it.[53] As with Benjamin's mourning, blues refuses to sound a retreat from the world, steadily conveying the notion of human worth in its very capacity and will to endure. An active politician, Sergei Mitrokhin, remarked in this vein on the earthly manner that he associates with blues.

> I like the idea of waking up with a terrible hangover, finding all my money and my woman gone, and thinking: "This isn't so bad." Blues is like that; experiencing terrible things but at the same time surviving them, and knowing that you are able to survive them. It makes you feel good about yourself.[54]

Vitalii Andreev recalled a moment that altered his life as a musician, mentioning a St. Petersburg performance in the early 1990s by English rhythm-and-blues singer, Arthur Brown:

> When I saw Arthur Brown on stage, especially when he was doing "I'll Put a Spell on You," I was seeing a man who had been involved with the blues for over thirty years, and I could see what it meant to play blues. I could see how everything depended on the internal arrangement of the person, on his internal side. When he went out on stage, he was another person. He had changed completely. I am not sure that I know how this happens, but I hope that people who leave the hall after we've been lucky enough to have played a good concert have that same experience and that same feeling with them.[55]

Finally, and from a quarter deep within the Russian tradition, St. Petersburg bass player Ivan Kovalev had this to say on the subject:

> I, myself, am an Orthodox believer. You can probably refer to blues as "music of the soul," but here there would be a sharp distinction between "music of the soul" and "music of the spirit." And it is the latter form that the Orthodox Christian would be in search of. I see it on a higher spiritual plane. People who don't have this kind of inner spiritual conviction and orientation, they search for their peace and satisfaction in other forms—in more ostentatious forms. And here, through the medium of blues, they find a kind of food for their souls. And this particular satisfaction of his soul that

an individual might get through blues music could perhaps well be a phase in a larger search for spiritual music and spiritual fulfillment.[56]

Cultural Resonances

The second part of the answer to the question—Why blues?—would involve locating those aspects of Russian culture that evince an affinity to the elements of the music just discussed.[57] The comparability between African American and Russian forms of folk expression derives in large measure from the particular mood or attitude with which cultural products are received and interpreted, a mood that designates the significance of their content as close to life or, through the prism of their respective artifices, as life itself. Just as the tradition of Russian folk epics (*byliny*) takes its name from the past tense of the verb "to be" (*byt'*)—suggesting that the events and personages recounted in the tales really "were"—so, as Henry Townsend points out, "the original name given to . . . [blues] music was 'reals.' And it was real because it made the truth available to the people in songs."[58]

Russian folk products of more recent vintage—the twentieth-century traditions of urban songs and songs from prison camps (*blatnye pesni*)—reflect this closeness-to-life mood as well, whether confessing the pain of unrequited love or reporting on events in the world from the wrong side of the law.[59] It appears that these genres today occupy a niche in that social stratum, the intelligentsia, which is also the country's primary audience for blues. As Aleksandr Dolgov—editor of the St. Petersburg musical magazine, *Fuzz*—has observed, "If you have an intellectual in this country who is oriented toward emotional music, and he has [the relevant] information, then he will likely be listening to *blatnye pesni* or to blues."[60] Along these lines, Aleksei Agranovskii recalled how his father—Anatolii Agranovskii, a well-known journalist with the newspaper, *Izvestiia*—used to play on his seven-string guitar and sing urban songs and *blatnye pesni* in the home.

> This music in the home was a kind of family tradition. And the expressions in these songs—the incredible naiveté and simplicity—[contain] elements that are very similar to what you sing in blues. A common theme in each would be the individual laughing at himself. There is tremendous humor and humanity in the Russian tradition of urban songs and *blatnye pesni*. This would be Russian blues in the commonly accepted meaning of the term. Many of the themes are parallel: being in jail, being unlucky in love, having no money, and so on.[61]

Agranovskii's band has included some elements from these Russian folk genres in their performances—usually by inserting a couple of verses into a standard blues number—while St. Petersburg's Big Blues Revival occasionally adds a Russian urban song to its set list. In both cases, audiences tend to warm to these efforts with enthusiastic appreciation.

Although a number of respondents remarked on the affinity that they detect between blues and these Russian genres—with respect to both the overall mood reflected in each and their basic musical structures—others have rejected the comparison outright. In their view, Russian folk music and blues would belong to "completely different" traditions. Usually, those professing this opinion back it up by pointing to the differences in rhythmic patterns—in blues, the second and fourth beats of the measure are accented while in the Russian folk tradition stress falls on the first and third beats—and sometimes complain that Russian audiences joining in spontaneously to clap time have unwittingly impaired their band's efforts on stage. This dispute would be worth noting insofar as it cautions against presuming the existence of some innate or objective similarity joining imported American blues to the body of home-grown music. Whatever similarity there might be in this regard would depend on the ear of the listener. Indirectly, Aleksei Kalachev raised this same question in describing the format of his radio broadcasts:

> The emotions that are laid into blues are not premeditated. They are expressions of what people have survived. They are a heavy, dramatic story of black Americans which is similar to the history of Russians . . . I don't want to pretend that this music, and even my radio show, are approachable for everyone. That is, I would say that maybe one out of thirty listeners would be able to appreciate it, to understand it. But that one-in-thirty, nonetheless, has a right to his own art, doesn't he?[62]

Turning to the issue of broader cultural proclivities that might resonate with blues style, mention might first be made of the common blues practices of testifying and signifying. Whether sung or spoken, these practices appear as a particular moment in song when the performer seeks to divulge to the audience some especially important information, usually about the trouble that he or she has been facing. Significance is signaled by marking off such a segment with imperatives such as: "Now listen," "Look here, people" or "Wait a minute." These suggest that, although that which is about to be related may strain credulity, it is the honest truth. But this stance is also mildly mockish, often intimating that a free pass for exaggerations has also been warranted. Exaggerations, too, are part of the story, part of the "effect of meaning" that the blues idiom conveys.[63] In this respect, Nancy Ries's study of Russian conversational practices and her descriptions of the extended tales of woe ("litanies") or mischief making that regularly inform them represent counterparts in Russian culture to testifying and signifying, respectively, in blues discourse.[64] Each pattern exhibits a bipolar structure based on the opposition of lament and exultation. For either testifying or litanizing, the mood is solemn and the content of expression tends toward the sorrowful. Conversely, signifying (as in Russian mischief tales) proceeds on a lighter note, undoing an inhospitable world through the devices of irony, mockery, and double-voicing. As is the case with testifying and signifying, litanizing, in particular, is cued—usually by the long, heavy sigh—that alerts the listener to the extraordinary nature of the personal episodes about to be recounted. Appropriately signaled, the ensuing narrative takes part in an identifiable discursive form that combines the mundane with the magical, themselves rough counterparts to fact and exaggeration in the blues idiom. It is within the intimacy attending these conversational practices that souls are revealed.[65]

During interviews, Russian bluesmen often remarked directly on the affinity that they detected between blues and their own cultural orientations. "In my view," explained bass player Sergei Mironov of Big Blues Revival,

blues is really close to the Russian personality. It's the soul, the soul. Everybody knows that Russian people are people who love to open themselves up before everyone. When I'm on stage, I am unable to disguise my feelings very well. I don't try to hide them. Say, I might be a little sad. That's soul, that's blues.[66]

His colleague, Vitalii Andreev, expanded on this point:

Just look at some of our poets—those who have died young, those who have died young by their own hand. In principle, a Russian person suffers, suffers always. Here we have that melancholy [toska]. The great poet, Mikhail Lermontov, would be a good example. He had that Russian melancholy, that Russian suffering, that Russian emotional free fall. As a Russian person, he was capable of quarreling with his best friend, just for the sake of provoking a duel. And all the time he knows perfectly well that he will not shoot. As a result, he gets killed. So, in my view, blues is actually, in the Russian context, a progressive thing inasmuch as the Russian person is condemned to suffer. Listen to Russian songs. They share the Russian soul. There are some really amazing songs you'll hear grandmothers sing in the countryside and these songs come directly from the people [narod]. They are about the external world but, most importantly, they are about the in-side of the person.[67]

Ries associates the proclivity to litanize tales of woe with the feminine dimension of Russian conversational practices. The masculine dimension, on the other hand, dispenses with direct statements of misfortune; it does not so much absorb the blows struck by unkind conditions as it does parry them, counterattacking with mischief making and mayhem. Whereas the response to misfortune in the feminine mode would be to dwell on it and to derive personal dignity through suffering, the masculine mode secures that dignity by laughing at trouble. In this respect, some of the remarks made by Kolia Gruzdev during an interview underscore certain affinities between Ries's "masculine" mode of expression and the blues ethos. "When you're playing," he said:

It's like an orgasm. You come to a certain point and you peak. That's what the Russian soul is like. Russian people are very unpredictable. They have a rebel spirit. It's inside. That's the way they act; how they present themselves to the world; the way they talk; the way they weave around. They do some stupid things or cool things, you know. And that's all about blues, because that's the way you live, the way you talk and the music is very close to what you do. I find this strong analogy with the Russian poet [Sergei] Esenin. He was always hanging out with prostitutes and bandits in the clubs and he's got very soulful poetry. It's about life, [both] modern and things past. And blues is like that. It's inside of us. And if you realize it, you can show it off.[68]

Ries's categories do not designate females as the sole bearers of the "feminine" discursive form, just as males are not the only ones to participate in the "masculine" mode of storytelling. Rather, as analytic concepts they aim to identify the poles of the conversational axis with which all members of society have direct experience. Taken as a whole, this discursive system appears quite congruent with its bimodal counterpart in the blues idiom: worries and trouble on one end, exultation on the other. What is more, both traditions have drawn their power from their ability to re-work in song or speech the materials that life has provided, either by inverting a miserable world through a moral valorization of suffering or by a jubilant leap beyond it. As Dale Peterson notes with respect to the religious roots anchoring both Russian and African American cultural practices, "in the midst of captivity and humiliation, true believers enact sudden, convulsive turns from lamentation to exultation; one is obliged not to let go a long-deferred dream of liberation."[69]

This transformational moment in the blues tradition appears to occupy an important place in the consciousness of many Russians who have been attracted to the music. For instance, Iaroslav Sukhov speaks of blues as containing a "radiant sadness. When I look around myself," he continues:

I see sadness, sad things. And that's not just because I'm getting older, but life makes it so that some of our optimism fades. But this is precisely where the blues comes in, to rescue our best hopes, to be able to face that sadness and not surrender hope. So in old blues songs you hear of some kind of dark drama that has unfolded, some unrequited love; and all that is taking place on the physical level, but the music transcends the physical level and transcends time. Blues music transcends that sadness and leads to hope.[70]

Along similar lines, Nikolai Arutiunov mentioned that:

The attraction of blues for me is hope and disappointment and energy, energy that keeps hope alive. You listen to Johnny Winter and he might be singing about disappointment, but the actual music that he is playing is full of hope. So blues has this division between sadness and disappointment that you hear in the words, and the power, the conviction, and the hope that abides in the music. In some blues you have the first verse that is something like "I don't have any money," and then a second verse "Because of that I lost my woman," and then the third verse, something like "That doesn't matter because I'm going to come out on top anyway." That's the optimistic side of this music that gains some adherents here in Russia.[71]

A second aspect of Russian communicative practices evincing an affinity to the blues idiom would be the valorization of ironic forms of hyperbole and understatement. Svetlana Boym has called attention to the ways in which "the facts," especially among educated Russians, are often regarded as resistant to direct expression. The supposition appears to be that a thorough verbalization of some important episode or event in which the individual is personally invested would somehow cause it to lose its full significance. Accordingly, speakers often tend to rely on indirection, suggestion, or meaningful silences in order to convey *podopleka* (the real state of affairs) or, in blues dialect, the "true facts."[72] This same discursive tactic is encountered in the blues practice of signifying, or double-voicing, which employs irony and double entendre to impart that to which the knowing listener is already attuned.[73] Signifying represents a non-European form of discourse that traces a charmed circle around those participating in the communicative event. It is "essentially a technique of repeating inside quotation marks in order to reverse or undermine pretended meaning, constituting an implicit parody of a subject's complicity."[74] Rooted in clandestine dialect designed to prevent the masters from understanding the communications of their underlings, signifying survives in contemporary blues largely as a double-voicing of (usually) sexual innuendo in which all manner of modern machinery and appliances—from trains and automobiles to washing machines and cross-cut saws—can be impressed into the service of the sexual imaginary. In Russian folk culture, the still popular *chastushka*—a song composed of short verses, often ribald and commonly containing a strong (but submerged) mockery of authority—is constructed along similar lines.

The rakish streak in blues music that takes aim at piety and pretension would appear to be particularly congenial to Russian audiences overfed on the promises of communism, perestroika, and, most recently, a democratic-capitalism heralded as the harbinger of material plenty, personal freedom, and, not least, a "normal" life.[75] As Greil Marcus has noted, by debunking the moral mouthings of authority, blues rescues the possibility to believe.[76] Belief, in turn, lies largely beyond the plane of verbal expression. It more inhabits the sonorous landscape of shrieks, wails, moans, and silences. This tendency in blues to go beyond the words themselves calls to mind certain counterparts in the world of Russian letters, whether the poetry of *zaum* (literally "beyond mind") or absurdist prose associated with writers such as Daniil Kharms, whose work in the 1920s and 1930s has enjoyed considerable popularity in Russia once the ban against its publication was lifted in the early 1990s.[77] As with these Russian literary trends, the blues idiom often employs words as gateways to worlds in which truth is uncluttered by verbal description. Summoned by the musical sounds heralding its occasion, truth emerges from the innermost quarters of consciousness where the memories and desires that bind it to the phenomenal world are stored. A number of performers brought up the truth factor in their discussions of the blues sound, its simplicity and directness. One, Vania Zhuk, a young St. Petersburg guitarist, contrasted it to other forms of music, saying that "when you play classical music or whatever else, you might enjoy the pictures that you draw in the air [with it]. But when you play blues, if you are drawing pictures you are lying."[78]

Transmission of Music and Culture

As cultural forms cross international frontiers, chain reactions are initiated when foreign objects and practices register an impact on the receiving culture. Simultaneously, individuals in that same culture play an active role in the process, consciously borrowing and imitating foreign objects and practices, and modifying or domesticating them in the act of reception.[79] The appearance of blues music and culture in Russia represents a clear illustration of this process in four respects. First, the foreign import has the potential for creating cultural distinctions. Its conspicuous consumption associates participants with something more momentous or significant—the modern, the West—than what might be associated with their everyday lives.[80] Second, and related to this point, transmitted objects and practices often undergo an inversion in their status as they traverse international boundaries. That which had been associated with "low" culture in its original milieu becomes transformed into a specimen of "high" culture in its new surroundings.[81] Third, successful transmission depends on extant conditions in the receiving culture, most especially the presence of existing networks of individuals prepared and poised to respond to the new cultural imports.[82] Finally, a certain concern attends this process—particularly in the incidence of musical practices—that speaks to the issues of cultural imperialism and the concomitant homogenization and degradation of cultures around the world. If a few multinational corporations control the airwaves, monopolize the recording industry, and saturate markets with their products, has not the global stage been set for the dominion of the West's "culture industry" and with it, the vapid sameness of a debased commercial culture?[83]

Taking this last issue first, the subject matter of this book does not much fall within the scope of issues—principally, does the global music industry drive out or encourage local musics and local musical innovation?—contested in the cultural imperialism debate. The reason for this is straightforward: blues produced in Russia can hardly be considered commercial music. Although blues bands make recordings, these usually are self-produced CDs or audiotapes recorded at concerts which mainly serve as promotion materials to secure live performance dates. Valerii Belinov's description of the difficulties encountered by his band in this endeavor would be emblematic of the experiences of many groups.

> We spent all of our money on promotion materials. First, it took us two years to get the money to make a good photograph for publicity purposes. Just to get the clothes to wear. The money for a tape was all contributed by sponsors, so there was a long process of meeting with people and trying to convince them of our project. It took 2,500 dollars to make [the tape], which for us was an enormous amount of money. We cut it over the course of about two weeks and got three hundred copies that we used for promotion, not for sale. David Goloshchekin played it on his radio program here in Petersburg and it was played on the radio in Moscow. The cassette accomplished what we had hoped; namely, it opened a lot of doors . . . We

had a legitimate, professional, first-rate blues group with a cassette that would get us gigs anywhere. But it didn't last. The bass player immigrated to Germany. Then the drummer turns very heavily to drinking and becomes a total drunk. So, with these two guys gone, our publicity is out of date. Our cassette no longer has these two people on it. We have to do everything again.[84]

Mikhail Sokolov confirms the standard nature of these practices. "As a rule, groups here make so-called discs with a maximum of two hundred copies. Our group cut a record, for instance, and only six copies were made."[85]

Although blues recordings are on sale at shops in large cities, almost invariably these are the work of U.S. and British artists. Some Russian blues is available at the Purpurnyi Legion Record Shop and its three branch stores in Moscow and at that city's flea market, Gorbushka. However, the selection is meager and availability is hit-and-miss. Even the most commercially successful band in the country, Crossroadz, derives the bulk of its income from live performances, rather than from the sale of its commercially produced recordings, and these performances overwhelmingly occur in small club venues where the pay is modest.[86] Consequently, the Russian blues community is relatively unplugged from the global music industry, although, as discussed more fully in chapters 6 and 7, that industry represents a noxious presence for most blues musicians who construct part of their identity around the idea of struggle against it. This musical community, then, tends to resemble those studied by Ruth Finnegan and David Coplan in which local artists in England and South Africa respectively reproduce and combine in their own fashion both imported and domestic music, usually with no larger purpose in mind than the pleasure of performing it before appreciative local audiences.[87]

The remaining three issues, however, are quite pertinent to the transmission of blues music to Russia, and they are taken up here in succession. First, there is little question that blues music—along with jazz and rock 'n' roll before it—is valorized by virtue of its association with the West. Russian conditions, as Katerina Clark has pointed out, have made this association particularly important due to the fact that effectively all domestic sources of otherness had been scotched in the Soviet period since the 1930s.[88] Social distinction, then, came to depend heavily on displays of Western goods (especially clothing) and Western cultural products (especially music). Judging simply by the photographs displayed on the walls of their apartments, today's Russian bluesmen—particularly those who have toured in Western countries or who have performed at festivals in the West—place great store on this association.

Second, considering the social origins of blues music in the United States and placing that same music in the context of its contemporary Russian audience, one encounters something of a textbook case of cultural inversion. Although Russian blues is performed at a number of venues—from up-scale supper clubs to down-at-the-heel bohemian joints—it is usually the case that bands playing the traditional Delta variant—a music "created not just by black people but by the poorest, most marginal black people [living in] virtual serfdom"—are the very ones to be found performing in the posh establishments.[89] There, one will witness sedate, smartly attired audiences responding to this rough, gut-bucket variety of blues with subdued and studied appreciation. Levan Lomidze—guitar virtuoso and leader of Moscow-based Blues Cousins—recalled the social composition of blues clubs during the city's blues boom, noting that:

> In the mid-nineties, [Foreign] Minister [Andrei] Kozyrev and lots of other big shots would come to the blues clubs. When we played, the audience was full of the new rich and the new class. And, of course, members of the intelligentsia. Until about 1996, blues was fashionable, it appealed to the elite.[90]

Similarly, Aleksei Kalachev observed that blues "has been established in Moscow as the music of young intellectuals of the middle class," a point echoed by Nikolai Arutiunov:

> When clubs opened in the early '90s, people with money began going there. At that time it was the so-called New Russians—the new business class—and a lot of members of the intelligentsia. In this respect there was definitely an element of snobbism. Snobbism, simply because blues was Western music. Some people were trying in this way to show that they were—and I use the English word—"cool." But snobbism has no place in blues, a music that is very simple and accessible. There is no snobbism around the blues in America. But here, for particular historical reasons—namely, that the people listening to it were largely from the upper layer of the middle class and felt distinguished somehow by their appreciation of this music—an element of snobbism surrounded it.[91]

The issue of cultural distinction—Arutiunov's "snobbism"—touches on the issue of musical authenticity: What constitutes "real" blues? This vexed question is taken up in chapters 6 and 7 which examine the ways in which this issue both establishes an identity for Russia's blues community generally and informs its internal status structure. Here, the purpose is to locate the links between the import and the importers. In so doing, it becomes apparent that blues and related musics have crossed the country's frontiers with considerable cultural baggage already in tow. Within the imported music a certain statement on authenticity had already been inserted, one acquired during the music's travels through American and British youth cultures decades prior to its arrival in Russia.

At bottom, the cultural associations appended to the blues import derived from the appropriation of African American music by youthful white audiences after World War II. In the United States, this appropriation has been associated with an expression of rebellion against mass culture and its premier musical form, pop. By the mid-1950s, a sea change had occurred in the musical tastes of American teenagers who began punching black rhythm-and-blues plays on their juke boxes instead of the familiar pop selections, and who tended to purchase black "originals" rather than the white cover versions of the same songs served up by major record companies.[92] In postwar Britain, too, young white audiences gravitated toward blues and jazz in search of an authentic cultural ground in which to anchor their resistance to both the old social order and the new commercialism.[93] Although the musical trajectories of these subcultures eventually charted somewhat different courses—a resurgence of rock 'n' roll in mid-1960s America infused with elements of the earlier folk revival, leading to the emergence of the folk-rock idiom; a blues explosion in Britain that laced the music with elements of rock 'n' roll, yielding a new variant, blues-rock—devotees of either hybrid putatively drew from their respective traditional music sources ways of positioning themselves against the superficiality and hypocrisy associated with the dominant culture.[94] By the end of the 1960s, the new rock in Britain and the United States had spun an ethos for these musical subcultures that was pitched around the virtues of sincerity, directness, honesty, and truth to oneself.[95]

This ethos appears to have traveled with the music to the USSR in the 1970s where, in a different sociocultural context these same values would be reproduced in Soviet rock.[96] The history of rock in Russia underscores its importance as an unstoppable cultural force during the late-Soviet period, despite all attempts by the authorities to suppress, and later to co-opt and contain it.[97] Regardless of official disapproval, by the mid-1980s, there were some 160,000 rock groups active in the USSR.[98] Much of the attraction of rock music at the time resulted from its capacity to channel youthful rebellion and protest, a factor that could help to account for the importance attached to rock lyrics and, accordingly, the replacement of English-language texts by those in Russian.[99] Rock music drew on subversive associations with an idealized and much valorized "West," channeling the energies of many millions of adherents into a cultural struggle against the officially proclaimed "Soviet way of life" and, of course, against the restrictions, pretensions, and hypocrisy associated with it in youth consciousness. As was true elsewhere in the former Soviet bloc, the collapse of communism was coincident with the decline and disintegration of this movement.[100] As Alexei Yurchak put it, this collapse represented a "mutation in cultural logic from which all nonofficial art drew its inspiration and on which it based its relevance. Suddenly, the official and nonofficial symbols and meanings became equally irrelevant."[101] As the rock movement disintegrated, it opened separate spaces for those types of music that had been alloyed with it in Soviet times; among them, blues.

This sketch of the prehistory of blues in Russia highlights the fact that the version of blues music that first reached the country overwhelmingly arrived in the form of the recordings of a cohort of white performers in Britain who had themselves learned the music by listening to the records of black bluesmen in the United States.[102] It would seem probable that the British variant, which had grafted elements of rock 'n' roll onto the blues form—especially strong, simple rhythms, and powerful guitar instrumentation—would have been more accessible than "deep" or "classical" blues to Russian performers and fans already immersed in the rock idiom. Groups such as the Rolling Stones, the Animals, Cream, Led Zeppelin, and Deep Purple, along with individual artists such as Eric Clapton and Peter Green, represented for Russian players in the late and post-Soviet periods the same objects of emulation that U.S. bluesmen had previously been for these same British performers. Consequently, the import of the music via Britain not only tended to define for Russians what blues actually sounded like; it also contained a particular gender bias inserted by the masculinist tendencies apparent in the British interpretation of the music that had erased from the genre a rich tradition of blues music performed by women.[103]

As charted in subsequent chapters, much of the history of Russian blues represents a backward movement in time, away from rock 'n' roll generally and from British blues-rock and toward the sources of these music styles in the older traditional forms played by blacks in the United States. The odysseys of individual musicians reflect that pattern. Aleksei Baryshev describes his musical journey as "looking for a kind of truth. Listening to all that rock 'n' roll naturally led me to search for its truth, its source. That's what I discovered in blues, the pivotal element in rock 'n' roll, the pivot."[104] With respect to specific sources, these comments from Vladimir Berezin—guitarist with the St. Petersburg group, The Way—are representative of many of those offered by Russian bluesmen during interviews:

All of us [in the group] were familiar with the Rolling Stones, Credence [Clearwater Revival], and Grand Funk Railroad before we came to blues.

This was probably a kind of bridge for us to blues music . . . But I became less interested in playing their music or in playing rock 'n' roll generally, because it struck me as just copying what Western groups were doing. I became more interested in playing blues because of the freedom to interpret it in the way that I would want to. Hendrix was then a bridge. Later, Stevie Ray Vaughn served as another bridge . . . He was the one who opened the door for us and, going through that door, we discovered the older bluesmen, such as B. B. King.[105]

A final aspect concerning the import of blues into Russia involves the presence of networks of performers and fans who had been prepared for the music's reception in the country in the postcommunist period. Above all, this cohort was composed of individuals who had been exposed to blues outside of Russia proper, and who brought it with them on their return home or when they repatriated to Russia after the end of communism. Certainly, some Russians had discovered blues during communist times without leaving home at all. A number of interview respondents spoke of B. B. King's concerts in the USSR in 1979 in terms that suggested musical epiphanies. And some blues recordings were traded on the black market despite state repression. However, the role of that particular cohort exposed to the music because of less restrictive circumstances and who then returned to or repatriated to Russia deserves particular mention. This group is represented among those interviewed for this study by Sergei Voronov, leader of Crossroadz, who discovered blues in East Berlin as a teenager in the 1970s (his father had been stationed there as a journalist); blues diva Inessa Kataeva, who listened to blues at an early age in Hungary (her father had been posted there by the Soviet army); Vovka Kozhekin, who attended a public school in England where he was introduced to blues in the early 1990s; Valerii Belinov, who grew up in Riga where Western music of all types was far more available than it was in the Russian Republic; Levan Lomidze and Giia Dzagnidze, whose younger years in Tblisi were likewise spent under conditions in which Western music was relatively available; and Edik Tsekhanovskii, whose naval service in the 1980s and subsequent peripatetic hitchhiking and palling around with sailors in port cities brought him into contact with the blues. Given the closed character of the Soviet Union it is not surprising that blues music, rather like most Western consumer items before communism's fall, was largely hand-carried into Russia.

CHAPTER TWO

First Encounters

The advent of blues in Russia could be likened to a stubborn match run across the striking pad a few times before finally igniting. Blues eventually would catch fire in Russia too, but only after some scratching. As early as 1928, blues sounds had been incorporated into some of the jazz arrangements performed in the USSR.[1] However, these elements—"blues as used in jazz," as they have been aptly called—remained just that, never breaking free of their jazz encasement to become a distinct musical form in the country.[2] In the early 1950s, the *stiliagi* ("style hunters")—a small clutch of hipsters in Moscow whose displays of outlandish dress and hair styles provoked the wrath of the authorities—favored the songs of Paul Robeson, the American artist whose performances in the USSR in the prewar period had been a sensation, as well as jazz music in general.[3] Rock music was performed at the Sixth World Youth Festival, which Moscow hosted in 1957. It electrified the audience and immediately began to reconfigure the musical coordinates of the youth subculture away from jazz and toward rock.[4] During this time Voice of America began to include some rock 'n' roll in the programming that it beamed to the USSR.[5] Songs such as "Sixteen Tons" became enormously popular among various circles of young music buffs and have survived today in the repertoires of performing groups. However, these early incursions of rock music in the 1950s would pale to insignificance when measured against the impact of the British invasion in the 1960s. Particularly because of the pronounced blues content in the music of such groups as the Rolling Stones, the Animals, the Yardbirds, and others, it was British rockers who first brought the blues to Russia.

Functioning as an import-export concern, the British bands not only served as a kind of bridge, making the blues accessible to an otherwise uninitiated Russian audience but, as already noted, they also put their own stamp on the music. As such, what counted for blues in the consciousness of most Russian performers and audiences for many years to come would be its guitar-driven, rockish variant perfected in the 1960s and 1970s in the United Kingdom. Valerii Belinov remembered the scene in Riga during the 1970s:

Myself and other musicians at the time did not much distinguish between the different styles played by, say, the Rolling Stones or the Animals—rock 'n' roll, blues, and so forth. I don't think that we distinguished at all. The main thing was the music itself, a new music for us, music from the West . . . It was just rock [to us], that's all.[6]

Nikolai Arutiunov recalled that time in this way:

I started listening to the Beatles in the latter part of the 1960s and I bet that there is not much separating me from many other children in Western Europe at that time. And I listened to the Rolling Stones and I think that is where my love for blues started. They became my favorite group because of the beat they had, and the Beatles were now secondary . . . My first real influences along these lines were British blues, particularly John Mayall, Alexis Korner, Graham Bond, and all these guys. It was only after that that I began to listen to black blues players. First we heard those people, and then we began to think about where they got their music.[7]

In the recollections of Vladimir Berezin, it was the blues-rock of Led Zeppelin and Deep Purple that inspired him to play. "But after a while," he remarked, "Deep Purple became less interesting to me. When I heard their 'Smoke on the Water' album [*Machine Head*, 1972], I said to myself, 'This is something that I'm less interested in.' Perhaps because I was already introduced to blues by Deep Purple's earlier music, I began to enjoy blues. When they changed direction, I didn't follow them."[8] Moscow DJ and blues critic, Aleksei Kalachev reflected on the same theme:

For the older generation of bluesmen in Russia today, their roots are in that particular music that was so popular in the 1970s: blues-rock. And that blues-rock was, of course, overwhelmingly [performed by] English groups like Ten Years After, Free, Eric Clapton, and Cream. To think about opening the country to real blues music at that time, the 1970s, was simply impossible.[9]

That moment would not arrive for nearly another two decades.

Early Exposures and Initial Trends

At the end of the 1960s, three Muscovites formed a group oriented toward blues-rock. The three were grandsons of Old Bolsheviks who had been members of the Soviet Politburo: Alik Mikoian and Stas Namin (both of whose grandfather was Anastas Mikoian) and Grigorii Ordzhonikidze (grandson of G. K. Ordzhonikidze). These young men resided in the well-known House on the Embankment, a massive structure positioned across the Moscow River from the Kremlin that had been commissioned by Stalin to house the top elite (many of whom would count their next address as the Gulag). Due to the privileges and contacts enjoyed by these scions of the Soviet establishment, the three were able to acquire things that were unimaginable for others; in this case, information about Western music trends, records, and electric guitars. Consequently, in the basement of the House on the Embankment, in the very bowels of the repressive communist state, Russia's first blues-rock band rehearsed the tunes of the Rolling Stones, themselves often covers of American blues songs by such greats as Muddy Waters and Howlin' Wolf. On a few occasions, the band managed to perform publicly for dances at student clubs.

In early 1970, a second blues-rock group formed in another quarter of the capital. Dubbing itself *Udachnoe priobretenie* (A Fortunate Acquisition), the group was led by guitarist and vocalist Aleksei Belov, and featured Vladimir Matetskii on bass and vocals, and Mikhail Sokolov on drums. Referring to the members' family backgrounds, Belov quipped: "You could have called us 'Children of the KGB,' because my mother was then a KBG lieutenant, Matetskii's mothers was a KGB captain, and the drummer's father was a KGB major."[10] Modeling itself on the British power-trio, Cream, Udachnoe priobretenie built its repertoire on rock 'n' roll and blues numbers that had been recorded on tape or "on the bones," an underground Soviet invention employing spent X-ray plates as a substitute for vinyl discs.[11] The singularly important influence on Belov's musical horizon was *Fleetwood Mac in Chicago* (1969), an LP put out by the fledgling British group recording at Chess Records with a number of their U.S. blues heroes: Otis Spann, Willie Dixon, Walter Horton, Buddy Guy, Honeyboy Edwards, and others. The group rehearsed songs from that album in a basement room of an educational institute, rounding out their repertoire with rock 'n' roll standards such as "Great Balls of Fire" and three original compositions sung in English. Later, in 1974, Alik Mikoian joined the band on harmonica and vocals.

The parental-political associations of the band's members enabled them to perform for a number of student dances in the 1970s sponsored by the Komsomol (Communist Union of Youth). These often riotous affairs were always packed and sometimes witnessed serious injury to disappointed entrance-seekers: young men bashing closed glass doors with their skulls; young women impaled on the spikes atop the fences that they had attempted to scale.[12] In these Komsomol venues, the band would blast rock and blues at audiences stunned and entranced by the effect of the music. Here were the rarest of instruments at the time, electric guitars, producing for Russian listeners literally unheard of sounds. Young men would push as closely as possible to the stage—in fact, as closely as possible to the guitar strings themselves—in order to catch a glimpse of the musicians in action. Unlike comparable scenes in, say, a U.S. blues club, they were not squeezing up to the musicians in order to steal licks from a hot guitar player: they simply wanted to see how the strange and wondrous sounds were made.

Fortunately, a tape has survived from one such performance and has been recently released as a CD.[13] "Fortunately," here, refers both to the fact that the recording itself was made unintentionally and to its subsequent recovery. Originally, a reel-to-reel tape recorder had been hooked up to the band's equipment at a Komsomol dance to produce an echo effect for the vocals. That effort failed, but the tape recorder remained on and inadvertently caught most of the performance. Belov took it home and stashed it in a cubbyhole above his kitchen door. There it had lain for some twenty-six years, lost and forgotten, until Belov—rummaging for some old Johnny Winter tapes—to his great surprise pulled it out of its resting place.[14] Naturally, the technical quality of the recording leaves much to be desired; but the energy, spirit, and full-tilt drive of the music impresses even today.

It was also during the 1970s that another version of blues music began to be performed in Russia—something in the local vernacular dubbed "hippie blues." This music can be described as a folk-inflected variety of country blues played on acoustic instruments. Initially, its principal inspiration seems to have been some of Janis Joplin's recordings. Igor' Vdovchenko became the leading exponent of this Joplin-style hippie blues, but he was followed by many others.[15] Vdovchenko's band—Blues Street Friends—derived its name from their itinerant performances on the streets of many of the USSR's major cities, not infrequently changing personnel due to chance encounters with other street musicians. This music represented for its devotees more than a sound. It intoned an entire lifestyle. Sonorously, it articulated much of their hippie philosophy, becoming one of the more pronounced musical currents coursing through that sizeable 1970s and early 1980s subculture known as *sistema* ("the system"). *Sistema* consisted of an archipelago of apartments, street scenes, and cafes whose denizens had turned their backs on the established order and sought to create their own society based on authenticity, trust, and freedom. Their resistance to the Soviet system was thus both indirect and total. Unlike political dissidents in those years, they mounted no overt challenges to the authorities, instead preferring to separate themselves as much as possible from the official world by means of such practices as "internal migration," the replication or creation within their immediate surroundings of some imagined locale better suited to the fulfillment of aspirations to live meaningful lives. With marked indifference to propriety and the trappings of success, the members of *sistema* sported their shabby attire as a countercultural badge of honor, resembling a "spiritual aristocracy that masqueraded as lumpen proletariat."[16] They could travel to effectively any large city in Russia and some other parts of the USSR and would be welcomed and housed by other members, regardless of the fact that they were total strangers. Hippie slang functioned as the indispensable badge of membership and password for admission.[17]

Hippies like music, and hippie blues proved a favorite in this subculture. Aleksei Agranovskii described those days with particular fondness:

> I began to play in a group while I was at university. It wasn't a serious group, but it brought me into contact with a lot of Moscow musicians. I would call them Moscow hippie musicians. We would just play in the kitchen—all night until the early morning. And the music we liked to play most, in fact the music that we always played, was blues . . . That atmosphere is just something that is not going to exist anymore. It was very intellectual, exceptionally friendly; people were always ready to help one another. There were long sessions discussing books—Tolstoy, Garcia Marquez, Dostoevsky, O'Henry. We talked about Buddhist philosophy, we talked about Jimi Hendrix, we talked about Led Zeppelin, we talked about Tchaikovsky . . . There was this one guy, Misha Guzhov, who was a completely crazy person, a real hippie. He just lived from apartment to apartment, didn't work and was always cooking up some new equipment— wah-wah pedals and stuff he made himself. He even played blues on the sitar. Now you won't find such people. Now people are more concerned with making money. We had this open and honest and uncorrupted relationship with the music. You find a few people around like that today, but few, very few.[18]

This style of blues was especially well represented in Leningrad, and is discussed in greater detail in chapter 5. Here, it will suffice to mark the convergence of the blues form with Leningrad's art-rock scene of the 1970s and 1980s when the city had effectively become the capital of Soviet rock. Hippie blues was represented above all in the repertoire of Leningrad's Zoopark whose leader, Mike Naumenko, composed a number of poetic lyrics in the genre of youthful exploration and protest that he set to simple blues musical forms. As with the compositions of another well-known Leningrader, Boris Grebenshchikov—who also employed some blues forms in his song writing—a serious engagement with blues itself was not evident in Naumenko's music. The instrumentation was weak and his music's rhythmic structures were undeveloped. Rather, Naumenko simply appropriated the blues form as a suitable vehicle for his music's principal component—self-reflective, satiric, and ironic verse. His style served as another bridge to blues music, especially for some in *sistema*, such as Edik Tsekhanovskii, who were residing in the provinces and effectively cut off from information about blues music itself.[19] Naumenko's poetic songs in Russian became favorites in the hippie underground, thereby accustoming those who played his music to some of the standard elements of blues.

Naumenko is remembered for the sincerity and authenticity of his music, aspects of blues that surface many times in this study. Vitalii Andreev remarked on Naumenko's influence during an interview:

> You could call him [Naumenko] a blues player or a rock 'n' roll player. He sang in Russian and he wrote his music in Russian. He was a prophet and in his work you will find "notes of language" that touch the soul—just like in blues. He lived as he felt, and this was not during the freest period of our history, but it is precisely these unfree periods that give birth to people who struggle against the current and who use their creative capacities to do it. And this concerns his own dignity as an individual and the dignity of so many individuals who, like him, died early.[20]

These thoughts are emblematic of the way in which many in Russia's blues community recall the importance that rock and blues held for them during the communist period. But it is not just the repression that they remember. Deprivation and a dogged determination to overcome it figure heavily in their recollections. Instruments for many of today's leading blues players were then simply unobtainable. During our interview Mikhail Sokolov appeared to take obvious pride in showing me the work bench in his bedroom where he learned to rebuild harmonicas and to rig up harmonica microphones. Valerii Belinov related a magical tale—set in guitar-barren Riga of the early 1970s—about serendipitously acquiring parts from a variety of unlikely sources, enabling him to build his first instrument.[21] Similarly Boris Bulkin, remembered his passion as a thirteen-year-old to acquire an electric guitar. "But having the wish," he pointed out:

> is one thing, and having the actual possibility, another. So what do I do? I decided to do it myself. I had a friend who knew something about this stuff and we built guitars together. In his case it didn't work—a big split developed in the guitar and it collapsed. I got lucky. My guitar sagged a bit, but it could still be played. Much later, at the end of the '70s, I bought a Czech

and then an East German brand. Then my trio entered a competition in which we took second place. From that I acquired a Korean guitar, which was an enormous help to me and my music.[22]

Some musicians mentioned their forays into the black market to acquire blues and rock LPs or cassettes. Nikolai Arutiunov remembered this experience:

In 1973 I managed to find that place where people would gather to exchange and sell black market records. Quite often the police would come and they would confiscate the records themselves and people would be arrested. In my case, they wrote a letter about my behavior to the institution where I was studying; engaging in black market activity, black market trade. Thereafter, things went badly for me at the institution. For all practical purposes, I was considered an American spy. This sounds like a joke, but I was understood to be a subversive agent. I didn't go to prison, but it is also very unpleasant when a policeman apprehends you and you face these consequences where you live and work.[23]

These adversities intensified the importance of the music for many of our respondents, a matter emphasized by Aleksei Belov in his description of those times.

It was then not so much the sound but the spirit. Playing that type of music could land you in jail or in the crazy house. But the thing for people then was that we lived, we lived close to one another. Not as casual friends but as comrades-in-arms. For us, a pair of blue jeans was not so much a pair of pants but an ideology, an entire world-view.[24]

Similarly, Aleksei Agranovskii recounts how as:

young guys, first-year university students, we got hold of a Jimi Hendrix album. We sat up the entire night listening to it and assessing every note. No one knew what he was singing about, no one could catch a single word. It was just the sound. We would assess every note, every sound, and we took our pleasure [kaif] from this. In those times, music was the most precious thing in our lives and when people began to listen to this music, they effectively would go into opposition against the authorities [vlasti].[25]

As Agranovskii's comments on Jimi Hendrix suggest, many Russians at this time got their first taste of blues music inadvertently, simply by listening to a variety of rock with a streak of blues in it. Some would seek out and pursue the blues sound that they heard on these recordings, remembering later how the work of one or another artist in particular led them across the threshold. Giia Dzagnidze recalled that when growing up in Tblisi—whose less restrictive atmosphere meant that Western music was relatively plentiful—he had listened to lots of British blues-rock. "But the person who just paralyzed me," he emphasized, "was Jimi Hendrix. When I heard his guitar on [the song] 'Red House', that made the difference for me. It was probably my first encounter with blues. After that, I started to listen to Muddy Waters."[26] Aleksei Kalachev's blues epiphany began in the 1970s as a search for the roots of rock 'n' roll. "This search," he explained:

> eventually led me to the home of a very well-known journalist, Vladimir Posner, who now does televised broadcasts on ORT [Russian Public Television]. He had spent the first part of his life in America, and he brought a large collection of records back to Russia. You have to remember that at the time, in the early '80s, there was only a small group of people, a few dozen, who had access to some blues records. Well, we were working together at the time and on one occasion he showed me this collection that he had. He lent me a few records—I remember in particular some by Big Bill Broonzy—and the effect was for me a real earthquake. I understood from this collection where rock 'n' roll had come from, as we say in Russian, "how the legs grow" [kak rastut nogi].[27]

B. B. King's Soviet tour in 1979 was a seminal event for a number of Russia's budding blues players, their first encounter with pure blues performed live by one of the genre's living legends. Both Belov and Arutiunov have remembered their reaction to B. B. King's performance as a "shock" filled with delight, a sound both immediately arresting and unfathomable.[28] It convinced Arutiunov to follow through on his idea of starting a blues group. Dzagnidze saw B. B. King in Tblisi and has recalled being "shaken" by the performance. "It was the way he communicated with people, not only with his singing—which is terrific—but with his guitar. It was the way that he spoke to people with his guitar."[29] B. B. King's tour, like that of Gatemouth Brown in summer 1979, was like another message in a bottle that arrived from abroad, bringing discrete bits of information about blues to an inchoate Russian blues community, which they would subsequently fashion into their understanding of the music and their own performances of it.

Incongruously, B. B. King's tour coincided with a period of political and cultural repression that pushed domestic rock 'n' roll and blues to the margins of public existence. Aleksandr Tsar'kov, a blues-rock musician who would be among the founders of Moscow's Arbat Blues Club in the early '90s, would date the start of the repression with that "clean up" that Moscow endured as part of the preparation for the 1980 Olympic Games.

> Cleaning up the city and Brezhnev's final years, too, were periods of cultural repression. It is actually funny to look back on those years now. The group, Bravo, which is very popular these days, playing light rock 'n' roll or twist music, was number one on the list of prohibited groups in the '80s. That's true of other groups that you can see performing on TV today. They were in no way whatsoever political, but nonetheless they found themselves on the list of prohibited groups . . . A lot of people put up their instruments during these times, the period of stagnation. They just took regular jobs.[30]

In the chilly political climate, Udachnoe priobretenie could no longer count on Komsomol connections to get gigs. The band managed to survive by taking jobs at restaurants which, under Russia cultural conditions, would represent a blow to any serious musician's status.[31] Another group, Liga bliuza had just formed amid these dispiriting circumstances. Its early history would be testimony to them.

In 1979, Sergei Voronov, who had recently returned to the USSR after spending his childhood and adolescence in East Berlin listening to and performing rock and blues, was introduced to Nikolai Arutiunov by a mutual friend, Sergei Mnatskanov.[32] They began to rehearse together—Voronov on guitar, Arutiunov on piano and vocals—a rock repertoire (with a few rhythm and blues numbers thrown in) at the Oil and Gas Institute's House of Culture, adding bass and drums along the way. Their patrons there liked the music and enlisted the four-piece group to play for their Revolution Day holiday concert—memorable for its lackluster reception and complete with an inebriate mounting the stage to tell the boys to stop playing Bach. Voronov, dissatisfied with the repertoire—Arutiunov was oriented to rhythm and blues but felt that they were not yet ready to play this music in public—left and formed another band, *Galleriia* (Gallery) with acquaintances from an art institute. Both bands played a few jobs together for another institute-based club directed by Mnatskanov, while Arutiunov's group continued to rehearse at the Oil and Gas Institute, occasionally performing at dances held at the Institute's "red corner," under the proviso that no blues was to be played. Christened Liga bliuza (Blues League) in 1981, the band found itself performing only soft rock. However, the urge to play rhythm and blues would not be stilled and the band became progressively less inclined to uphold its end of the bargain. Within a few months, they were expelled from the premises. Mnatskanov rescued the group by securing them a venue at the youth club attached to the Kalibr factory. There, they performed a combination of blues and rock to a small (fifty to one hundred people) but steadfast audience for some four years. As the situation began to deteriorate politically even more, in 1984, the authorities at the Kalibr factory turned to censoring the band's lyrics, a prelude to terminating their performances altogether.

Perestroika Blues

When the Soviet regime launched perestroika in 1985, its opening to the West and the concomitant relaxation of domestic repression released an explosion of popular music throughout the USSR. Unmistakably, this explosion concerned rock first and foremost. Yet it also kindled for some an interest in blues music that would contribute directly to Russia's blues boom in the next decade. Two aspects of perestroika are of particular importance in this respect: the political tilt away from the repression of Western popular music and its domestic exponents, and toward official sponsorship for those performing it; and the curtailment of state censorship, such that streams of information about various types of contemporary music, blues among them, began to flow into and throughout the country.

With respect to the expansion of the opportunities to perform in public, Aleksandr Tsar'kov remembers, in particular, the relative novelty of music festivals that sprung up throughout the country during the perestroika period.

> Groups would come to Moscow from Belarus, from Ukraine, from the Baltic republics, and we would play at their festivals, too. And there was lots of music played on the street. At that time, everyone was filled with the idea of new music and new possibilities for expression and for just making new friends. Since I was playing keyboards then with the group, *Zolotaia seredina* (Golden Mean), I got the chance to travel a lot, to the Baltic, to Georgia, all over the country. These were usually big events with many thousands of people attending. Prices were ridiculously low in those days.[33]

The improvement in conditions meant that Udachnoe priobretenie was able to leave the restaurants where they had been playing. Soon, they found themselves performing frequently and in huge halls, so crowded that "you couldn't even fight your way into them."[34]

A good illustration of the changing climate and of the new possibilities opened for blues music can be taken from the history of Liga bliuza in this period. Particularly evident in this instance would be the association between professionalism and the commercial opportunities afforded by perestroika. Leaving the underground to perform in large venues, to tour at home and abroad, to record, and to have their songs popularized over radio, as well as to appear on television—all of these new endeavors made possible by perestroika naturally stimulated the group to raise the level of their musicianship and to perfect their showmanship on stage. Inasmuch as a number of prominent Russian bluesmen of the nineties honed their skills while playing in Liga bliuza in the 1980s—in particular, Boris Bulkin, the group's guitar player from 1981 to 1986, and his replacement, Sergei Voronov, who played with the band from 1987 to 1989—this group was of seminal importance for the blues boom to come. However, in the early years of perestroika, the nature of the new opportunities remained altogether unclear and it was anyone's guess how long they might last.

Early in 1986, Liga bliuza got its first sizeable public exposure at a rock show staged at the concert hall attached to the Dinamo factory. Although the group's hard-driving delivery of rhythm and blues electrified the audience, the authorities took a dimmer view of the proceedings.[35] Midway through the band's seventh number, the management pulled the plugs on their amplifiers and expelled them from the stage, claiming it necessary to call a halt to the "*bezobrazie*" (literally "without form," this Russian word connotes rank deformity, unbridled outrageousness, and running amok beyond all limits). Nonetheless, heartened by the crowd's enthusiastic response, the group decided that it was time to record. Arutiunov, then working in a division of the state's recording monopoly, Melodiia, was able to secure studio time for the band which completed the recording of an album in fall in 1986. It was not released, however, until five years later, all the songs rerecorded with new personnel.[36] At that time, however, with success both tantalizingly close and yet frustratingly out of reach, the band disintegrated. (see fig. 1)

At roughly the same time, Voronov returned to Moscow from his sojourn with the Stas Namin Group, having toured the United States, Europe, and Japan, as well as the USSR. Armed with a bottle of vodka, Arutiunov paid him a visit and spoke plaintively of his band's untimely collapse. The two decided that the time had arrived to restart the blues project that had brought them together some eight years earlier, especially because of Voronov's close association with Stas Namin who then, as the impresario of Soviet rock, maintained a veritable stable of the country's best players at his musical center and recording studio in Gorky Park. Namin made good on his previous promise to Voronov to assist him in as-

Figure 1. The mockish cover of Liga bliuza's 1991 album parodies the pomp and circumstance of Communist Party gatherings, a favorite target for the times. Here the band, led by Nikolai Arutiunov with mike in hand, performs amid the transformed surroundings of a Party Congress: the placard on the left asserts "Long Live Rhythm and Blues" (attributed to Muddy Waters) instead of the customary "Long Live Communism"; the towering figure of Lenin has been replaced by that of Muddy Waters, just as the heads of Paul Butterfield, Jimi Hendrix, and Eric Clapton occupy the places previously reserved for Marx, Engels, and Lenin.

sembling a band devoted to blues, supplying a reincarnated Liga bliuza with a seasoned rhythm section, a sax, and keyboard player and putting them on the concert circuit. After performing at the First Moscow Festival of Blues and Rock 'n' Roll in 1987, the band set off on tours of the USSR, Sweden, Columbia, and Peru. Soon they hit the airwaves. In March 1988, their demo got some play on Radio Yunost'; in August, they represented the USSR on the international television event "Save the Children"; in September, they performed on the USSR's most popular television show, *Vzgliad*.

In 1989, the band's *"Iiul'skii bliuz"* ("July Blues") became a hit, receiving copious radio play around the Soviet Union and boosting sales of the Melodiia anthology LP on which it appeared. However, the excessive touring schedule had caused some personal difficulties in the group. Voronov left, and was followed by others. The band reformed in 1990 to recut their unreleased LP and then devoted itself to covering old Cream material. In 1992, Liga bliuza went through another reincarnation, appearing now as an eleven-piece unit, complete with horn section and a group of female backup vocalists. With this contingent in place, the group redirected their energies toward performing straight rhythm and blues (with great success).[37]

In addition to the opportunities provided for public performances, the perestroika period represented an unprecedented influx of information about blues music that laid much of the foundation for that music's development in the 1990s. When the first video rentals opened in the USSR in the late 1980s, three recent U.S. films appeared that quickly caused a sensation among budding blues performers and fans. One was a live concert, *B. B. King and Friends* (1991) (with Paul Butterfield, Stevie Ray Vaughn, Albert King, Eric Clapton, and others), that introduced innumerable young Russians to the sight, as well as the sound, of blues music. This video was copied and recopied endless times, instantly becoming a standard point of reference for those attracted to the music. More than a decade later, it could still be seen on wide-screen TVs in Russian blues clubs, filling the dead time between sets. Likewise, the films *The Blues Brothers* (1980) and, especially, *Crossroads* (1986) captured the imagination of numerous aspiring musicians. In the words of Vania Zhuk, *Crossroads* was "a milestone for every bluesman in Russia, especially of the younger generation."[38] Sasha Suvorov has recalled that after working as an artist for some eight years, he "saw by complete accident the film, *Crossroads*, and heard that harmonica in the movie along with Ry Cooder's guitar," realizing immediately that his life's desire was to play blues.[39]

In the late '80s, blues recordings began to become generally available to Soviet listeners for the first time. In St. Petersburg, Edik Tsekhanovskii had his initial encounter with blues in 1988, thanks to a pirated copy of a Muddy Waters album. As he tells it:

He made a very, very strong impression on me. That was right away what I wanted to play, what I wanted to learn. I can't say that I could play it on the guitar from the very first. That took a long time to learn. But my immediate reaction to the music was very positive and very strong. Then I came across a whole series of blues discs put out in Bulgaria. All Chicago blues: Big Joe Williams, Memphis Slim, and some old blues players, too. Like Son House—oh, he is really terrific.[40]

In far-off Novosibirsk, Mikhail Mishuris was surprised one evening in late 1986 by a friend who had just returned from a Finnish publisher's exhibition in town where he had purchased a bundle of LPs put out by a Finnish firm, all reissues from the Chess Records Blues Masters series. "The first one that I heard," Mishuris would later recall:

was Howlin' Wolf. It was incredible. And, after that, Melodiia brought out its own series: Howlin' Wolf, then Muddy Waters, Buddy Guy, and Otis Rush. I bought them all immediately. The jacket of the Howlin' Wolf album is still on my kitchen wall.[41]

The growing availability of blues recordings made possible a popularization of the music that itself increased exponentially once it became possible to play blues over Soviet radio. Combining his interests in Latin culture and blues music, Aleksei Kalachev began narrating a weekly program that included blues, rock, and Spanish music.[42] In 1987, Andrei Evdokimov developed the first radio program devoted exclusively to blues. Nationally broadcast in hourly installments twice per month on Soviet radio's Channel One, his "About Blues"—soon rechristened "All This Blues" (*"Ves'etot bliuz"*) when Evdokimov decided to ignore the admonition of his editor and appropriated the right to name his own show— brought this music to countless new listeners scattered over the USSR's eleven time zones. In Leningrad, Volodia Rusinov became devoted to the program. "It meant a lot to the blues community," he remembers:

many of Evdokimov's radio broadcasts were taped and they are still around in my house. We learned from the records that he played. We would tape and transcribe them, and then play these songs. The show created a great atmosphere. You would have your friends over on a Saturday or some weeknight and listen to the blues show on the radio. Afterward, things would be a little different. You found yourself playing better, more in tune with the blues atmosphere.[43]

Mishuris and his bandmates listened to the show faithfully in Novosibirsk; in Donetsk in Ukraine, the popular rock group, *Dikii med* (Wild Honey), tuned into Evdokimov's blues show and altered their musical direction accordingly. From Sakhalin Island in the Soviet Far East, a letter reached Evdokimov reporting that because of the eight-hour time difference from Moscow, appreciative young fans were forced to miss their Monday morning lessons in order to catch his broadcasts. They remained faithfully truant. In 1989, Radio Maiak also signed Evdokimov for an hour-long national broadcast featuring blues and commentary on a weekly basis. Within two years, similar engagements with Radio Rocks and SNC Radio brought to four the number of radio stations featuring "All This Blues," airing as often as five times per week. In 1991, Radio Maximum, a joint Russian-American venture on the FM dial, also added an hour-long blues show—"Blues Bag"—to its weekly programming.

During perestroika, the problem was no longer that radio stations were unwilling to play blues—plenty of new stations looking for programming were happy to include it—but the relative dearth of material to play. Evdokimov, having exhausted both his private collection of blues records and tapes, as well as the collections of his friends in Moscow from whom he had been borrowing, was replenished from abroad. The U.S.-based music magazine, *Living Blues*, published a letter sent them by Evdokimov in early 1992 and readers from the United States and Australia responded to it by mailing him ample supplies of blues on CD and cassette. Commercial firms responded as well: Alligator Records sent him all their latest releases; Mike Kappus of Point Blank Records came through with a hefty package of their CDs; and Yazoo Records contributed three LPs of early Delta blues, a great rarity for Russia at the time.

Russia's exposure to blues that occurred during perestroika signaled a watershed in the country's apprehension and appreciation of this music. Contrary to a widespread (mis)understanding—one enshrined in the *Great Soviet Encyclopedia*—blues turned out to include a great deal more than "the lyrical songs of American Negroes [played] in a slow tempo."[44] Blues was neither jazz improvisation nor rock-guitar fireworks. It was more than British blues-rock—although it was that, too—and had its own deep and rich history that invited exploration. To the amazement of its organizers, these new understandings came together in unanticipated ways at the First Moscow Blues Festival, convened within weeks of the USSR's disappearance.

CHAPTER THREE

Moscow Blues: Musicians and Their Music

During the Soviet period and afterward, Moscow has been the country's capital in the political, economic, educational, and cultural spheres. To use an American analogy, the city could be regarded as Russia's equivalent of Washington, D.C., New York, and Boston, all rolled into one. With respect to the blues, this concentration of activities supplied a niche for the music, making Moscow something of a Russian Chicago as well. At the beginning of the 1990s, Moscow had the country's largest cohort of blues-oriented musicians and it attracted many more from other parts of the former USSR as the decade progressed. The city also had by far the largest contingent of U.S. and European residents whose numbers were expanded enormously by the influx of young men and women from the West in the 1990s who had come to seek their fortunes in the new business opportunities afforded by the introduction of capitalism, and in the numerous Western aid agencies that had set up shop in town, offering advice and training, and administering research grants and startup funding for successful Russian applicants. In their home countries, many of these young people had participated in the 1980s blues revival that had introduced a new generation of Americans and Europeans to the music. Their patronage of Moscow's new blues clubs helped to sustain these fledging enterprises both financially and socially. During the early 1990s, a sizeable group of Westerners frequenting a given nightspot would connect it immediately to an imaginary social register consulted by status-conscious New Russians. Whether signaling by their very presence which clubs trend-seekers should visit or simply bringing their Russian acquaintances along for an evening of music, Westerners played a critical role in supporting Moscow's emerging nightclub economy which provided dozens of venues at which local blues bands could perform.

In the following chapter, we examine that nightclub economy, along with other media through which blues music has been transmitted in Russia. Here, our attention turns to the musicians and their music. The discussion begins with the First Moscow Blues Festival (17–19 January 1992), an event which represented, among other things, a gathering of bands from Russia and the western regions of the former Soviet Union at which various small groups of people—engaged in similar projects but scattered across the country and thus largely unaware of what others had been doing—came into contact with one another for the first time. In this respect, the festival would be reminiscent of similar conclaves of political and social activists held some five years earlier. In either instance, encounters with hitherto unknown others who had been pursuing comparable projects and interests in relative isolation proved exhilarating. It validated one's own efforts, induced a spirit of camaraderie and a feeling of participation in a common enterprise much larger than previously imagined, inspiring many to redouble their commitment to projects whose meanings were underscored by the fact that they now seemed parts of a larger whole.[1]

This chapter charts the musical directions of Moscow bluesmen across the 1990s and into the new century. In this respect, we outline a progression in their music: first, "backward" toward a deeper appreciation of blues traditions and roots; later, "forward" toward new syntheses of blues with other musical forms, among them, native Russian idioms. Throughout, the intention is to represent the Moscow blues scene as a community, one composed of individuals and distinct groups whose separate directions were profoundly influenced by the actions, decisions, and projects of others around them. These musical interactions took two general forms: mimicry and emulation, on one hand; the construction of difference and the search for distinction, on the other. Taken together, they accounted for a steady expansion in the number of blues styles performed by Moscow bands and for palpable improvements in their renditions of them.

The First Blues Festival

The principal organizer of the First Moscow Blues Festival was Aleksandr Demidov, a young naturalist, explorer, and blues fan from Moscow, who got the idea of staging a festival while having a kitchen chat with guitarist Sergei Voronov, by then leading his own band, Crossroadz. Demidov teamed up with television editor and talent scout, Elena Karpova, who knew a number of Moscow bluesmen personally and who put out the call to invite others by word of mouth. Additional players, who had heard about the festival third- or fourth-hand, just showed up and asked to participate on the spot. They were also accommodated. In all, about twenty-five groups played at the festival, thirteen of which appeared on the double LP—and eleven on the CD—recorded at the event.[2]

Not a few factors combined to hamper the organizers' efforts. One was the weather. On the eve of the festival, heavy snows hit the capital, accompanied by arctic blasts that sent the mercury plummeting. The event was staged in north Moscow at the Izmailova Sports Complex, constructed for the 1980 Olympics. Reaching this relatively remote venue in the face of the inclement weather called for some effort, especially because the copious snowfall had stilled surface public transport. But long treks over tundra-like terrain did not appear to chill the fans' enthusiasm. On opening day, about five thousand people trundled into the gelid Sports Complex.

Another problem was the organizers' complete lack of experience in staging such an event. This was apparent in their choices for situating ticket booths without any thought of using them as choke points to restrict access to the premises. As a result, as many as half of the fans were able to revive that longstanding practice celebrated in the days of the Soviet underground: free admission. Likewise, arrangements for paying the musicians were haphazard. Widespread gate-crashing had left a hole in the expected receipts that was not at all filled by the modest contributions from the festival's sponsors, the Russian Industrial-Trading Company and the Tiumen and Moscow Exchange "Hermes." As a result, only a fraction of the bands could be paid in cash. Fortunately, another sponsor, Tverskoe Beer, delivered a few truckloads of their product—a prized commodity at the time, owing to the fact that the only beer then available in Moscow was prohibitively priced imports. Consequently, many unpaid Moscow bluesmen were able to console themselves by trucking home cases of the beverage, stacking them high in their small apartments as liquid reminders of the event. A shortage of funds had also meant that the festival proceeded without any advertising. There was a mention of the event on radio, but the greater part of the turnout seemed entirely due to word of mouth.

Inside the hall, fans experienced three days of delight at the novelty of blues performed in a "normal" venue, rather than in private apartments, as had been the rule. The crowd's high spirits, however, were not always matched by a high level of technical proficiency or blues acumen among the performers. Heavy rock rhythms dominated the sound of most groups. Moreover, it would be more than a stretch to describe some of the performances as belonging to the blues genre at all.[3] The group, Ultimate Thule, for example, played in a hard-rock style just short of heavy metal, while Veto Bank performed in a pop vein. Nonetheless, the center of gravity and the center of attention was the blues. Crossroadz, Udachnoe priobretenie, and Liga bliuza scored the biggest successes, even though prevailing conventions still mandated a reserved reaction from the listeners—polite applause to express the appreciation of a serious audience listening to serious music.

Aside from the combination of so many groups in one event—all of which were at least nominally performing blues—the biggest novelty of the festival was the harmonica playing of Mikhail Sokolov, Udachnoe priobretenie's drummer, who had recently taken up this quintessentially blues instrument. Because the electric guitar had previously been the only lead instrument in rock and blues ensembles, Sokolov's harp created a sensation. Hammering blues notes to an enchanted audience—effectively none of whom had ever heard blues played live on harmonica before—he both captivated his listeners and mapped some new territory in Russian blues that others would be quick to explore.

The results of the festival included the double LP (with an issue of five thousand copies) and a related CD (in smaller edition) that were recorded on site. The LP sold out quickly. NTV television, Russia's new independent channel, covered the event, broadcasting half-hour segments of performances and interviews with musicians, organizers, and fans over the three-day span of the festival. Demidov tapped his acquaintances in the world of journalism to cover the proceedings, resulting in a few newspaper articles on the performances that broadened the music's public exposure. Nonetheless, the festival generated more enthusiasm than it did commercial possibilities for the bands involved. In the Moscow of that day, there was still—outside of the occasional concert hall appearance or the odd gig at a newly established punk/biker bar—no place to play. The next stage of development came, after a yearlong hiatus, with the opening of the Arbat Blues Club, an initiative indirectly traceable to the festival's success.

Early Bloomers

We can assemble the individual groups participating in Moscow's blues boom of the 1990s into a kind of mosaic, each band forming one piece of the whole. Such is the attempt in figure 2, which situates eighteen of Moscow's leading blues groups according to their respective orientations to various blues styles (vertical axis) along a time line running from 1991 to 2000 (horizontal axis). The vectors appended to some groups connote a change in their musical directions over this period. We begin with those groups flush on the left-hand column of figure 2—our "early bloomers"—that represent the first generation of Russian bluesmen, dividing by means of the vertical axis those eight bands into two subsets according to their respective styles, whether rock-oriented or based more on traditional blues genres.

The bands appearing in the lower-left column of figure 2—Udachnoe priobretenie, Crossroadz, Liga bliuza, and Chernyi khleb i Doktor Agranovskii—were all heavily influenced by British blues-rock, perhaps above all by the Rolling Stones. Instrumentally, they fashioned their sound after the guitar wizardry exhibited by players such as Jimi Hendrix, Eric Clapton, Peter Green, and (early) Johnny Winter. Heavy guitar drive would thus define these four groups. Their exposure to blues had come from British bands and, as individuals who had taken up the music during Soviet times, they had little, if any, opportunity to seek out the sources of the music that the Stones and others were playing. Without much opportunity to hear the recordings of the original artists whose songs the Stones had covered—much less to listen to those same artists in live performance—the tendency among these Russian bluesmen could be characterized as mimicking those who mimicked the originals. Consequently, this segment of the first generation of Russian bluesmen began by reproducing in their own music the same rock-based sound that they had heard on British records. As information on the sources of blues music became more accessible in the 1990s these Russian bands changed directions accordingly. Nonetheless, in many cases the transition was not a smooth one. These groups had already been playing the blues as they knew it. And what they thought that they knew could constitute an impediment to further development. Sometimes, information revealing the limited nature of their enterprise came as a disquieting and unwelcome shock. For example, Mikhail Sokolov recalls sitting down with his longtime friend and former bandmate, Aleksei Belov, to have a listen to a Bukka White album that he had just acquired. Belov was nonplussed. "'What's that?' he said. 'That's not blues. B. B. King is blues, but that's not blues. Johnny Winter is blues. I can't even listen to this stuff. I don't even think that the guitar is tuned. In general, it's not even music.'"[4] The limits of Moscow's received wisdom were also apparent in the case of Alik Mikoian of *Serebrianyi rubl'* (Silver Ruble) (placed in the upper-left quadrant of figure 2) who had performed Robert Johnson's "Love in Vain" for many years, but along the lines of the Rolling Stones' rendition of the song. Curiously, the particular Stones LP from which he had taken it incorrectly listed another composer. Only in the early 1990s did it come to Mikoian's attention that it was Robert Johnson who had written and recorded this song in the 1930s. As a conscientious student of the music, Mikoian sought out the original, only to be grossly disappointed by what he heard. The sound seemed alien and unintelligible. Conscientiousness prevailed, however, and Mikoian began to explore Johnson's music more.

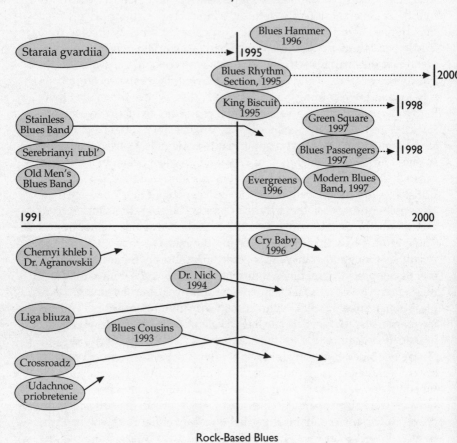

Figure 2. Leading Moscow blues bands in the 1990s. Arrows with solid lines connote changes in musical direction. Those with broken lines indicate the lifespans of the bands.

A change in the direction of each of these four bands was noticeable over the 1990s. Although it would be impossible to account for all of its sources, some factors can be mentioned with confidence. First would be the sheer variety of blues available for listening. Radio broadcasts, regularly tape recorded by musicians at home, along with an enormous influx of cheap, pirated cassette tapes and CDs, added immeasurably to the common stock of blues music and styles. Second, visual materials—such as the video cassette, *B. B. King and Friends,* along with instructional videos by guitarists Johnny Winter, B. B. King, and Otis Rush—contributed new stylistic techniques. Even the film *Crossroads* played a role in this respect, due to the way in which it spotlighted Mississippi slide guitar playing. Would not the Russian player, identifying with the young hero on his pilgrimage to the Mississippi Delta, notice the dichotomy in the film's dénouement between the rockish style of the Devil's exponent and the traditional forms favored by the hero? At some level of apprehension, the thought could easily emerge: "That's what we play, and here in opposition to it is a guy playing real blues." And, of course, B. B. King's two appearances in Moscow in the 1990s had an impact. Both were opened by Liga bliuza, whose singer, Nikolai Arutiunov, joined B. B. King's band for a guest vocal on each occasion. These and, doubtless, other influences propelled all four of these groups in the direction of a more traditional blues sound.

A more traditional blues sound, however, would be a notion admitting to a number of variants. In the case of Udachnoe priobretenie, we can observe an evolution in their repertoire and style from the music of, say, (early) Johnny Winter and (early) Fleetwood Mac—showcasing long, rockish guitar solos, the specialty of their leader, Aleksei Belov—toward a more tasteful and sophisticated variety of blues. Belov's guitar work remained the hallmark of the group, but over the 1990s he began to include more plaintive and lyrical passages, toning down the flash and thunder. Similarly, material borrowed from the Rolling Stones dropped out of their repertoire, while the heavy rock style featured in most of Jimi Hendrix's songs gave way to his more bluesy numbers: "Red House" rather than "Foxy Lady." It was not the addition of new personnel but Belov, himself, who was responsible for these changes. He drew up the set lists, dictated the style, and determined the group's direction. Although to a significant extent Udachnoe priobretenie was Belov's band, his sidemen were themselves outstanding musicians with opportunities to earn appreciably more money playing in other groups. That fact would speak to his status as one of the top two blues guitarists in Russia at this time.

The other was Sergei Voronov, who had left Liga bliuza in 1989 in order to found a group oriented exclusively to blues music. After experimenting with different combinations of musicians, in early 1990 Voronov hit on the right mix and formed Crossroadz. As with Udachnoe priobretenie, this band was built around its leader, Voronov, whose vocals and guitar solos were backed by a second guitar, bass, and drums. Likewise, Voronov set the band's directions—determining its repertoire and overall style—albeit with less definitude than that exercised by Belov. The band's name, taken from Cream's version ("Crossroads") of Robert Johnson's classic song ("Crossroad Blues"), indicated something of its orientation: from blues-rock toward blues roots. As such, the repertoire was replete with the songs of Muddy Waters and Howlin' Wolf. Although this wasn't rock anymore, it equally wasn't the blues of Robert Johnson or even Muddy Waters. Rather, the group interpreted their music in the form of power blues dominated by the lead guitar. This format connected with audience preferences and the band's popularity soared immediately. In 1991, Crossroadz performed at a Moscow hockey stadium—sharing the bill with ZZ Top—to a crowd of some ten thousand. In the following year, they played a rock gala at the spacious Kremlin Palace. Steady engagements in Moscow clubs during the 1990s were punctuated by domestic and foreign tours, as well as by some recording.[5] Over the course of the decade, however, the wind, blowing blue at first, shifted some and sent the group in more rock, even pop, directions.[6] By the late 1990s Crossroadz was arguably the most popular blues group in the country, only to be overtaken in that respect by Blues Cousins at the start of the next decade. In each case, popularity in part has seemed to be a function of the bands' readiness to include rock elements in their sound, thus making it more available to broader Russian audiences unaccustomed to blues in its purer forms.

In the early 1990s, the indefatigable leader of Liga bliuza, Nikolai Arutiunov, propelled his band to the forefront of Russia's blues scene. Their music began to shed its rock influences and veered into rhythm and blues, and blues standards. The group grew in size as well, becoming a veritable blues review, with female backup vocalists and, at times, a horn section. They appeared frequently on TV—a singular achievement in itself for Russian blues bands—performing on television variety shows, and producing music videos that were broadcast with some regularity. Only Crossroadz could compete with them in this latter respect. Inasmuch as the band performed a number of original songs in Russian, it would seem plausible to suggest that it was their readiness to break the language barrier that contributed to their popularity. The reputation that they built for themselves in Russia resulted in an invitation to play at the 1994 Montreux Jazz Festival in Switzerland where they were awarded a certificate for Outstanding Performance. Even more than the other two groups already discussed in this section, Liga bliuza was a leader-dominated band. Past members recall that Arutiunov would not only "select the songs that we would play and set the arrangements, he would rate the musicians. After a concert we would each receive a score."[7]

Strong leadership was not a characteristic of the last of the four groups under discussion here, Chernyi khleb i Doktor Agranovskii. As with the other three groups, the band—which took various names in the 1990s coincident with musicians coming and going, until it settled on its present appellation in early 1999—was built around its front man, Aleksei Agranovskii, who sang and played the guitar. However, Agranovskii had honed his skills in Moscow's hippie underground. Thus, he retained that subculture's casual approach to life, as well as to music, despite being a rather prominent biologist at Moscow State University whose published work in virology has appeared in some of the world's top scientific journals. Agranovskii's research commitments, which took him abroad in the 1990s for long periods, meant that the group existed episodically with a revolving membership. Although the band was more inclined to good-time music than to a disciplined professionalism, they have taken their music seriously enough to perfect a strong blues sound. A typical performance by this group in the 1990s would take place in a student club attached to an academic institute. The atmosphere there would contrast sharply with that found in Moscow's more upscale nightclubs: casual, friendly, and solely given over to having fun. Agranovskii would sing for long spells, not always strictly in key, until drink and the evening's merriment had exhausted performers and patrons alike. At the beginning of the next decade, however, the band began to refine its sound, producing one of Russia's finest blues CDs on a shoestring budget of less than two thousand dollars, which covered both studio time and production costs. Albeit somewhat uneven in content and quality, this collection contains some fine pieces of music—in particular, the barrel-house sound that the band gets on "Good Ole Wagon" and "Train Station Blues"—that reflect in relaxed, modulated tones the group's easy-going approach to the blues.[8]

The four bands assembled in the upper-left quadrant of figure 2 were all composed of seasoned musicians sharing broad backgrounds in blues and, in some cases, jazz and swing. What defines these groups collectively, in opposition to the first four bands that we have discussed, would be the fact that their sound was neither dominated by the electric guitar nor bore any strong traces of rock 'n' roll. Beyond that, the common element shared by these bands would be their respective tendencies to explore elements of the music that were underrepresented in Russia's blues scene at the time. Above all, these factors would characterize *Staraia gvardiia* (Old Guard), which took its name for this very reason.

Some in Staraia gvardiia had played in Altanta, a legendary Soviet-era underground rock ensemble, while others came from *Samotsvety* (Gems), an officially sanctioned vocal/instrumental group that in communist times was featured at many Komsomol concerts and dances. At nineteen years of age, the piano player, Denis Mazhukov was the youngest; others were in their late forties while the remaining members fell somewhere in between.[9] The combination of musical styles represented in the group's membership was synthesized as an urban blues sound that the band developed in the early 1990s, from classic Chicago blues of the 1950s to a more sophisticated version of this music with jump and swing elements. These changes in style reflected changes in personnel. When Mazhukov and Mikhail Sokolov left the band around 1993, the harp and the honky-tonk piano left with them. The group then added female vocalists and a horn section, becoming a jump-blues orchestra backing the lead vocalist, Alek Sikorskii. Staraia gvardiia was a highly professional outfit, something of a musical counterpart to Liga bliuza. Both featured female backup vocalists and used their horn sections to great effect, experimenting with complex and sophisticated musical arrangements. Yet, although a market for Liga bliuza's rhythm and blues existed, the same was not true for the more polished sounds that Sikorskii and his ten-piece band were perfecting. In order to thrive, this big band needed to tour. But circumstances were hardly propitious. The national booking agency Roskonsert collapsed at the beginning of the 1990s, and new private firms were reluctant to book these doubtful moneymakers.[10] This was an outstanding band that found itself playing on fewer and fewer occasions—sometimes in concert halls and sometimes in nightclubs—and the money was not sufficient to keep them going. They ceased performing in 1995.

Sharing some of the problems, as well as a bit of the style and name-image of Staraia gvardiia, was the Old Men's Blues Band, initially formed in 1977 as a school band performing a pastiche of Beatles, Stones, blues, and compositions written by band members.[11] They played festivals in the 1980s with flute and sax, along with piano, drums, bass, and guitar. In 1992 the group reformed with new personnel: three Russians and three foreigners. One of the latter was John Anderson, an economist attached to the U.S. Embassy in Moscow, who fronted on vocals and harmonica and steered the band toward a jump-blues repertoire. In the early 1990s, the Old Men's Blues Band became a favorite at the Arbat Blues Club which, as discussed in further detail in chapter 4, was also founded with Anderson's influence. When Anderson's Moscow posting came to a close in 1994, the band reformed again, adding a horn section and featuring a female vocalist—at first Michel Garcia, from the United States, and later Liga bliuza's backup vocalist, Lada Kolesova. By the latter part of the 1990s, the band had developed a driving yet sophisticated sound, usually with the horn section on top. The variety of their material—"Route 66," "Dr. Feelgood," and some tastefully rendered blues ballads—and their polished delivery rivaled the performances of Staraia gvardiia. It clearly set them apart from the remaining two bands under consideration in this section.

Both the Stainless Blues Band and Serebrianyi rubl' fashioned their sound in the 1990s from key elements of the Chicago blues tradition of the 1950s: a driving rhythm section undergirding the soaring wails of the slide guitar and harmonica. Theirs was clearly the rawest blues delivered by any of the bands discussed thus far. Serebrianyi rubl' had been formed at the close of the Soviet epoch for the specific purpose of conducting foreign tours. Although the necessary organizational infrastructure for touring had been put in place, their manager abruptly quit and the group was stranded in Moscow. When the prospects for touring before large audiences evaporated, Serebrianyi rubl' decided to drop the rock 'n' roll numbers from their repertoire and to concentrate on playing the music that they most enjoyed: Chicago blues. Almost immediately, they earned a favorable reputation in Moscow for their proficiency with this idiom. Alik Mikoian's growling vocals—rendering the English-language lyrics with a flawless pronunciation—along with his tasteful slide work anchored the band's sound squarely in the Chicago tradition. However, owing to a second passion in Mikoian's life—race car driving, at which he is quite adept, as victories in numerous Russian and European races would attest—the band went through a number of dead periods in the 1990s. With Mikoian back from the races, the band would reform, only to fall idle again when he returned to the speedway. At this writing, Serebrianyi rubl' has become active again, with the proviso that this will be their last time out.

The final group under discussion in this section, Stainless Blues Band, was formed by four experienced players: Ales' Popov on bass (but himself an ace on acoustic blues guitar); Pavel Zhdankin on drums; Boris Bulkin, a guitarist lately of Liga bliuza and Hot Style Band; and Mikhail Sokolov (known in blues circles simply by his patronymic, Petrovich), a veteran player from Udachnoe priobretenie and, later Staraia gvardiia, who had dropped his drumming in order to pick up the harmonica. Bulkin recalled the band's inception in this way:

> After playing with Hot Style Band, I became acquainted with Ales' Popov and Anatolii Podvigintsov, who is still our manager. These guys invited me over once and we had a lot of vodka. They were praising me as a great guitar player. Petrovich was there, too. We started to jam and I was really taken with the way that Petrovich could play the harmonica. It was out of that jam that we decided to get a group together, and within a month we had a program to play.[12]

The band took the name "Stainless" as a reference to razor blades, connoting that although they might be old, they were still capable of cutting it, and smoothly. This band featured a broad repertoire of blues from the Mississippi Delta to Chicago, playing both acoustic and electrically amplified sets. In order to dig a bit deeper into the blues bag and pull out the older sounds, the groups found it necessary to manufacture some of its own instruments—a guitar in the style of the famous National, and for Petrovich, a harp mike and, indeed, rebuilt harmonicas. They often played the deeper version of the blues at the Arbat Blues Club—drawing appreciative responses—but the band was forced to play electric with a less traditional blues set list in order to get gigs elsewhere in town. In 1995, they appeared on an hour-long show on Russia's ORT network in which they played traditional numbers on acoustic instruments and discussed blues music generally, explaining how they fashioned not only their own sound but their own instruments. The show caused a minor sensation in blues circles, but club owners were less impressed and still demanded the electrically amplified urban blues if the band were to be hired.

Some conflicts began to smolder within the band, kindled by the very success that they were enjoying. Petrovich—who already been a professional musician for over twenty years—stepped into the role of front man for the first time. He quickly warmed to the task and argued for a larger share of the vocals.[13] He also believed that the band should confect a better stage presence by dressing in an appropriate blues style. However, Bulkin—burley, bearded, and above any suspicion of being a clothes-horse—would have none of that.[14] (see fig. 3)

In 1996, Petrovich left and Bulkin became the leader and primary vocalist. His guitar dominated the band's instrumentation until Roman Gegart, the leader of King Biscuit, joined with his harmonica a few years later. As with effectively all of the groups discussed in this chapter, Stainless Blues Band produced a homemade recording of their own. Its technical quality was relatively good, and the musicianship on it was even better, fusing traditional acoustic blues with elements of swing. However, the band's strong suit has not been organization. The homemade CD, for example, took over four years to complete. On one occasion, when radio Ekho Moskvy scheduled them for a live national broadcast in studio, they let a golden opportunity slip away. The second guitarist got drunk and failed to show. The band's efforts suffered accordingly, as Bulkin attempted to cover both guitar parts and wound up making his share of mistakes. On learning the reason for the truancy, however, all members readily concurred on its validity and immediately forgave their errant brother.

Figure 3. Mikail Sokolov (Petrovich), patriarch of Moscow blues, growls a vocal—harmonica in hand—at a Moscow club circa 1999. Photo by Andrei Evdokimov.

Blues Boomers

The six groups bunched around the vertical axis of figure 2—Blues Cousins, Dr. Nick, King Biscuit, Blues Rhythm Section, Evergreens, and Cry Baby—were all formed during the peak years of the Moscow blues boom. Among the three bands appearing below the horizontal axis, Dr. Nick and Cry Baby serve as good examples of the many bands that picked up blues material because it was in vogue and relatively rewarding. Members of the blues community today look back ruefully on that aspect of the mid-1990s boom. Petrovich, referring to the forty or so bands playing blues in Moscow at the time, speaks of "a lot of flotsam and jetsam, not all of those forty bands were playing pure blues."[15] Aleksandr Tsar'kov remarks on the period as one in which:

> we had more blues bands in Moscow than we needed, if you get my meaning. When good money was being paid for blues in the mid-1990s, a lot of

these blues groups were composed of musicians who tried to reproduce this music that they had learned note-for-note from records . . . Some of the bands of this type would come to us [at the Arbat Blues Club] for work. They would say, "This is a blues club and we are a blues band. How about a job?" We would listen to their tapes, and the singing and instrumentation would be impeccable. Not a single false note; but at the same time, no music. When we didn't hire them, they would say, "That's blues, we play blues, what's the problem?" It was very difficult to explain to them, good musicians, that they should just play the music to which they were given—rock or jazz or whatever.[16]

Although Dr. Nick and Cry Baby were not of the mercenary ilk by any means, they featured blues in large part because of the times. Both bands have had varied repertoires—rock and blues for Cry Baby, funk and blues for Dr. Nick—and when the boom subsided, they stepped away from their blues numbers, accentuating in one case 1950s and early-1960s rock (Cry Baby) and, in the other, funk (Dr. Nick).

The story of Blues Cousins is more complex and requires a little telling.[17] On the simplest level, it is about Levan Lomidze, vocalist and guitar player *extraordinaire*. Drummers and bass players in the trio have come and gone, being no more than a rhythm section backing that volcanic Stratocaster with which Lomidze has dazzled many an audience. After beginning his musical career in the Georgian Republic of the USSR, Lomidze moved to Hamburg in 1991 to play on the street. On learning that a blues scene had developed in Moscow, he headed there in 1993, found a bassist and drummer to back him, and hit the burgeoning club circuit, playing as many as twenty-five dates per month. In the commercially oriented clubs, Blues Cousins was well received, but in the venues haunted by more serious blues aficionados, their reception was much more measured. Both Lomidze's overpowering guitar and the constant turnover among sidemen would seem to have had something to do with this. When the band was on, however, they electrified audiences, even with overplayed standards such as "Hoochie Coochie Man." Lomidze's guitar style has been that of the shredder: brilliant fireworks and difficult techniques, effortlessly played. His voice, although adequate, has served largely as a respite between volleys of guitar cannonade. Nonetheless, more than pyrotechnics would characterize his style; on slower numbers his solos have demonstrated a remarkable and subtle lyricism. In the mid-1990s, however, Lomidze was struggling. On one occasion, he played live on radio RAKUS, showing up at the studio with a guitar whose guts dangled out the back, and with a frayed cord that kept buzzing despite all efforts to control the noise. Nevertheless, his nine-minute version of Albert King's "Personal

Figure 4. Georgia boys Levan Lomidze, on left, and Giia Dzagnidze, on right, perform some laid-back acoustic blues with members of their respective bands at Moscow's Le Club on a sleepy Sunday evening in July 1999. Photo by Mike Urban.

Manager" was rendered eloquently, the guitar solo packed with a drama and intensity that gave the music an almost operatic turn. (see fig. 4)

Although few in Moscow in the mid-1990s might have guessed that Lomidze would emerge as the guitar player of choice for Moscow's blues cognoscenti, by the end of the decade he had become the acknowledged leader in circles of blues fans. Marginal improvements in his playing would not account for this unexpected outcome. Rather, his standing would seem due to the attention that he affords to his audience, the way that he employs certain techniques picked up from observing other blues performers in Paris where, since the late 1990s, his band has played a number of festivals and large shows. Although these elements of blues showmanship would be more or less commonplace in the West, their novelty in Russia has made Lomidze a real favorite with audiences there. He has learned the craft of the blues performer, the ability to reach his audience and to include them in the performance. Sometimes this is accomplished by Lomidze stunting, playing the guitar behind his head, while his drummer exits the drum kit, pacing around the stage tapping rhythm on all available objects before descending into the audience to do the same. Alternately, Lomidze involves the house with the clap-along technique, goes into the audiences and strolls around while playing, or he will stick the microphone into attentive faces, allowing the listeners to sing a phrase or two. Verbal call-and-response techniques are frequently employed, sometimes with the threat that "If we can't hear you, we're leaving." This bag of tricks is under constant renovation, and Lomidze's shows always seem to have something unexpected to throw at the audience.

Lomidze has been one of the few bluesmen in Russia who has composed blues songs in Russian. His purpose, again, has been to reach his audience, in this instance, by overcoming the language barrier. However, because audiences had given these Russian language songs a rather chilly reception, he has rewritten them all in English. Two CDs recorded by Lomidze, one at the beginning of his popularity, the other two years along, show the marks of his trial-and-error approach. On the CD *Dozhd'* (*Rain*), the title appears in Russian, as does the group's name, with Latin script under the Cyrillic. Two of Lomidze's compositions contained in it are in Russian, four of them are in English, and the remainder of the CD is filled out by a variety of tunes made popular by Muddy Waters, Louis Jordan (whose "Caldonia" is misattributed to Albert King), and the Beatles.[18] On the follow-up CD, *Hoochie Coochie Man*, Lomidze powers his way through six blues classics, including Johnny Guitar Watson's "Johnny Guitar" that Lomidze adapted from Johnny Winter's high-energy version of the tune, just as on his first CD he recorded Watson's "I'm Tired" in its racing Gary Moore rendition rather than in that of the original.[19] This CD also includes two of Lomidze's own compositions, both written in English.[20]

Lomidze has paid close attention to rhythm and its relation to the audience. The band has mastered Muddy Waters' signature beat, delayed rhythm with a heavy beat behind the pulse. Although they were quite satisfied with the musical results, they gauged audience reactions to be less than fully appreciative. Consequently, the band dropped the delay and returned to a straight beat. Reasoning that Moscow audiences may not be either attuned or much interested in the rhythms of pure Chicago blues, Lomidze had adopted a philosophy of "Give them what that can understand and enjoy." As he has remarked, "I'm from Georgia. So I'm a bluesman, yes, but a businessman, too." He seems to have succeeded in both roles. On the business end, his heavy schedule of appearances in Moscow and frequent performances abroad, his CDs that bristle with advertisements for beer, cigarettes, mineral water, and FM stations, his booking of bands for various nightclubs—all testify to his talents. On the musical side, these achievements have been matched with the recognition accorded the group by *Blues Magazine*—which in 2000 awarded four stars to the *Dozhd'* CD—and by the judges and organizers of the Paris Blues Festival of 2000 who included the band's "Nobody Knows," a Lomidze composition, on the anthology of festival performances that they commissioned.[21]

The three bands on the upper-middle portion of figure 2—Blues Rhythm Section, King Biscuit, and Evergreens—all formed during the boom with the idea of playing straight blues. These bands also featured the harp rather than the guitar as the principal solo instrument. However, each group has approached blues from a different angle. Evergreens—whose name symbolizes the undying music of their core repertoire—was formed by five college students attending various institutions of higher education in Moscow. Although when playing electric instruments the band performs songs from many genres—swing, reggae, rockabilly, rock 'n' roll, boogie-woogie, and rhythm and blues—blues has represented their center of gravity. Their version of the music is unvarnished by rock rhythms and style. None of the members has a formal musical education and, after their student days, each has entered into a professional career. But they have stuck to their music, playing and rehearsing with considerable discipline, perfecting their sound over time. Taking their performance cues from the film, *Blues Brothers*, the four-piece band (drums, bass, guitar, and harmonica) features step and gesture routines while the singer, Pavel Melkin, wears the heavy dark suit and shades iconocized in the film. As semi-professional musicians, the group plays infrequently, but regularly. The music is upbeat, danceable, and tends to please club audiences. A good-time band, Evergreens sometimes travels to venues outside of Moscow just for the fun of playing before appreciative audiences.

Blues Rhythm Section developed out of a chance encounter between Aleksandr Bratetskii—a self-taught harp player who, like his counterpart in Evergreens, Sergei Sorokin, took up the instrument after hearing Petrovich blowing on his harmonica in the early 1990s—and slide guitarist Evgenii Il'nitskii. Bratetskii was busking solo on the Arbat (something of a Moscow equivalent to Chicago's old Maxwell Street), and the deep resonance that he was pulling out of his harp caught Il'nitskii's attention. The two decided to put together a group devoted to playing Delta blues. As Bratetskii has recalled:

> We decided that blues was what we wanted to do, but not the blues that you would be likely to hear in Moscow at the time. We were trying to distinguish ourselves by removing the rock influences as much as possible and by attempting to produce that feeling in classic blues—that kind of primordial energy—which is the basis of the music itself.[22]

A second aspect of this group's self-conception would also distinguish it among the bands in our mosaic. Blues Rhythm Section—as its name would indicate—formed in reaction to the leader-dominated groups populating the Moscow scene. This group of young sidemen playing drums, bass, (slide) guitar, and harmonica, would provide the backing for others. However, when no would-be frontmen appeared, the group—whose rehearsals had raised the level of their skills as well as their self-confidence—decided to strike out on their own. As had others, they ran up against the sound barrier in nightspots, and were forced to abandon their acoustic instruments and to go electric. This changed the direction of their repertoire some, away from Delta blues and toward the Chicago style.[23] When Il'nitskii left to play in Italy, he was replaced by Aleksandr Kazankov, a folklorist and ethnologist lecturing at Moscow State University who was about twice the age of the other members of the group. At the time, Kazankov was convinced that the idea of playing deep blues successfully in Russia held little promise, and so he approached the matter as a kind of ethnographic experiment. He soon discovered that his doubts were ill-founded. Contributing his extensive stage experience gained over a number of years as a singer in Russian folk ensembles, Kazankov also insisted that the band expand its repertoire to include a number of the ancient and obscure Russian folk songs with which he was well acquainted. The band's new format thus became Delta and Chicago blues, performed alongside fifteenth-century music from deep in the Russian provinces. These traditions are both represented in Kazankov's composition, "Mr. Sherling Blues" which finds the singer pleading with his employer not to sack him from his job as night watchman.[24] The song is a simple blues shuffle performed in English but it is laced with humor, pathos, and double-voicing—elements equally common to the blues and Russian folk traditions.

This composition was emblematic of the band's style: serious blues played with plenty of tongue-in-cheek humor. A good example of this in live performance would be bass player John Sanchillo's rendition of the Jimmy Reed classic, "Bright Lights, Big City." Sanchillo, a young man in his mid-twenties, had been hitchhiking around Europe with his standup bass, busking on the streets and gathering information about blues music. When he joined Blues Rhythm Section, he brought with him a version of the Reed tune that he would sing in the exaggerated voicings of an old man reduced to near infirmity by what had apparently been a pretty tough life. His accompanying bass lines departed from his classical training, completing the effect with some very low-down licks.[25] The many styles and influences flowing through the group eventually led its members to go their separate ways. Harp player, Aleksandr Bratetskii, however, remains much in demand as a session player for other groups in Russia and often works as a sideman gigging around Moscow. He frequently sits in with Chernyi khleb i Doktor Agranovskii, and is a member of Agranovskii's acoustic trio, Blues Spinners.

Perhaps the most interesting band to emerge among the second generation of Moscow bluesmen is King Biscuit. Formed in autumn 1995, King Biscuit consisted of five, and sometimes six or seven players who came mainly from Dans Ramblers and Cry Baby. The core included: Kirill Gutskov, a young bass player and vocalist; Dmitrii Krasivov, a guitarist whose T-Bone Walker–style approach set him apart from all other Moscow pickers of the day; Mikhail Rebrov, a sax player with much experience gained while playing in European jazz clubs; and harmonica player Roman Gegart. Although the group had no leader at first, Gegart's steady improvement on harp and his original musical ideas pushed him to the fore. Completely self-taught, Gegart quickly began to dazzle his peers and audiences, winning the Hohner company's 1996 Russian harp competition, sharing formal honors with Petrovich but nosing him out as the person selected in Russia to play Hohner's Marine Band model at the ceremony commemorating its one-hundred-year anniversary.

King Biscuit would epitomize the tendency among these three second-generation groups to tame the guitar, and to spotlight the harp. At the time this was a major development, revealing the gulf between the orientations of the first generation of Moscow bluesmen and that reflected in this new wave. Appearing on the scene while the blues boom was in full swing meant that distinction—not only from the older bands but from the many groups who had gone over to a blues-rock repertoire purely for the sake of gainful employment—could be won by burrowing deeper into earlier forms of the music. King Biscuit was particularly adept at both building a repertoire exclusively based on classic Chicago blues, and muting and reshaping the guitar's timbre to produce an overall blues-band sound with the harp out in front. Their arrangements became more complex and jazzy, but remained solidly in the blues mode. The band regularly played Moscow's top three blues clubs—Arbat Blues Club, B. B. King Blues Club, and Forte Club—and developed a devoted following. When sax player Rebrov left to play in European clubs, he was replaced by Leonid Darmostuk, whose jazz experience and blues feel represented an overall improvement in the band's sound, especially when he moved from tenor to baritone sax. Toward the end of the 1990s, the band stopped rehearsing and began to perform much less frequently. Perhaps the downturn in activity reflected the fact that they had started out with instant and growing success, only to run up against the question—What next?—for which they could not find an answer. Heavy drinking—for which bluesmen generally maintain

a certain reputation that their Russian brethren have more than upheld—
also took a serious toll. In 1998, the band broke up. Gegart joined Bulkin's
Stainless Blues Band, Gutskov returned to Cry Baby, and Krasivov gravitated into the computer field after briefly playing with Serebrianyi rubl'
and Blues Passengers, but even then as just a hobby or sideline.[26] King Biscuit's demise represented a great loss for Moscow's blues scene. No young
bands with equal skills in the areas of musicianship, creativity, and blues
feel have emerged to replace them. With perhaps one exception.

Late Bloomers

An element defining the four bands that complete our survey—Blues Hammer Band, Green Square, Blues Passengers, and Modern Blues Band—is
the fact that none of them represented a development from rock to blues.
By the time these groups emerged, that development had already run its
course and blues was now the point of departure. But the trajectories issuing from a blues approach were quite different in these four instances.
Blues Hammer Band got its start in 1996 when Petrovich, while playing
with Stainless Blues Band at the Arbat Blues Club, was asked for harmonica lessons by a mild-mannered and unassuming Nikolai (Kolia) Sadikov.[27] After an initial hesitation, Petrovich agreed, and Sadikov dropped
by his flat a few days later. As Petrovich recalled the event:

> Kolia comes to my place with a National [guitar], sort of like John Ham-
> mond, like someone from the basic roots of that musical style, the blues.
> We forgot all about the fact that I was supposed to teach him some harp
> and we just started to play, he on guitar, myself on harmonica. I realized
> pretty quickly that this was the person I had been looking for. It felt like we
> were in a movie, you know. As we played, the feeling quickly arose that we
> had known each other for a long time and had been doing this for a long
> time. We both felt the same style. We were both playing in other groups,
> but we decided to put together our own thirty-minute acoustic program of
> Delta blues. When we performed, nobody understood the music. They'd
> say, "Hey, what is this? I thought you were supposed to be playing blues."
> Then we got a bass player and I would play the snare drums sometimes,
> trying also to sing and play the harp on a holder. We played acoustically,
> trying to master traditional blues music step-by-step, starting with Robert
> Johnson. Gradually, we began to realize our dream of playing the same mu-
> sic electrically.[28]

The rhythm section backing Sadikov's guitar and Petrovich's harp consisted of Nikolai Vtorov—a slap bass specialist then gigging with rocka-

billy groups whose love of the instrument meant that he would undergo the formidable tongue lashings of control ladies on the Moscow metro in order to transport it around town—and a young Aleksandr Grechanikov on drums who was extensively tutored by Petrovich in the polyrhythmic idiom of the Delta, early West Helena, and Memphis styles.

When Blues Hammer began performing in 1996, Petrovich was probably the single most popular blues player in Moscow. As such, the others in the band basically comprised his backup unit. However, Sadikov began to develop as a vocalist as well as a slide guitar player and by 1998 the group had become a well-balanced ensemble—Petrovich's growling vocal alternating with Sadikov's smooth and melodic deliveries. Their sound was quite original and certainly unique in Russia. The guitar and harp provided accomplished solos that were propelled by an exceptional rhythm section whose complex, polyrhythmic structures would set the room jumping. Particularly on up-tempo tunes such as "Dust My Broom" and "Shake Your Hips," the band's impact was exceptionally powerful. In more demure venues, such as Forte Club where the band has been performing weekly for some years, patrons might be able to resist the temptation to dance. But they are observable at their tables, absorbed, if not spellbound, by the music.

In 1996, Petrovich participated in Hohner's harmonica competition in Trossingen, Germany, and received a rating of "very good." He returned in the following year with the full band but they played below their potential—a case of nerves—in the formal competition, scoring "excellent" but not "outstanding." However, after the official program had ended, the jury, musicians, and organizers held an informal session at which the band was asked to perform. There, they cut loose. After burning up the twenty-five minutes initially allotted to them, the group was asked to carry on for an hour. Which they did, bowling over the audience with the same driving polyrhythms and soaring solos that had made them favorites among Moscow's blues cognoscenti.

Green Square and Modern Blues Band represent quite opposite directions in blues music. The former is led by Mikhail Vladimirov on harp and vocals. He had been working as a stagehand at the Helicone Opera House, a children's theater, where he met Aleksei Kuz'min, a young guitar player. The two began jamming together on Mississippi Delta songs at the theater after hours. Adding a bass—and only later, drums—the group set out to play a variety of blues saturated with subtle rhythms: strong enough to be felt but not stressed. Soon, Green Square's music began to move away from the Delta style and toward the danceable jazz of the 1930s. A few blues standards have remained in their repertoire (for instance, Robert Johnson's "Red Hot") but these are heavily inflected with ragtime. In time, Tamara Kozhekina—wife of Vovka Kozhekin, who is discussed later in this chapter—joined as vocalist and the band turned to the songs and style of Bessie Smith, Ma Rainey, and others.[29] Their showstopper became Nat Adderly's "Work Song," sung by Kozhekina in a plain voice soaked in deep feeling.

Modern Blues Band plays in the style of Memphis and Chicago blues with an extraordinary ring of authenticity. This four-piece group—drums, bass, piano, and guitar—is fronted by Giia Dzagnidze whose career as a singer and guitarist began in his native Tblisi. There, he played in a number of jazz and rock combos before joining a big band in 1981 which was attached to the Polytechnic Institute where he was studying to become an engineer.[30] In 1983, Dzagnidze formed his own rhythm-and-blues band, toured with them for a while, and then vacillated between careers in engineering and music until moving to Moscow on a permanent basis in 1996. In Moscow he landed a solo job playing blues in a bar, five hours per day, six days per week. He remembers that experience as a threshold. Playing publicly on such a demanding schedule forced him to focus on the ineffable feel and tone of the music. "Soon," he remarked, "each note began to sound a little clearer, a little more precise." After his stint at the bar, Dzagnidze hooked up with some players whose groups had just broken up and, in late 1996, they formed Modern Blues Band.

This band features Dzagnidze's husky voice and piercing guitar, supported by solid accompaniment. Its repertoire consists primarily of Chicago blues standards, with a few Jimi Hendrix and Eric Clapton songs tossed in for crowd-pleasing measure. At their regular weekly performances at Forte Club, as well as their occasional appearances at other Moscow nightspots or at festivals, Dzagnidze treats his audience to tasteful guitar solos, delicious bends, and exceptionally soulful renditions of blues music. Were there a prize for the most underrated blues band in Moscow, this group would be the frontrunner.

The final group in our survey, Blues Passengers, arrived in Moscow in 1997 when Novosibirsk's veteran blues band, *Novaia assotsiatsiia bliuza* (New Blues Association), migrated to the capital and adopted a new name in order to distinguish themselves from Liga bliuza which, as far as the young Siberian bluesmen knew, was one of only two bands playing blues in Moscow at the time. The group's leader, Mikhail Mishuris, had visited the United States earlier that year to attend the Chicago Blues Festival. The impact of that event caused him to extend his stay and to enroll in Chicago's Old Town School of Folk Music where he received training on blues vocals and harmonica. That experience transformed him as a musician. Recalling those times, Mishuris remarked:

> I wanted to put all that experience into practice in Russia, especially I wanted to play with my Siberian friends because I had learnt a lot of things.

And when we started to play back in Siberia, it was as if we were another band entirely. We played more authentically. It was the right kind of blues.

Inspired by the results that they were getting, the band moved to Moscow, where Mishuris bought a small flat for himself and his wife, installing the band's remaining five members in one of its two rooms. Despite the absence of a place for rehearsing, Blues Passengers achieved a degree of success in the capital until the band dissolved in 1998 when some members decided to return to Novosibirsk.[31] The significance of the group for our mosaic consists in the fact that they brought two things to Moscow: first, certain elements of the Chicago blues style that were previously absent from the Moscow scene; and, second, a formidable vocal talent, Mishuris, who quickly gained recognition as the country's top blues singer.

Afterword

Our survey of Moscow's principal blues bands in the 1990s has mapped the trajectory of the music's development across the first decade of its existence in Russia as a separate, identifiable genre. Above all, the 1990s were marked by a disentangling of blues from rock with which it previously had been tightly bundled. As we saw in chapter 2, these musics had not been hitherto much distinguished in the country, even by those performing them. That changed in the 1990s, both as a result of the formation of new bands oriented specifically toward blues and because of the fact that many established blues-rock players set off to explore the roots of their music. With the advent of a second generation of blues musicians at mid-decade, that turn had been more or less completed. Moscow now hosted a number of bona fide blues bands performing the genuine article, unalloyed with either rock or jazz. Once this had been accomplished, the question would pose itself: What next? What stylistic changes would players, especially those relatively new to the scene, adopt in order to distinguish themselves in the field of Moscow blues?

One new direction in the development of this music would be represented by Mishuris and His Swinging Orchestra, a group formed in April 2001. After Blues Passengers dissolved in the summer of 1998, Mishuris turned to another genre, Russian sailors' songs. He recorded a CD in this style with a backup ensemble drawn from various groups—Aleksandr Grechanikov and Nikolai Vtorov from Blues Hammer Band along with others from top-flight blues and country bands in Moscow.[32] The overall effect replicated the sound of the music heard in Russian sailors' bars, but all the material was original—most of it composed by Mishuris himself—and often contained an edge reminiscent of a Nick Cave murder-ballad.

Adopting the name *Necha* (Standoff), Mishuris's group began gigging around Moscow, playing one set of sailors' songs in Russian and following it with another set of blues performed in English. The blues portion of the program proved the more popular, and Mishuris returned to that genre exclusively, recruiting various sidemen for the Mishuris Blues Band that thrived on the strength of his booming voice until a new project was hatched in spring of 2001.

That project, Mishuris and His Swinging Orchestra, emerged from a combination of musical reflection, stylistic fusion, and pure serendipity. On the reflective side, Mishuris remarked that:

When I started to play in Moscow, everybody was playing the same songs. Every band. This kills blues potential, it kills the feeling. So we started with some Willie Dixon songs like "Howlin' for My Darlin'" and "Hidden Charms," which are unusual because they have more harmony than does traditional blues. Then we added some other material and other elements: old jazz, Dixieland. I think that New Orleans is close to Odessa. Lots of minors. And the other thing was what I learned in Chicago: how to make a show. Nobody was doing this in Moscow. So I just started to sing sometimes without a microphone, sometimes I started jumping up and down on stage, sometimes doing call-and-response. This helped to involve the audience, they seemed to hear the music better and the music is itself the language for communicating with people.[33]

With respect to their music, the band represents a fusion of distinct genres reflected in the backgrounds of its members. Drummer Evgenii Lomakin and bassist Nikolai Vtorov have come from the rockabilly tradition, although the latter was well acquainted with the blues owing to his two-year stint with Blues Hammer Band. These players had comprised the rhythm section for Upbeat Band, which featured Denis Mazhukov's Jerry Lee Lewis–style piano, until conflicts sundered that group. On clarinet and piano were two classically trained musicians: Sergei Shitov and Oleg Garchekov. The former had been playing a heavily jazz-inflected blues with Green Square, while the latter's experience as a performer and composer had been exclusively in the classical vein, aside from the boogie-woogie riffs that he had worked out at home for his own amusement. The blues contingent in the Swinging Orchestra would be represented by Mishuris himself and by guitarist Vadim Ivashchenko, who moved from Rostov-on-Don to Moscow on the eve of the band's formation.

The serendipitous aspects contributing to the formation of this group were many, and perhaps best exemplified by Ivashchenko's experience. Ivashchenko had visited Moscow in the late 1990s to scout out the prospects for relocating his band there. During an interview, he spoke about visiting the Forte Club where Mishuris happened to be singing with Blues Hammer Band that night.

> I had never heard that kind of voice before, nor had I ever heard the kind of slap bass that Kolia [Vtorov] was playing . . . I returned to Moscow in 2001, hoping to hook up with some musicians. But I didn't know anybody. I just remembered that in Moscow there is Misha [Mishuris] and there is Kolia, so there are some prospects. I called Petrovich and he told me that Mishuris was putting a band together. I didn't know any Mishuris, I just knew this guy Misha who was doing such a good job singing at the Forte Club. I called this Mishuris person and it turned out to be the same Misha whom I had heard earlier and who had so impressed me. We agreed to meet at the Tretiakovskaia metro station, but that failed. There are three distinct stations there and I stood with a guitar at one for an hour, two hours, no Misha. So I rang him again and he said just come to the rehearsal, which was in some guy's apartment. When I knocked on the door there, who answers but Kolia, the bass player from Blues Hammer Band that I so admired . . . Of course, I was really nervous. And I didn't know that these guys were planning to play '40s and '50s music because no one in Moscow was doing that. Well, this was the very music that I had been listening to in Rostov, thanks to the local deejay, Vitalii Khachin'ev, who would let me listen to his old records. I had been playing Chicago and country blues, but I suppose that my real love is for that jump blues that I heard on those old records. That's what Mishuris's group wanted to play, and after the rehearsal they told me that I was the very guitar player that they had been unable to find in Moscow.[34]

The sophisticated rockabilly sounds of Brian Setzer's Swing Orchestra had already reached Moscow on CD, thus preparing an audience for Mishuris's new group. They have become an instant success, performing upward of twenty dates per month. However, his "orchestra" consists of only five instruments and, necessarily, their arrangements are attenuated. But they are also enormously inventive. The band has recast the songs of, say, T-Bone Walker, Howlin' Wolf, and Louis Jordan in a jump-blues motif all their own. Atop the thumping rhythms of rockabilly bass and drums glide guitar and clarinet duets punctuated by Garchekov's boogie-woogie piano. Mishuris's powerful vocals and playfully animated stage presence provide the center of gravity, holding together the mix of musical elements as a single sound, even while its components retain their distinct identities that provide the music with a remarkable color. To the American ear, it sounds like *Russian* blues, laced with lilting clarinet lines that suggest

Figure 5. Mikhail Mishuris calls his reed player, Sergei Shitov, up for a bow, on the stage at Moscow's Forte Club in 2002. Vadim Ivashchenko is playing guitar, other musicians unidentified. Photo by Andrei Evdokimov.

the plaintive music of Odessa dance halls. To the Russian audience, it is infectious. Those who aren't dancing are tapping time at their tables, taking in every moment of a first-rate show. (see fig. 5)

A second vector into the future of Russian blues would be represented by Vovka Kozhekin and his Petersburg partner, Vanya Zhuk (whom we discuss further in a subsequent chapter). Kozhekin heard his first blues while a teenager abroad for schooling in Britain. He returned to Moscow in the early 1990s with a harp given him by a school chum, and set about mastering the instrument, learning from records, and from local harp players Roman Gegart and Mikhail Vladimirov.[35] Rejecting the commercial blues scene then blossoming in Moscow—and, in particular, its strictures against performing blues in the Russian language—Kozhekin joined the hippie alternative. While busking on Arbat Street in 1995, he met Umka, a folk singer and veritable Russian hippie legend who had not been performing for some seven years. Kozhekin persuaded her to make a comeback, performing Russian language blues songs that they would compose themselves.[36] For over two years the shifting personnel of *Umka i bronevichok* (Umka and the Little Armored Car) toured the former USSR, hitchhiking through St. Petersburg, the Baltic states, Kiev, the Crimea, Rostov, and Siberia, and playing for whatever monetary contributions that listeners would drop in the hat. Along the way, the band picked up Vania Zhuk and his guitar. When the band's peripatetic rambling ceased in 1998, Kozhekin and Zhuk formed a duet that played small clubs in St. Petersburg and Moscow, sometimes with the support of their acquaintances on drums and bass.

In late 1999, the duo got together with a virtuoso accordionist, Fedor Chistiakov, and a supporting rhythm section to record a collection of material fusing blues with Russian folk songs, sometimes inflected with rock, jazz, and Latin elements.[37] This is the vector that Kozhekin and Zhuk have been subsequently pursuing, a blues performed in the Russian language which simultaneously draws on the country's folk traditions. Their project has been both to make the music more available to Russian audiences and to create something new and distinctive in the process. In this respect, their apprenticeships on the hippie circuit have served them well. Kozhekin and Zhuk's performances are especially casual and heavily larded with humor and Russian slang, thus enabling listeners to catch the double-voicings and comic asides that occur in songs such as Lightnin' Hopkins's "Itchy"—which they deliver in Russian—integral to both the blues and Russian folk traditions.

A few issues that have surfaced in the narrative are worthy of note in concluding this chapter. First, there is the matter of language. Almost all performers sing the blues in English, thus making the lyrics unintelligible to their audiences. Would not Russian renditions of the blues add to the music's appeal, promoting the popularity of the genre and its performers alike? Second, as instantiated by the popular theatrical showmanship displayed by Levan Lomidze and Mikhail Mishuris, we are left wondering why more of the country's bluesmen pay so little attention to involving audiences in their performances. Finally, as witnessed in the conflict between Mikhail Sokolov (Petrovich) and Boris Bulkin over dressing for the stage, why are most performers averse to adopting attire that would help to create a style associated with the music, thereby attracting more attention to themselves and, in the process, to the music that they play? As will be shown in subsequent chapters, each of these issues—language, showmanship, and style—is thickly entangled with the norms and mores prevailing in Russia's blues community. To varying degrees, community members disdainfully recode these practices as base and commercial, opposing them to the celebrated authenticity found in blues music. Assuming the identity of a bluesman in Russia, then, tends to eclipse these elements of blues.

CHAPTER FOUR

Moscow Blues: Sites and Sounds

Musical logistics is our topic here, with the focus falling first on Moscow's postcommunist innovation in leisure activities: the nightclub. This institution represents a site on which an imported set of practices has been refashioned by Russians in accord with both extant cultural norms and new commercial opportunities. For those clubs featuring blues music, our interest is in their manner of organization, their respective clienteles, and their layouts. The second concern is with the ways in which blues has been publicized in the mass media, particularly in the instance of radio where a few devotees of the music make a sustained effort to reach and cultivate a Russian audience. Finally, this chapter concludes as the previous one began, with a discussion of blues festivals; in this case, those occurring in Moscow during the spring of 2000 and 2001, separated from the winter gathering at the First Moscow Blues Festival ("Blues in Russia") by more than eight years. We begin with the nightclub, the mainstay of blues performers in the capital.

The Nightclub Economy

Although blues has been performed at concert halls and festivals in Moscow—and, for that matter, elsewhere in Russia as well—the nightclub has become the music's premier site. Under communism, such clubs—where people could gather to relax, eat, drink, and immerse themselves in live music—were simply unknown. Indeed, the whole idea of combining these practices initially seemed to Russian musicians to be both strange and even humiliating. Prevailing norms in the musical world dictated that serious music required a suitable venue where listeners could appreciate it, undistracted by the bustle of waiters, the clanking of plates and glasses, and oral diversions that interfered with audial concentration. Indeed, these were the hallmarks of the restaurant, a place where people came primarily to eat, drink, and relax in leisurely and lengthy conversation. A visit to a Soviet restaurant would consume the entire evening. Of course, dancing to the music provided by a live band was a popular activity in restaurants too, but that music itself was, in effect, "canned," amounting to a standardized format of pop or *estrada,* there to create the proper atmosphere and to provide the necessary accompaniment to those on the dance floor. Consequently, these sites were stigmatized in the community of musicians as "low" culture. Musicians would play there only for the money, and used terms—as they still do today—such as "restaurant music" or "a restaurant band" to signal their contempt for the entire enterprise.[1]

The collapse of communism and the advent of commercial possibilities rapidly reconfigured the ensemble of Soviet practices in the area of musical entertainment, combining in new mixes various elements of the cultures of restaurants and of youth clubs found at factories or educational institutes, with exotic new forms imported from the West: the nightclub and the bar. On one hand, underground Komsomol culture surfaced at the new nightspot, *Forpost* (Outpost). There, the proprietors of a concert and dance hall simply partitioned the premises, enclosing thereby a smaller venue supplied with cheap beer and nightly entertainment. On the other, nightclubs emerged from Soviet restaurant culture, their owners targeting affluent foreigners as the principal clientele and, soon, the new Russian "middle class." In 1992 alone, as many as one hundred of these nightclubs opened in Moscow, the great majority of them folding in very short order. Aside from the stiff competition in a relatively restricted market, the problem for the owners lay with management. Who in Moscow knew how to organize and run a nightclub? Indeed, who had even been to one? Without any local personnel experienced in nightclub management and its economics, owners sometimes turned to expatriates from the West to direct these new enterprises. However, although this option yielded some successes, it was not without its own problems. For instance, New Yorker Mike Osley came to Moscow in 1993 to take over the management of the club, Metelitsa, converting it from an almost bare room equipped with a dilapidated and unreliable Soviet-era tape recorder into a rather stylish spot with good acoustics and live music. During an interview, he remarked on the frictions that dogged the relations between Russian club owners and their Western managers.

The Russians really don't understand anything about how to run a club. The better ones just stay out of the way but, unfortunately, most of them want to be the boss, to make the decisions. The result is that they get into quarrels with the foreign managers and, the foreigners get fed up with that and leave after a month or two. Sometimes, foreigners are hired—without their knowledge—as people that the Russians will learn the ropes from. After a while, they're fired and Russians are put in their place. Then these guys screw everything up and the club goes bust.[2]

It has also been the case that the opening and closing of Moscow's nightclubs has been due directly to the influence of organized crime. Some proprietors could not or would not make protection payments to criminal groups and, accordingly, either left this line of activity or were forced out of it. There have been (and still are) other clubs—notable for their low revenues and sparse patronage—which were opened to provide a *krysha* ("roof" or, in Western parlance, "front") for illicit activities such as money laundering and prostitution.

Initially, rock and pop dominated Moscow's new nightclub circuit. Except for rare performances at Sexton Fost—a hard-rock biker-bar that opened in fall of 1992—the blues was not to be heard. With time, however, club managers began to notice that there was an audience in the capital for blues music—especially among resident foreigners with money to spend—and that local blues bands would play for appreciably less money than the sums commanded by Russian pop-rock groups. They also were instructed on these counts by the success enjoyed by Moscow's first bona fide blues club, which opened on January 30, 1993.

By recombining extant practices in a manner favored by musicians themselves, the Arbat Blues Club represented a unique addition to Moscow's emerging nightclub economy. Much credit, in this respect, has been given to John Anderson, the U.S. Embassy economist who was singing and playing harp at the time with the Old Men's Blues Band. As one of the club's founders, Aleksandr Tsar'kov, remembers:

> John came up with the idea. At the time, there was simply no understanding of such a musical club in Russia. Our whole concept of a club was different from yours. It had to do with groups of people united by a common interest. Some people might want to dance, others might want to perform acrobatics—those would be clubs. We had no idea that in places like America such clubs existed—two hundred people or so in small halls. We found a good place and John explained to us how we could use this hall by dividing it up—one place for dancing, over here a stage and, of course, tables for sitting and listening to music. But people don't always just want to sit and listen. Anderson explained how we should set up a small eating area and a bar, away from the stage and the dancing. We would sell beer and have this area away from the music so that people could talk and drink there.[3]

This spatial innovation was then combined with elements of Soviet musical culture. Tsar'kov continues:

The club never had any financing. There was this hall that we took over and some equipment that I had access to because of my days as a musician. And we knew people with technical skills, so they could do the lighting and so forth. At the time, there wasn't a very strong conception in our country about things like property and rent. There was a word, "base," that musicians used. It concerns the actual physical composition of what you need to perform. It was something that nobody would actually pay for. It was just the equipment, and the hall and the lighting and so forth. We secured our base through the institution of barter, another word that wasn't very well understood or even used in those years. We bartered with free evenings of music for various institutions to which we were indebted in one way or another. But the concept "to rent" with documents and contracts and all of that, played no role in our activities, although later we did have to pay a certain amount of money for the premises. We can put it this way: we occupied this building on Filippovskii pereulok under conditions that were not very concrete.

This combination of practices inherited from the Soviet era with the format of a Western-style blues club proved an immediate success. The Arbat Blues Club sold out on its very first night and continued to do so with some frequency at both its twice-weekly performances and twice-annual festivals until business began to dry up in the wake of Russia's financial crash in August 1998. Today, Moscow's bluesmen often reminisce about the halcyon days of this nightspot, recalling its excellent sound system, its enthusiastic and appreciative audiences and its easygoing ambience—just as they relished the chance to perform there earlier, despite the fact that their pay was always leaner than that which they had been accustomed to earning at other establishments. Since the club disdained any sort of glitz, it did not draw big spenders from Moscow's new moneyed elites. And, as a semicommercial project, it never became a suitable target for gangsters in the protection industry.

The strategy for attracting patrons employed by the club's management would appear to have had much to do with the interpersonal tranquility—not a single episode of fisticuffs—that prevailed in a downtown Moscow joint featuring loud and raucous blues music. After a year of relying on word of mouth, the Arbat Blues Club began to advertise its shows exclusively in the English language. Naturally, this suited a large contingent of its clientele—Westerners, especially from the United States, who comprised most of the audience during the first year or two, until Russians began to frequent the club more heavily—but its primary purpose was to discourage the "wrong people" from showing up at the door. English-language advertising functioned as a kind of code, signaling who would be welcome. As such, it screened out both the nearby hippies on the Arbat as well as gangsters and their molls, while inviting in a "cultured audience" from the ranks of the intelligentsia and the young professional classes. Pricing and amenities likewise played a role in constituting the club's clientele. The admission fee—usually about eight to ten dollars—kept out the hippies, while a fare of only light snacks eliminated the possibility that the nouveaux riches would turn up to indulge themselves in acts of conspicuous consumption.[4]

Taking these various factors into account, we can situate the Arbat Blues Club in the upper-left quadrant of figure 6 which graphs Moscow's fifteen premier sites for blues performances in the 1990s according their priciness (vertical axis) and their relative stocks of cultural capital (horizontal axis). The term "cultural capital" in this context refers to both performers and audiences, and might be interpreted as familiarity with, knowledge about, and sophistication with respect to blues: that is, a certain refinement evinced by an appreciation of pure, highly emotional, even gut-bucket blues music. In addition to the Arbat Blues Club, three other establishments employed an exclusively blues format—B. B. King Blues Club, Cactus Jack (during the period 1993–95) and Club Beliaeva (which opened in late 1995 and closed in early 1997)—while the others hosted blues bands regularly. The fifteen clubs listed in figure 6 were by no means the only places to hear blues music in Russia's capital during the 1990s. Scores of other clubs booked blues at one time or another, but not often enough to be included in our sample.

Each of the three remaining clubs devoted exclusively to blues occupies a distinct space in figure 6. Cactus Jack's had been functioning as a bar and grill where many types of music could be heard. In 1993, when Moscow's blues boom was gathering steam, Levan Lomidze came to town and soon became—in Russian parlance—the club's art director (booking agent), converting it to a strictly blues format. When he left that position in 1996, Cactus Jack's reverted to the multigenre musical fare that it had previously featured. The B. B. King Blues Club, however, opened with the intention of being an exclusively blues establishment and has stuck to that program. Located just inside Moscow's Garden Ring, the club occupies a large basement decked out with all manner of blues paraphernalia, including life-sized figures of the movie characters, the Blues Brothers, that one encounters in the entrance way. Mike Osley, who managed the club for some eighteen months in the mid-1990s, has reported that when he arrived there it was largely a place to see and be seen, with lethargic audiences more absorbed by cell phone conversations than by the music being performed. However, by enlisting a number of his rowdy U.S. friends as role models, he introduced stolid Russian audiences to a more appropriate mode of behavior and the club's patrons thereafter have been responding to performances with suitable levels of shouting, hand-clapping, and foot-stomping.[5] The B. B. King Blues Club is situated slightly to the right on the horizontal axis in figure 6, connoting a relatively low level of cultural capital. This judgment is not based on the club's musical fare so much as it is on its visual trappings—which give the impression of a kind of blues Disneyland—and on a segment of the clientele that it attracts who complete the masquerade by dressing in stylized blues costume. In short, the elements of a commercialized cult would diminish the club's stock of cultural capital. (see figs. 6 and 7)

Club Beliaeva reflected quite the opposite orientation. It was founded in 1995 by Aleksei Kalachev who used his radio program and its attendant fan club to popularize the new establishment. As he remarked:

> I knew my audience very well at the time and I understood that a large percentage of it consisted of students. They had a serious problem with access to blues music because going to a club was expensive—cover charge, drinks, and so forth. So the task was to make a club that would be accessible for those people. Through love and, I could say, even knowledge of the blues we kept this club alive purely by volunteer work. It was something that I would imagine American coffee houses or juke joints to be like: a very democratic place and, at the same time, very sympathetic . . . We had concerts once or twice per week and we always sold out. Literally every figure in Moscow blues played there, with the exceptions of Arutiunov and Voronov who, perhaps because of their fame, declined our invitations to perform. Even today I often encounter people who first became acquainted with the blues precisely in this club.[6]

Club Beliaeva's appointments were bare-bones. It consisted of a basement that had housed a *stolovaia* (a Soviet-style, low-end cafeteria) in a large apartment building that had ceased functioning years earlier. The club appropriated the junk furnishings left over from the room's days as a *stolovaia* and installed a simple bar serving only the cheapest beer—although a few bottles of better varieties were kept on hand in case an honored guest or two was in the house—and comparably priced light snacks. Admission fees (about fifty cents) were set deliberately low in order to enable impecunious students and hippies, the club's only clientele, to attend. The club's bylaws were informality and enjoyment. Often, bands would perform until 4 or 5 a.m., owing both to the verve of the musicians and to the fact that the patrons were too poor to afford cab fare home and needed to wait for public transportation to resume operations.[7] In the end, the sapping of the volunteer spirit spelled the club's demise. As Kalachev reported:

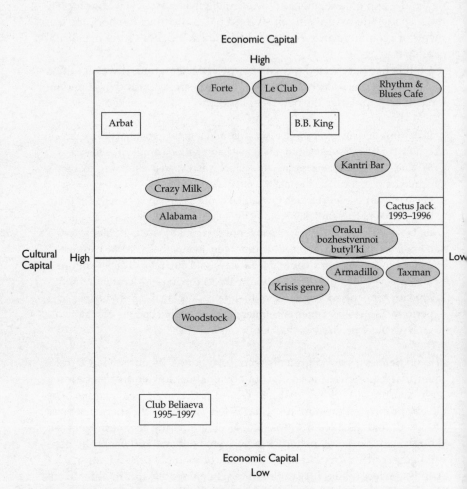

Figure 6. Principal Moscow clubs featuring blues in the 1990s. Ovals indicate blues performed occasionally, rectangles indicate blues performed exclusively.

Figure 7. Participants and fans at the 2002 Efes Pilsner Blues Festival gather for an after-hours jam at the B. B. King Blues Club. From the left: Louisiana Red (on guitar), C. J. Chenier (pointing), an unidentified harp player, Lil' Ed (on guitar), Sergei Voronov (with black hat), Tamara Kozhekina and Mikhail Mishuris (behind Voronov), and Mikhail Vladimirov (on harp, back to camera). Photo by Andrei Evdokimov.

I have many mixed feelings from those days—sometimes delight, sometimes warmth, sometimes horror. To put together a juke joint in Moscow involves a lot of risks and a lot of waste . . . There was a lot of work involved and, gradually, I found that I wasn't getting any help. It had become a full-time job for me and it was just too difficult to continue. Certainly, there are no business people who wanted to get involved in such an enterprise: a cheap, student music club. Anybody who is going into the club business wants quick returns. In fact, all the clubs in Moscow are under the control of gangsters or of people who—from vodka or from narcotics or from prostitution or discotheque dances—expect to receive big money. Certainly, Club Beliaeva did not fit their picture at all.[8]

Inasmuch as the remaining clubs in our survey have featured blues music on an irregular basis, we shall not discuss them all individually. Rather, we conclude this section with a few general observations on blues in the context of Moscow's nightclub scene, relying on the twin axes in figure 6 to coordinate our comments, illustrating these concretely with typical examples. First, the remarkable variation in ambience across those venues where blues is performed should be noted. At establishments such as Forte Club and Le Club, the visitor encounters posh surroundings: waiters in tuxedos, table cloths and silver, up-scale restaurant fare, and fashionably dressed patrons, occasionally with children in tow. There, audience reactions are appreciative but reserved. People dance, but infrequently; a strong harp or guitar solo might elicit a few shouts of encouragement, but these generally come from the tables occupied by the musicians' friends. At the other end of the spectrum, we encounter various forms of abandon. At Gentleman Jack's (not included in figure 6), blues is rare, but when played it is often accompanied by pantomime sex acts, performed by the male staff and exotic female dancers.

A second distinction among these clubs would directly concern the matter of social status: the criteria according to which would-be patrons select one or another nightspot as suitable for the presentation of the self. In this respect, we observe a clear social divide separating—at the poles—Club Beliaeva from Forte Club, Le Club, and Rhythm and Blues Café, with the remainder of the clubs falling somewhere in between. The three clubs occupying the top row of figure 6 are not just expensive but sumptuous, especially Rhythm and Blues Café. This club was opened by rock-impresario Stas Namin and Andrei Makarevich, guitarist and vocalist with the Russian rock band, *Mashina vremeni* (Time Machine), which still enjoys the legendary status that it achieved in Soviet times. Indeed, in those times it would have been imaginable that had these two individuals undertaken the founding a music club, it would likely have resembled the spartan décor of Club Beliaeva. However, as exponents of what many native bluesmen disdainfully call "Russian show business," their establishment is of quite a different order. As a gathering place for the wealthy and chic, a place to see and be seen, it is occasionally graced by celebrities from the world of entertainment and cultural production not unlike the proprietors themselves. As such, Rhythm and Blues Café is sharply distinguished from less pretentious haunts of the Russian "middle class" such as Crazy Milk (formerly Moosehead, a Canadian bar) or even *Orakul bozhestvennoi butyl'ki* (Oracle of the Divine Bottle). The latter, named for the Rabelais novel, is tastefully decorated with thematic representations from that work, including Gargantua's soliloquy on colonic hygiene (in an age prior to the advent of toilet paper) that graces the club's restroom walls.

A final distinction involves an incongruity that occasionally obtains between the signifiers incorporated in a club's furnishings and those associated with the style displayed by its patrons. Sometimes the patrons appear dominant, filling a club's space with their signs; sometimes it is the club's décor and ambience doing most of the signifying, while the actual club-goers, sitting passively at their tables, seem more or less inert by comparison. To illustrate, consider the contrasting cases of Club Alabama and *Kantri bar* (Country Bar), both located in central Moscow. Club Alabama's owner, Nikolai Kalandareshvili, describes the conception behind his establishment as that of an "art club."[9] Accordingly, the club's spacious interior is simply and very sparingly appointed. A few photographs adorn the walls in keeping with Kalandareshvili's taste for jazz. However, rather than icons of the greats, these are photographs of jazzmen who have actually performed there. Once Kalandareshvili had made the acquaintance of fellow Georgian Levan Lomidze—who persuaded him that blues would also be appropriate for his enterprise—the club began booking blues bands two or three nights per week. On blues nights, colorful crowds are likely to appear and a kind of masquerade might ensue. For instance, at a performance by Mishuris and His Swinging Orchestra on August 22, 2001, about half of the crowd was in costume: women wearing full skirts or pedal pushers, puffy blouses and hair in pony tails; men, with oversized trousers, rolled-up short sleeves, and butch cuts or pompadours for hairdos. The club's atmosphere crackled with a kind of electric charge as the band cranked out high-energy jump blues while the costumed portion of the crowd threw itself into the jitterbug. The spectacle seemed to drip with nostalgia, a reenactment of fashion and fad from the 1940s and early 1950s. But in this respect, a second incongruity asserted itself. This was, after all, neither New York nor even London, but Moscow. Here were young Muscovites displaying "nostalgia" for something that the country had never actually experienced. It would appear that they were, in a sense, borrowing someone else's nostalgia, trying it on for size as a set of visible and audible markers signifying their association with some larger community. For these young club-goers, entrance into that community would require a leap in time and space, catapulting the imagination into some other "here," some other "now." Curiously, that "here" and "now" represented the contemporary West, which projects itself to them through stylized images of its own past.[10] These young Muscovites, then, were constructing themselves as modern individuals by participating in one of the West's constitutive cultural practices, the art of nostalgia, even if they needed to appropriate someone else's appropriated memories in order to do so.[11]

At Kantri bar, things are quite different. There the copious décor follows an American West theme—a cowboy analogue to the B. B. King Blues Club—complete with stuffed figures of cowpokes, cactus designs on the walls, and the implements of ranching scattered about. Blues nights do not tend to draw many of Moscow's cowboys, and on these occasions the customers in their everyday apparel sit much like tourists in a theme park. Moreover, Kantri bar occupies the first floor of a two-storied complex that houses a sex club and bordello on the floor above. Inasmuch as the women working there apparently have been instructed not to use that establishment's front door, they enter and exit their work site through Kantri bar, following an itinerary that cuts across the dance floor separating the stage from the tables, and winds around the bar to a staircase leading to the second floor. On one occasion when I was present, Stainless Blues Band was on stage and the space for dancing was unused at the time. At roughly ten minute intervals, fashionably dressed young women would enter and exit through the bar's front door, sauntering to or from the stairs that went up to their workplace. This constituted a different type of spectacle: in one corner, a band in rag-bag attire belting out the blues; at the tables young, middle-class patrons, respectably dressed; and, between these two groups, a steady parade of voluptuous young women turning all the heads in the house with each pass through the empty dance floor.[12]

Blues in the Mass Media

Since the late 1980s, radio has been the singularly important medium for bringing blues to a wider audience. The country's longest running blues program, Andrei Evdokimov's "All This Blues," which began in late 1987, moved from one to another radio station in the 1990s and, at this writing, can be heard weekly on both *Ekho Moskvy* (Echo of Moscow) and Radio Arsenal. The program's emphasis during its initial years was pedagogic, aimed at conveying to listeners the idea that blues was both deeper in its origins and more varied in its content than the conceptions held by most Russians would then allow: blues was not just Eric Clapton and Gary Moore but, more importantly, Muddy Waters, Willie Dixon, and Robert Johnson. This format proved popular with a radio audience getting its first tastes of the music and, doubtless, curious about its roots and development, its various styles of performance, its idioms, lore, and significance. For instance, a listeners' poll conducted in 1992 by the radio station SNC [Stas Namin Center]—where "All This Blues" was then housed—revealed that the program placed second in popularity among all shows broadcasted by the station, nosed out of the top spot by a show devoted to Beatles music, the most beloved of pop music groups in Russia then and probably today. Letters and phone calls to the stations carrying "All This Blues" usually expressed a combination of amazement and gratitude. Not knowing that this music existed, some were happy to have their cultural horizons broadened, others simply fell in love with the sound. However, as the program evolved, its focus tightened on particular themes: Did Led Zeppelin play real blues? What is country blues? And so forth. In the mid-1990s, when the show was broadcast by a number of stations on different days of the week, it employed the commemorative format of a "Blues Birthday Party," featuring—in line with hallowed and longstanding Russian practices—the music of bluesmen whose birthdays fell in that week.[13] On a few occasions beginning in the late 1990s, the radio stations carrying the show permitted live performances in studio by Moscow blues bands. These broadcasts were generally well received, but some listeners phoned in to insist that this format be terminated, because in their view only black musicians from plantations or inner cities in the United States can perform "real blues." As might be expected, the outlook and attitude of listeners have changed since the program's early days, reflecting both the accumulation of knowledge about the music and, relatedly, a more discerning and critical appreciation of it. Yet, if anything, the opportunities for blues broadcasting have contracted, perhaps indicating that audience saturation, at least from a commercial standpoint, has been reached.

In 1994, Aleksei Kalachev—whom we met in the context of his efforts to launch and sustain Club Beliaeva—began weekly broadcasts on Radio Rossiia of his show "Dr. Blues," which likewise has continued to the present day. Kalachev selected his fare according to the criterion of popularity which, "in the early 1990s [meant] blues that featured strong guitar playing," but he has also included some of the songs of his favorite old bluesmen in the program. During its early years, "Dr. Blues" sometimes played the recordings of Russian blues musicians and invited them to perform live on the air, the apotheosis of which was a twelve-hour marathon in August 1994 featuring most of Moscow's top players. However, over time Kalachev has come to the conclusion that playing Russian blues on his program has amounted to a rather feckless undertaking. "You have a high quality of authentic American blues," he commented, "and this is an American art—they know how to play it. Not only play it, they breath it, it is in the air. What is done in Moscow with respect to blues is something quite different. It is a reflection or copy."[14]

Elsewhere on the radio dial, blues has been hard to find. Occasionally, some blues numbers might be included in the programming of FM disc jockeys working within a rock-based format but, since Alek Kasparov's weekly "Blues Bag" left the airways in the mid-1990s, there has been a dearth of blues on that radio band. Kasparov's show, itself, had begun airing in 1991 on Radio Maximum, a joint Russian-American venture. "Blues Bag" derived its name from the sack of blues CDs that Kasparov toted into the studio, unpacking them at the mike, and spinning those that he felt like playing. Reflecting, perhaps, the tastes of the station's young listeners, this show tended to play the music of contemporary artists. Evdokimov and Kalachev—as well as Kasparov while he was in the picture—have been swapping tapes and CDs, along with musical and biographical information on blues artists that they use in their commentaries. Moreover, toward the purpose of raising both the quality and approachability of program content, the broadcasters have not shunned the old Soviet conventions of mutual criticism and self-criticism.

Much like FM radio, television has not figured much into the dissemination of blues music in Russia, other than the already mentioned few televised performances by Liga bliuza and the videos that they, Crossroadz, and Blues Cousins have produced. The one exception to this spotty record would be the program *Prosto bliuz* (*Simply Blues*) which aired for ten weeks on the cable station NTV-plus from December 1996 to March 1997. With Petrovich in the role of emcee, each installment of this hour-long show spotlighted one of Moscow's top blues bands, bracketed by film clips from the movie *Crossroads* or by shots of jam sessions on a sharecropper's porch somewhere in the Delta. Because the sparse studio audience—when there was one—was composed of musicians, music critics, and cultural figures, the show often resembled a seminar.[15] No band would be able to gather a head of steam before its performance would be punctured by commentary on style and genre or by the replies to the questions phoned in by viewers: "What is the difference between St. Louis and Chicago blues?" "Why are they singing in English rather than in Russian?" Somewhat ironically, because the show aired on a cable channel, the vast majority of Muscovites had no direct access to it. However, reception elsewhere was far more extensive, especially in Russia's Far East where this blues program inopportunely aired in the early morning. The only televised blues available to Moscow's residents on a more or less regular basis has been over the Culture Channel, leaking into its weekly program *Jazzophrenia* in the form of a "Blues Corner": five-minute spots showing clips of artists such as Son House, Muddy Waters, and Leadbelly that would be accompanied by brief commentaries.

With respect to the popular print media, the record for blues music has been, again, sparse and spotty. Both local and national newspapers have published articles on blues music in Russia, and more extended essays on the music have appeared in various music magazines. Some in this latter group have been nourished by the blues-oriented radio shows, using the remarks of, and replies to, telephone callers as ready material for their texts.[16] Although a few pieces on Russian performers have appeared,[17] the bulk of the coverage that music magazines have devoted to blues consists of profiles of famous foreign bluesmen with discussions of their music and its influence on the genre.[18] Rather incongruously, the longest article on blues music published by a popular journal in Russia has appeared in a magazine devoted to audio equipment.[19] Although information about blues, both at home and abroad, has not been particularly easy to come by in Russia—there are no Russian equivalents, for instance, of the many blues magazines published in the United States and Europe—a rudimentary knowledge of the music and its practitioners can be acquired by any resourceful fan. This is especially true for individuals with access to the Internet where, along with a host of blues web sites created in the West, one can also find a Russian one at www.blues.ru.

Finally, with respect to recordings, two generalizations can immediately be offered. First, a sizeable influx of blues CDs and tapes into the capital has occurred since private trading has become legal (to the extent that the adjective "legal" can be used in the Russian case). One can find a limited selection of the music in a few of the capital's record shops—limited because of the fact that commercial pricing under copyright regulations sets prices for blues CDs in these establishments above fifteen dollars. In Moscow, this represents nearly 10 percent of the average monthly wage; in the provinces, of course, the percentage would be considerably higher. The solution to this problem has come from black market operations which supply the country with pirated editions of all manner of contemporary music, blues included. Pirated blues recordings are usually produced in batches of five hundred and sell for between two and three dollars per copy. They have been available in ample supply at Moscow's Gorbushka, an open-air public market that commenced operations in the mid-1990s, moving in 2001 to a large new indoor facility maintained by the city government. Because the editions are small and the trade is brisk, one can find CDs by almost any Western bluesman at Gorbushka if one is both patient and prepared to act with dispatch when the desired items appear in the stalls.

Second, cheap, pirated versions of foreign blues recordings have driven the Russian article out of the market. How many Muscovites would want to spent their money on a CD produced by a local group when they can buy one by, say, Otis Rush or John Mayall for the same price or even less.[20] Accordingly, the commercial potential for Russian blues recordings that was present to some extent in the early 1990s, has been scotched by pirated imports.[21] As a result, the commercial strategies of Russian bluesmen much resemble those of their African American forebears: rather than using live performances as a means to promote their records—which is the norm for many artists in the United States today—the goal has been to get jobs performing in clubs, using recordings for demonstration purposes and, thus, as a means to that end.

Festivals

In the aftermath of the highly successful "Blues in Russia" festival of January 1992, no successful attempts ensued to restage such an event in Moscow in the 1990s. To be sure, its organizers hatched and rehatched plans to put on another event of that type, but economic conditions—drastic price increases and the consequent impossibility of convincing potential sponsors that it would be commercially viable—militated against it. However, in June 2000, organizer Adam Beliaev from Lithuania managed to restart the festival machinery. At an open-air venue in north-central Moscow—the neoclassical Hermitage Park and concert grounds—a blues festival ran for three days, complete with almost all the leading Moscow groups, a few blues bands from the provinces, and representatives from Poland (Blues Night Shift, a veteran band with some twelve years of experience), Denmark (Ken Lending Blues Band, another veteran group), and headliners Paul Lamb and the Kingsnakes from the United Kingdom (arguably Britain's top blues group at the time). Although Beliaev had plans to make this an annual event, it failed the first time out; the advertising was scanty, ticket prices were exorbitant, attendance was consequently sparse, the sound quality was cut-rate, and some bands were not paid. Very soon afterward, Beliaev left town. On the heels of this disaster, however, local organizers decided to put the burden on themselves and to try again the following year.

To that end, Andrei Evdokimov and Vovka Kozhekin joined up with Timofei Sakhno, an experienced manager and entrepreneur on Moscow's club circuit with a soft spot for promoting noncommercial music. Together, they devised a plan intended to surmount the difficulties encountered last time out. Working on a shoestring budget, foreign invitations could not be issued. Therefore, offers went out to groups in St. Petersburg and the provinces with the proviso that they would perform at their own risk; payment could not be guaranteed. There were sponsors, but their contributions—advertising and Internet space—came only in kind. *Tochka* (The Point), a large club with ample room for one thousand patrons, agreed to house the event. Its owner put up two thousand dollars to cover the payment for musicians, hoping to reimburse himself from the door should ticket receipts actually reach that figure. Discouraged by the financial situation, Sakhno left town, but not before he had agreed with Tochka's owner to push the opening date up by one day: Thursday and Friday (April 19–20), instead of Friday and Saturday. Inasmuch as a better turnout could be expected on a night not followed by a working day, this untimely change had Evdokimov and Kozhekin wondering whether they were about to repeat last year's commercial debacle. Their fears were

Figure 8. Fifth Moscow Harp Festival, Moscow 2002. From left: Blacky Chernov (amateur harmonica player), John Sorokin (in dark glasses), harmonica player for the group Evergreens, Vovka Kozhekin (waving), Aleksandr Bratetskii, Aleksei Agranovskii, and Mikhail Sokolov. Photo by Andrei Evdokimov.

compounded by the fact that ticket prices, although more sensibly set at about five dollars in advance, six dollars at the door, still remained out of reach for many blues fans. (see fig. 8).

Money problems turned out to be just one of the headaches confronting the organizers. In addition to the unfortunate change of dates, the festival's opening was delayed by a fire that broke out in an adjoining building. Although the club itself was undamaged, the blaze knocked out the building's electrical power. By 9 p.m., when a generator had been located and hooked up, the sizeable crowd that had arrived for the scheduled 7 p.m. start had dwindled to a small fraction of its former number. Then there was the matter of replacing the headliner, Crossroadz, whose leader, Voronov, had fallen ill on the previous day. The organizers turned to Udachnoe priobretenie as a replacement, but were confronted by the money problem again: the diminished revenues from the first-day's proceedings were insufficient to pay the five hundred-dollar fee that Belov's band commanded. Luckily, at the last minute, a solution appeared. Song-writer and publisher Margarita Pushkina, who had just sold one of her songs, offered to use part of the proceeds to pay Belov's band. Belov agreed to lower his band's pay rate for this occasion and Udachnoe priobretenie performed on the festival's second day.[22]

Although the events surrounding the opening played out much like that series of contretemps which inform a standard blues lament, the festival proved a success. With the exception of Crossroadz and Liga bliuza—which had recently suspended operations—all of Moscow's veteran bands performed.[23] They were joined by three groups from St. Petersburg, three from the provinces, and six Moscow blues ensembles of more recent vintage.[24] Canadian Robin Harp, a seasoned blues singer and harmonica player who happened to be visiting Moscow at the time, rounded out the lineup as special guest, demonstrating a showmanship that both delighted the crowd and set a lesson for Russian performers. After the setbacks of the first day, which reduced paid admissions to about 150 people, attendance rebounded and over four hundred fans forked over the price of a ticket for the second day's performances. Along with the musicians, their guests and some fifty representatives of the press—all of whom were initially skeptical about the authenticity of blues played by hometown boys, never mind lads from the provinces—this composite crowd numbered around one thousand.

On opening day, the festival's logistical disarray was furthered reflected in the proceedings on stage. The intervals separating performances were long and disorderly, as musicians and roadies casually tore down and set up equipment, lazily tuning their instruments and bantering with one another before an impatient audience. Either inspired by the music coming from the bandstand or simply intoxicated from the drink consumed during the two-hour postponement, some musicians brought their instruments on stage while other bands were performing and attempted to join in as uninvited guests. These impromptu appearances produced no positive musical results, but did add to the desultory air of the event, stopping the music while band members and organizers cajoled the interlopers to return to their seats. A certain crisis developed along these lines when the festival's special guest, an inebriated Robin Harp, climbed on stage to add an unsolicited harmonica to the performance of Modern Blues Band. When initial entreaties failed to dislodge him, the organizers shut off the sound system, narrowly avoiding an unsightly international incident by mustering enough diplomatic skill to persuade Harp to leave the stage without undue commotion. On the second day, three simple rules were introduced that appreciably improved the proceedings. Tuning was to be accomplished before taking the stage; the volume on the amplifiers was to be tuned down while instruments were being plugged in, thus sparing the patron's ears; and no drunks would be allowed on stage.

Using the experience of the 1992 festival as a convenient benchmark, performers at the 2001 gathering indicated unmistakably that Russian blues had made considerable progress over the course of the past nine years. In addition to obvious improvements in the quality of the musicianship, the music itself had been distilled as a purer form of blues. Repertoires were no longer cluttered with rock and pop songs, while blues numbers were performed in a blues style, free of rock rhythms and overpowering guitar solos. The city's conception of blues music seemed to have expanded well beyond the blues-rock that had dominated the scene in the early 1990s. A number of distinct styles within the blues idiom were on display at the festival: traditional Delta blues; blues in its Chicago and Texas variants; the smooth, loping delivery of the music associated with T-Bone Walker and, relatedly, the jump and swing arrangements of West Coast blues; and, apparently, an emerging Russian variety of blues. The festival also demonstrated that Russian bluesmen had begun to perfect the knack of communicating with their audience, thus adding to their performances that intangible but critical component of the blues tradition which accounts for the music's capacity to generate and to sustain a palpable sense of community. As both emcee and performer, Mikhail Mishuris acquitted himself especially well in this respect, joking and clowning with the audience, and conjuring up a relaxed, intimate atmosphere. Levan Lomidze got the club jumping with call-and-response, clap-along, and singalong techniques that emptied the back rooms, with those in the house who were not dancing packed around the bandstand, rocking to the music, and shouting their approval. Because they performed in Russian, Kozhekin and Zhuk were greeted with considerable hostility from the crowd. This, they gradually overcame with self-parodying humor and patient explanations about the way in which blues is rooted in the moment and, above all, in the concrete. Illustrating their thoughts with some original talking blues reporting scenes of misfortune, stupidity, and frustration drawn from everyday life, they transformed their icy reception into sustained cheering. The original stylings of St. Petersburg's Big Blues Revival also proved immensely popular at the Festival, earning for the group the best press notices appearing in its aftermath.[25] The band's success would be in part due to the way in which they have married certain Petersburg traditions to the basics of blues performance, the subject under discussion in the following chapter.

CHAPTER FIVE

St. Petersburg and the Provinces

Outside Moscow, live blues music can be found in several of Russia's provincial capitals and large towns. Nevertheless, this would probably require some searching. With the exception of St. Petersburg—where a lively blues scene began to develop in the mid-1990s—a handful of groups scattered across the country's expanse have been performing the music in relative isolation, commonly in a ratio of one city: one blues band. Indeed, during Moscow's mid-1990s boom, the number of blues bands in the capital would have easily outnumbered their combined total in the rest of the country. This imbalance reflects Moscow's central position, which in the particular instance of blues music carries two important implications. First, cultural influences from the West tend to reach the capital first, before radiating out to the rest of the country with a more or less predictable lag in time. Thus, exposure to blues—whether simply information about the music, the opportunity to purchase blues recordings, or the chance to hear it performed live—has been a relatively rare occurrence in the provinces. Likewise, with few exceptions, provincial bands tend to be "behind" their Moscow counterparts, playing in the late 1990s the rock-based style of blues that had been dominant in the capital at the beginning of the decade. Second, ambitious Russians have been known to move to Moscow to advance their career prospects, and bluesmen have been no exception to that rule. As a consequence the magnetic force of the capital has drawn to it numerous blues musicians, thus depleting their already limited supply in the remainder of the country.

Despite these imbalances between Moscow and the provinces, blues has been marking progress in what Russians—or, at least, Muscovites—call "the periphery." Indeed, by the end of the 1990s, the vector of the music's proliferation had been reversed: the number of working blues bands in the capital declined after reaching the saturation point in the mid-1990s whereas elsewhere in the country their numbers have been on the rise. In this chapter we offer an overview of these developments, focusing first on

St. Petersburg and then turning attention to those pockets of the blues community that dot the remainder of Russia's urban landscape.

St. Petersburg Blues

The history of blues music in Russia's "northern capital" is split into two distinct epochs whose association one with the other would be supplied by memory rather than in the person of living performers. As in Moscow, elements of blues had made their way into St. Petersburg's flourishing rock scene during Soviet times; yet, unlike the pattern that developed in the capital, none of the Petersburg rock groups would chart a musical direction toward the roots of rock music and metamorphose into a blues band in the postcommunist period. Obvious differences in the material conditions attending these cities would provide one reason for their divergent trajectories. With its sizeable community of affluent expatriates and disproportionate share of the country's nouveaux riches, Moscow has been cast in the role of Russia's Babylon where disposable incomes have fueled a nightclub economy sustaining a host of performing bands. In contrast, St. Petersburg, where life has been far more spartan, has not afforded such remunerative opportunities to performers. However, the material factor would seem to be only a part of the picture here. Aesthetics have mattered as well.

During the final two decades of the USSR's existence, Leningrad (St. Petersburg) had emerged as the capital of Soviet rock. This feat was accomplished by a remarkably talented collection of musicians who forged their own sound and style by redirecting their efforts away from mimicry of Western rock 'n' roll and toward the perfection of a patently Russian product. Leningrad underground rock first asserted itself in the early 1970s when musicians began to compose original lyrics in the Russian language.[1] This innovation led both to an emphasis on lyrics over instrumentation—with rockers regarding themselves as poets, in Thomas Cushman's view—and to experimentation that would expand their music's circumference by including elements from a number of genres: Russian folk, Eastern music, classical music, and blues.[2] This music was regarded by performers and fans as something more than rock. It was "art-rock."

Leningrad's rock scene was every bit a piece of Russia's *sistema* that we have described previously: a hippie/bohemian underground characterized by a creativity contemptuous of convention and by a sociability centered around its emblematic beverage of choice, port wine. Alla Gladkikh, a musician who worked as an organizer of underground rock concerts in

Soviet times has recalled the halcyon days of Leningrad art-rock with ironic affection. "The leading groups—*Akvarium* (Aquarium), *Mify* (Myths), *Mashina vremeni* (Time Machine), and *Rossiiane* (Russians)—all played some blues then," she recounted:

> not classical American blues but songs they had written themselves in a blues form. In the underground, blues and rock were mixed together very closely, just like music and life. In those days, our favorite drink was port wine, the cheapest port wine. We drank it whenever we gathered, no matter the time or place. Of course, nobody ate anything—well, sometimes we ate. For instance, Rossiiane worked in a bread factory. The whole group worked there. They would bring home these big, round loaves of bread, open them up and tear out the bread in the center. Then they would pour port wine into the hollow crusts. And that is pretty much the way Rossiiane lived. Their diet consisted of these hollowed-out loaves filled with port wine, except in the morning when they would use milk instead.[3]

Although the influence of blues was apparent in the music of many of Leningrad's top art-rock groups, it was Mike Naumenko, leader of Zoopark, who delved deepest into the blues idiom. His compositions appropriated a number of blues and rhythm and blues styles—the classic Delta variety, the blues lament, and Chuck Berry—to which he would add poignant, socially critical, humorous, and satirical lyrics. Many of his songs were arranged in standard twelve-bar blues form, sometimes relying on the deep blues pattern of three-line stanzas in which the second line emphatically repeats the first. However, Naumenko borrowed from other styles as well, performing some of his compositions in the folk idiom or in that of urban songs whose themes run parallel to those of the blues tradition. In this respect, Naumenko's work, which had gone the farthest toward introducing blues elements into Leningrad art-rock, might supply an explanation on the musical plane for the absence of a cohort of musicians in St. Petersburg poised to adopt blues music wholeheartedly at the beginning of the 1990s. In fact, two explanations might be enclosed within it. On one hand, there may not have been enough blues *music* in Leningrad's art-rock to sustain a blues direction when that scene began to disintegrate during perestroika.[4] Musicianship for the Leningraders came second to poetry, and the few survivors of the art-rock genre, such as Boris Grebenshchikov, have continued in that tradition. The vessel for the lyrics may be a blues form in a given case, but it could just as well come from another genre. On the other, as far as blues was concerned, Naumenko in particular may have achieved a certain premature synthesis. That is, his combination of a blues style—however rudimentary and unpolished—

with contemporary themes sung in Russian and replete with images of everyday life anticipated the efforts of Kozhekin and Zhuk to create a "Russian blues" many years after Naumenko's early death. In that respect, Naumenko would be remembered as a forerunner. His recordings have been posthumously reissued and his songs in the blues vein have been recorded recently by two of Russia's top guitar players.[5]

If perestroika depleted the cultural capital of Leningrad's art-rock community by making it possible to voice public protests concerning the very things that the underground's bards had been singing about for years, then it also opened a new venue for performance: the street. Artists such as Vitalii Andreev and Edik Tsekhanovskii—whom we discuss later in this chapter—first honed their craft as bluesmen by busking in the city's public places. Both remember their experiences as rewarding in many ways. Tsekhanovskii recalled the remunerative aspect, noting how "people would throw money at us. At that time, there was very little on which to spend money, so people would spend it on us."[6] In the same terms, Andreev remembered how "people had money and they would throw it at us," but he also called attention to the liminal nature of this period.

> During the flowering of perestroika, there was also a real flowering of street music. For instance, on the sidewalk by Kazan Cathedral on Nevskii Prospect, a lot of people would gather to exchange opinions and to argue. So, we would go down there and to play on the street. Sometimes the police would come, and sometimes OMON [paramilitary police] would appear there too. They didn't know whether to beat us or not. On one hand, it would seem okay for us to do this—to play on the street—but, on the other, it wasn't clear to them why we would want to do this. That's how things are. If society begins talking and discussing, then pretty soon you don't need the *vlasti* [authorities] anymore, they don't have anything to do.[7]

Both the good times for street musicians and the authorities' preoccupation with street-level tranquility ended simultaneously. The new capitalist Russia would be a place in which playing on the street did not invite blows from the policeman's truncheon, but also a place in which the vast majority of people had no room in their tight family budgets for tipping buskers. Moreover, the emerging commercial sector was loath to take on a project as dubiously rewarding as blues music. As Alla Gladkikh related:

> After communism a new kind of audience began to appear and clubs were opened that would appeal to it. Kids and grandmas were what you would see in those clubs and you would hear a new thing there called *popsa*. The

club with which I was associated was guilty in this respect. We did nothing to advance the musical upbringing of these kids; we just put in the music that they wanted to hear and we did it just for the money. So, these kids now had places where they could hear music that they liked, this *popsa*, and a lot of the players from the underground days were just sitting at home—especially the ones who played blues—or they left the country or, at least, the musical profession. . . . The new show business would fill stadiums with teenagers by putting on their idols and selling lots of tickets. . . . When the more or less informal underground network of musical relations in Petersburg was replaced by this music business, there was simply too small an audience—people familiar with blues—to support the kind of show business that followed in communism's wake.[8]

Without commercial outlets for blues in the early postcommunist years, the music was initially kept alive only in the haunts of the hippie counterculture: apartments, some busking on the street, and the occasional performance in clubs, usually of the seedy, underground variety. Edik Tsekhanovskii and his itinerant group, Hoodoo Voodoo, managed to keep body and soul together by making regular trips to Sweden, Denmark, and Germany where their street performances would often attract the attention of club owners who would book them for small sums that appeared princely by Russian standards. These profitable informal tours have remained the cornerstone of Hoodoo Voodoo's financing, allowing the group to live and to perform—for as little as two dollars per night—in St. Petersburg during the greater part of the year. Trips to the West are facilitated by Tsekhanovskii's many friends and acquaintances in the hippie and punk countercultures who provide lodging in communal flats or abandoned warehouses. When renting accommodations have been necessary, the group has permitted itself the relative luxury of a hotel room on Hamburg's Reeperbaun.

Tsekhanovskii is himself a talented slide-guitar player and singer who delivers his version of Delta blues with an arresting authenticity and freshness. His near-impeccable pronunciation and intonation of the lyrics that he sings is made all the more remarkable by the fact that he effectively speaks no English. Tsekhanovskii also lives a life not unlike that of his storied forebears in blues lore, in which a happy-go-lucky spontaneity has cohabited with the demons of alcohol and drug addiction. He tells of his adventures on the road with a certain passion that reminds one of the Russian reluctance to verbalize deep and important truths, lest they be diminished by confinement to mere words. For example, during an interview, Tsekhanovskii would convey to me with verbal asides, gestures, and enigmatic smiles, the fact that he was not telling me everything straight out. If I were to catch his drift, then I would have to listen to him very closely, supplying those measures of sympathy and imagination required to reach understanding. Slapping his thigh for emphasis, he tells of being set upon by hoodlums while spending a summer's night camped with his woman in a city park somewhere in Poland. Becoming quite serious, he says that "from the first, they promised not to touch the woman. That was good. And then," he pauses as a big grin sweeps across his face, "they lit into me." As he reaches for another cigarette, the light streaming through the single window in his one-room communal flat reveals the outlines of extensive, reconstructive surgery on the right half of his head. The grin is still there as he lights up. Is it saying, "And can you see for yourself what those bastards did to me?" Or were they some other bastards, such as the eight policemen in Hamburg he mentioned who had picked him up one night and, obviously drunk themselves, pummeled him with their night-sticks and smashed up the best guitar he had ever owned?

Vladimir Golovanov was another Petersburg singer-guitarist perform-ing blues on the city's hippie circuit during the lean years. As with Tsekhanovskii, Golovanov has been surrounded by a number of acolytes that comprise his support group, *Kliuch* (Key). The shifting composition and instrumentation in the band has been as varied as the venues that it has played—from underground walkways beneath Nevskii Prospect to the stylish tourist restaurant, Chaika, on the Griboedov Canal, with all manner of bohemian basement establishment in between. Unlike Tsek-hanovskii, however, Golovanov's music is not deep blues. Rather, one strand of it—self-compositions sung in Russian—would be reminiscent of Mike Naumenko's appropriation of blues forms as a vehicle for con-veying his verse.[9] However, depending on the actual complement of mu-sicians enrolled with Kliuch on a given night, the band would be likely to dip into any number of other styles: reggae, rock, or jazzy free-form in-strumentals led by flute and mandolin. Vania Zhuk, whom we have dis-cussed in chapter 4, completed his apprenticeship with Golovanov's band, as did Dima Lin'kov, an inventive blues guitarist who formed the group Contraband in the late 1990s after spending years on the hippie circuit in Moscow and Vilnius, as well as in St. Petersburg.

In a number of ways, the second coming of blues music in St. Petersburg during the mid-1990s can be traced to the efforts and influences of two in-dividuals: Nikita Vostretsov and Valerii Belinov. The former, a burly, na-tive Petersburger, was a musician himself, who sang and played blues on guitar, sometimes performing his own compositions. But he has been bet-ter remembered after his early death in 1996 as a tireless campaigner for the music, whose infectious love for blues had pointed other individuals in that same direction. During the blues hiatus of the early 1990s, Vostretsov opened Indie Club, an underground establishment where blues was featured. He managed to supplement the paucity of Petersburg performers by importing some low-wage bluesmen from England. In addition, he worked as a disc jockey on both Radio Rocks and, later, Radio Katusha, hosting a weekly two-hour blues program. Vitalii Andreev recalled how Vostretsov was so committed to the music that "he actually purchased with his own money two hours of live air-time on two occasions, just so there would not be any commercial interruptions. His program was pure blues, and there was not any dirty money around to spoil it."[10]

Vostretsov has also been remembered in the song "Blues for Nikita," composed by the other major figure promoting blues in St. Petersburg in the mid-1990s, Valerii Belinov.[11] Having toured widely with the Soviet rock group, Radar, Belinov emigrated from his native Riga in 1991, taking a job with a band playing on a riverboat for foreign tourists that deposited him on the banks of St. Petersburg's Neva River in 1993 when that gig had come to an end. A self-taught guitarist, Belinov displays an impressive musical range that spans rock, jazz, and fusion, as well as blues. Falling in love with the sound of the guitar at the age of thirteen, he tells a magical tale about acquiring his first instrument.

> In those days, you couldn't find any guitars in the shops. Just rolls and bad sausage. So I had to build my own guitar. This started when my brother returned from Georgia with some strings. I didn't know much about what this meant, but here were these strings. Next, I went up into the attic and, rifling through the things there, I came across the body of a guitar. It had a picture of three women on it. Of course, it was as tremendous shock to find it there. With the strings and the body, I already felt that there was some kind of intrigue going on. Then it remained to find a neck for the guitar. As it turned out, my mother took me to a winter camp just before the New Year's holidays and there I met Sasha Petrovskii for the first time. Almost immediately and for no apparent reason, he mentioned to me that he had some kind of guitar neck. You can imagine how excited I became. We agreed to meet ten days later at a particular place. On that day, this Sasha Petrovskii roared up on a motorcycle—vroom, vroom. He handed me the guitar neck and said, "No problem. She's yours forever." . . . I immediately forgot everything else, school, sports, all of that. I gave birth to that instrument by assembling the different parts. If you can't buy it, can't get it, then you must give birth.[12]

That experience laid a foundation for the design of subsequent instruments—guitars and Belinov's own inventions, the savitar and pizicator—built for him by some of St. Petersburg's master craftsmen.[13] Belinov's previous work as art director in a Riga club also prepared him to take part in the design and organization of two of St. Petersburg's best musical venues: JFC, a jazz club that opened in 1996 which regularly features blues music; and Jimi Hendrix Blues Club, which opened in 1999 and, due to the problem of filling its fourteen openings per week with primarily local musicians, also puts on jazz, Latin, reggae, and other music.

After gigging with a number of Petersburg's jazz and rock musicians in various groups, Belinov founded BBB (Belinov Blues Band) in 1994, a four-piece band with piano, bass, and drums backing Belinov's vocals and guitar. They found steady employment at the recently opened New Jazz Club in the Tavricheskii Gardens and soon attracted the attention of the reigning impresario of Petersburg jazz and artistic director of the city's Jazz Philharmonic Hall, David Goloshchekin, who invited BBB to perform on Tuesday nights. As Belinov explained:

> We played there a few times and it was a huge success. On one of these occasions when Goloshchekin was introducing us to the audience, he crowned me "King of the Petersburg Blues." He began to publicize this name for me, saying that I was the only person in the country who had mastered this genre. This was a paradox, because I had never aspired to nor imagined myself in such a role. Moreover, I had never directed my attention to blues as some kind of pure form that I should master unto itself. I was simply playing the things that I wanted to play, blues included, but not endeavoring to become a blues artist. However, at that moment when I was crowned "King of the Blues," I divided that music off as a zone removed from other kinds of musical expression and began to dig deeper into it, to isolate and concentrate on the blues itself.[14]

Adopting the stage name King B, Belinov began playing straight blues sets with his band at several clubs in the city. They also did some touring around Russia and participated in various music festivals, thus attracting both a following of fans and the attention of the press.[15] BBB performed live on radio broadcasts from St. Petersburg and Moscow, while clips of their performances in St. Petersburg were aired on local television. The cassette that they recorded helped boost their public standing once Goloshchekin began to play it on his prestigious radio program.[16] However, amid this success, personal conflicts—to which Belinov has been no stranger—set in. BBB lost its Tuesday night dates at the Jazz Philharmonic Hall; JFC (the successor to the New Jazz Club) instituted a ban on the group following Belinov's outré antics on their stage; and some of the other musicians in the group began to go their separate ways in spring of 1996. Belinov remembers those forlorn days with a rueful smile.

We had put all of our money into making the cassette and now jobs were drying up. My wife and I were able to survive thanks to the potatoes that our relatives in the countryside would give us. Once in awhile we would make a little money, but it didn't amount to anything. For instance, I didn't make enough money in those years to be able to take the metro regularly. We lived far from the center then and carrying the equipment wasn't easy. It was a struggle to get the money to ride the metro [then about twenty cents per ride] and sometimes we would have to resort to counterfeit tickets or student passes to ride the bus. It was embarrassing.[17]

BBB's composition shifted around its leader until the group finally jelled as a trio that included a driving rock drummer, Igor' Perebaev, and a gifted bass player schooled in traditional jazz as well as in rock, Ivan Kovalev. Until Belinov's emigration to the United States in late 2000, this slender ensemble represented St. Petersburg's premier blues group. Although their repertoire remained effectively frozen and no rehearsals were ever called, BBB exhibited an extraordinary versatility, range, and creativity, enabling them to play quite distinct versions of the blues, depending on the house and the mood. At *Mankhetten* (Manhattan) Club, where people came to cut loose, they would amply oblige by blasting out a Texas-style blues with rock overtones that would keep the roof raised well above its moorings until three or four in the morning. In the more sedate surroundings of the Jimi Hendrix Blues Club—where people would come to dine and to listen more than to get tanked and dance—they would play the same songs but in a form unrecognizable from other performances. These occasions held audiences spellbound with jazz-inflected guitar virtuosity that led the listener on extensive musical excursions wrapped snugly in a rhythmic accompaniment that effortlessly followed Belinov's improvised changes in tempo, tone, and mood.

In addition to his own performances, Belinov advanced St. Petersburg blues by training a number of young local guitar players who formed their own groups. The most outstanding guitarist among his protegés has been Kolia "Hands" Gruzdev, who picked up the guitar at an early age, learning, like the great majority of the country's bluesmen, the music of the Beatles, the Rolling Stones, Led Zeppelin, and Jimi Hendrix before discovering the sounds of Muddy Waters, John Lee Hooker, B. B. King and T-Bone Walker.[18] Returning from a year of high school in Colorado and some exposure there to the music in live performance, Gruzdev began to frequent the New Jazz Club and the Art Clinic in the mid-1990s to hear BBB. Belinov took him on as a student and soon made room for his guitar on stage, allowing the young gangly Gruzdev to sit in for a set on certain nights. In 1997, Gruzdev put together his own group, Blues.com, consisting of three young Petersburgers (the eldest was twenty-one years old) who had committed themselves both to mastering the blues idiom and to doing something original with it. Inasmuch as the limitations of a three-piece band militated against the realization of that second objective, Gruzdev and his bass player, Sergei Mironov, formed a larger ensemble three years later, adding a horn section, a rap vocalist, and a vinyl-scratching deejay. This group, Soul Power Band, performs original compositions with Russian lyrics that blend blues and funk, relocating Gruzdev's fluid guitar work within a larger band sound. However, Gruzdev entered the military in 2000—using his university training in psychology to counsel Russian servicemen traumatized by their experiences in the Chechen War—and, as a consequence, Soul Power Band's experimental project has been placed on hold.

Inessa Kataeva is another performer whose blues career has been influenced by Belinov. After singing with a number of *estrada* and jazz orchestras in Tashkent and Khabarovsk, Kataeva found her preferred voice performing hard rock, thereby crossing one of the gender lines of the Soviet period that has remained largely intact even today. Her musical possibilities, constricted in Tashkent by the same ethnic conflict that nearly took her life there in an unprovoked assault on the street, Kataeva managed to immigrate to St. Petersburg in 1994 where she sang with an assortment of rock groups whose seemingly promising projects never panned out. She even joined the circus for six months, attempting to learn the art of the clown before leaving when reassigned to the acrobatic corps as a catcher. While in and out of one group or another and working various low-paid jobs to support herself and her young son, Kataeva accepted Belinov's invitation to sing a couple of songs with his band that was performing at the Art Clinic. As she recalled the event:

> I got there straight from work and I was just frozen. I was working construction at the time, working outdoors in the middle of winter. They asked me if I were going to sing and I told them no, that I didn't have any clothes. I was still in my work clothes, quilted jacket and pants, a scarf tied around my head under my helmet. They said, "Just sing like that." I couldn't believe it, but as I sat there and listened to the music in that warm room, all my difficulties seemed to melt away. So I got up to sing and said, "Just play something slow." They began to play and I just sang one phrase and repeated it. And I sunk my teeth into it and began to improvise. There was a great reaction; the people started to shout. After this concert, Valerii [Belinov] began to invite me more often to get up and sing, especially at Mankhetten Club. I would often sing without using any of the words. I

Figure 9. Inessa Kataeva performing with Valerii Belinov at St. Petersburg's City Club, July 1999. Photo by Mike Urban.

would just improvise sounds, drawing on the various musical styles with which I was familiar: jazz, rock, trash, and Eastern music. But Valerii would berate me for that and he would insist that I learn the text.[19]

At the end of the 1990s, Kataeva quit hard rock and devoted her energies to becoming a blues vocalist. Performing under the name "Ines" with a succession of backup bands, she has won the reputation of Russia's Janis Joplin, changing her stage apparel from sequined evening gown to jeans and fringed leather jacket to fit that image. She has also developed an engaging performance style, using her powerful voice in prolonged series of shrieks, screams, wails, and growls to pulverize audiences, to induce them into all manner of crazy dancing and to elicit their echoes to her raspy shouts of "bay-be." Although her career as a blues singer has registered relative progress, we would be remiss not to record the fact that this remarkable talent has continued to live a life—even measured against the poverty characteristic of effectively all Petersburg blues players—that could be called penurious.[20]

It was also Belinov's suggestion that led to the assembly of what would become St. Petersburg's top blues band, Big Blues Revival.[21] The group is led by singer Vitalii Andreev who, in formidable spectacles and perched behind a music stand on stage, looks every bit the part of a would-be maestro (although the music stand supports not sheet music but typed copies of English language lyrics that Andreev, who does not speak English himself, uses as a prompt). Two players—drummer Evgenii Bobrov and mandolin and dobro player Sergei Starodubtsev—have come from a country/bluegrass band, Fine Street; another, guitarist and harmonica player, Sasha Suvorov, from the rock group, Resistors; bassist Sergei Mironov joined after learning his blues with Gruzdev's Blues.com; and slide guitarist Aleksandr Rozhdestvenskii has also come from a blues background, having completed a four-year apprenticeship on second guitar with Tsekhanovskii's Hoodoo Voodoo. In 1999, the first year of the group's existence, Big Blues Revival struggled to forge an original sound from both the band's unusual instrumentation and the discrepant styles issuing from its members' musical backgrounds, surviving on the pay— at little as thirty dollars for the group per performance—earned at infrequent engagements. Only the drummer, Bobrov, has maintained a day job; the others have been content to scrape by with the meager remissions from their musical careers, devoting their energies to developing the group's unique blues sound.

From the first, the plan had been to perform Delta and early Chicago blues in a subdued, mellow style. To that end, only acoustic instruments were employed and the drums were limited to a trap set played with brushes. This yielded a remarkable string sound with guitar, slide, dobro, and mandolin complementing one another in a resonant variety of subtle timbres and shadings overlaid on a polyrhythmic base. Andreev's deep vocals blended nicely into that musical mix. In its second year, however, Suvorov's acoustic guitar imploded and the band was forced to introduce electrical instruments (although Starodubtsev has continued to play acoustic mandolin and dobro, using a stage microphone for amplification). Although the group has gone electric, no gadgets or electrical effects have been employed, and the band's forte—a pure, string sound—has remained largely intact.[22] With time, Suvorov has begun to play more in the jazzy, swing style of Django Reinhardt, his guitar serving as an inventive counterpoint to Rozhdestvenskii's Delta-blues phrasings on the slide. Along with the perfection of its style and sound, Big Blues Revival has been experiencing more commercial success, performing in some of Moscow's top clubs and at festivals in Russia and Norway. In 2001, the band produced a CD of its songs recorded at various venues in Russia.[23] On it can be heard their rendition of Arthur Crudup's "That's All Right Mama" on which the band repeats a figure in descending key changes on the refrain, creating thereby an arresting effect that suggests things coming apart and wheels falling off while Andreev's growling vocal continuously assures his would-be interlocutor that "that's all right."

A number of other groups playing blues appeared in St. Petersburg during the mid-to-late 1990s, among them: the Russian Blues Band, the Rusinov Blues Band, Blues Time, Splash Point, Underground Blues Band, and Underground Sunburn. These groups either did not stay together long or have had only one foot in the music so they will not concern us here. However, two other groups formed in this period merit some attention. The first of these got started in late 1994 when Jerome Jeffrey, a Canadian country singer and guitarist, accompanied his wife to St. Petersburg where she had just found employment with a nongovernmental organization. Jeffrey had decided to try his hand at blues and toward that end recruited local jazz and fusion players for his Blues Project. Beginning with covers of blues standards, the band gradually began to include a number of Jeffrey's own compositions in the blues vein and developed a sound of their own, one slightly inflected by their leader's background in country music. The fact that Jeffrey's native language was English added much to the group's overall presentation and cast Jeffrey in a role somewhat analogous to that of John Anderson in Moscow's Old Men's Blues Band: an experienced player at home in the idiom who introduced his bandmates to many of the finer points of blues performance. A quip from the band's harp player, Sergei Nekrasov, captured Jeffrey's influence on those in the group: "he played in the same language in which he thought, and this opened doors for us musically,"[24] Due to the dearth of blues venues in St. Petersburg in those years, the Jerome Jeffrey Blues Project rarely played local dates, earning their way as musicians by training to Moscow. They played in clubs there with some frequency once Sergei Voronov had brought them into the city's circuit for blues bookings. When Jeffrey left the country in 1997, the band broke up.

The second group under consideration, The Way, formed in that same year, soon becoming St. Petersburg's hardest working blues band. This trio was composed of vocalist and bass player, Sergei Semenov; and exceptionally rhythmic drummer, Sergei Kuznetsov, who has an extensive background in jazz, especially Dixieland; and guitarist, Vladimir Berezin, who plays in the fluid style of Stevie Ray Vaughn. An exchange among them underscored the combination of motives that led to the group's formation.

Semenov: Around the mid-1990s new clubs began to open and this gave us the chance to play the music that we actually liked to play.

Kuznetsov: Yes, there had been a kind of hole. There was a lot of rock 'n' roll around in the '80s and '90s, and certainly jazz has a much longer history

Figure 10. Big Blues Revival on stage at St. Petersburg's JFC Club in July 1999. From left: Evgenii Bobrov, Sash Suvorov, Sergei Mironov (partially obscured), Aleksandr Rozhdestvenskii (partially obscured), Vitalii Andreev, and Sergei Starodubtsev. Photo by Mike Urban.

in the Soviet Union and Russia. But for blues there was this void. It simply wasn't represented on the musical landscape.

Berezin: We didn't begin to play this music just because there was someone who wanted to listen to it.

Kuznetsov: But that was also one of the reasons that we began to play, wasn't it? You can't play to an empty hall, can you?

Berezin: Once you start playing this music, people will come to listen to it.

Kuznetsov: Maybe. But the moment arrives when it becomes necessary to feed the family.[25]

Following that compass, The Way has maintained a heavy performance schedule, playing as many as twenty-five dates per month in St. Petersburg's clubs, halls, and casinos. Inasmuch as their lineage cannot be traced to either of the two principal sources of Petersburg blues—the hippie underground personified by Tsekhanovskii, Golovanov, and their acolytes on one hand, and the groups formed under Belinov's wing on the other—a certain social distance has been present from the first between this band and other bluesmen in the city. The Way's willingness to play often and anywhere has widened it. Some blues musicians deride various venues in which The Way has performed as a "discreditation" of both the musicians and the music that they play. Others point to the group's near-nightly performances as a practice that kills creativity and turns the music stale. As a consequence of that social distance, The Way was not offered a spot at a small blues festival held in St. Petersburg in 1998. However, in the following year, they were asked by other bands to participate in the musicians' strike at the Jimi Hendrix Blues Club, but they declined the invitation. Semenov, speaking for the group in a press interview, acknowledged the grievances motivating the strike, but claimed that "there would always be a band who would offer their services [to the club owner and that] . . . it is better for musicians to work on the quality of their playing than to spend time in idle chatter."[26] We turn now to that strike and to the organization that it spawned, the Association of Blues Musicians.

Clubs, the Strike, and the Association

Since the advent of nightclubs in the mid-1990s, blues can be heard in St. Petersburg at a variety of sites. At the low end, it is played in bohemian haunts such as *Priiut strannykh* (Odd-Balls' Refuge) and Fish Fabrique; at the other end of the sociocultural scale, it is performed in concert halls such as the Jazz Philharmonic and the New Jazz Club; and, in the middle-brow range, a number of establishments offering restaurant service and bars—such as *Korsar* (Corsair), Jam, City Club, and the Beatles theme club, Liverpool—have booked blues bands on either a regular or intermittent basis. Naturally, the diversity of venues has created a considerable variation in the ambience at performances. At JFC, for instance, patrons in sport coats and ties or in modestly fashionable frocks sit comfortably amid the tastefully appointed décor of a jazz club whose weathered-brick interior, chromed railings, and stately bar remind the foreign visitor of any number of similar establishments found in metropolitan areas from Berlin to San Francisco. The atmosphere is restrained yet casual; the conversation is hushed, intent on serious listening. At Taxi-Drive, on the other hand, customers come to immerse themselves in the revelry. There, performances have been punctuated by wiggling g-stringed damsels—an innovation apparently inspired by the combination of this species of lusty entertainment with blues music as portrayed in the U.S. film, *From Dusk Till Dawn* (1996)—who administer lap-dances to enthused young men.

In spring of 1999, the first St. Petersburg club devoted exclusively to blues music opened its doors. At its founding, the Jimi Hendrix Blues Club was greeted by blues musicians as an important breakthrough. Now, just as in Moscow, St. Petersburg would have a "real" blues club, a home for them and their music. With a central location on Liteinnyi Prospect, midway between Nevskii Prospect and Liteinnyi Bridge, this cozy cellar club—which stayed open around the clock, seven days a week—could provide both steady employment for musicians and serve as a congregating point for the city's bluesmen and blues lovers alike. The pay was modest—about thirty-two dollars per performance for an entire group—but slightly above standard club scale. Moreover, since the club put on fourteen shows per week, the opportunity to play there occurred both frequently and regularly. For the city's bluesmen, this represented a considerable improvement in their commercial prospects. With Valerii Belinov serving as the club's art director, their access to the means of performance seemed secure.

Early on everything went splendidly. Patrons came to drink and chat against the background sounds of classic and contemporary Chicago blues, or to watch videos of Muddy Waters or B. B. King performances on a wide-screen TV, thus keeping the club at least half full, regardless of the hour. Each of the club's two daily shows was usually sold out. In July, the Wynton Marsalis Orchestra played a date in St. Petersburg. Rather unexpectedly, they actually turned up at the Jimi Hendrix Blues Club after their scheduled performance, responding positively to an invitation to jam there that Belinov had managed to extend to Marsalis over the phone. For Petersburg bluesmen the ensuing event was almost unimaginable, representing the realization of some dream that one might only entertain in the category of the impossible. Here, in their very own blues club, stood the full complement of the Marsalis Orchestra, performing shoulder-to-shoulder with the city's best blues musicians and blowing the sweetest blues that one could hope to hear—till 5:00 in the morning. This occasion became an instant legend in blues circles and marked the club's musical apogee. Within a matter of weeks, however, matters at the club had degenerated into a series of rancorous conflicts that culminated in a strike staged by four of the city's best blues bands and led by Belinov himself.

Monetary matters constituted a portion of the grievances expressed by BBB, Big Blues Revival, Blues.com, and Ines and Blues Time. The strikers were upset by the fact that the club management had introduced a cover charge of about a dollar and a half per head, yet continued to pay the same small fees to performers. They reckoned that the musicians, who were responsible for the packed houses, should be compensated accordingly, and that the management should be satisfied with the enlarged receipts from the restaurant and bar yielded by their performances. They were particularly incensed by the fact that they were allowed to invite guests to their concerts who, although not stopped at the door to pay admission, would later find the cover charge added to their bill for refreshments. Taken together, these grievances suggested a deeper motivation for the strike—a perceived lack of respect for musicians on management's part, an indignity that they would not suffer. At their meeting on August 11, 1999, the representatives of the four striking bands emphasized the issues of dignity and respect, and framed monetary matters in those terms. They claimed that the management had regularly and publicly spoken to them in deprecatory language, just as they had insulted them by offering them no discounts on drinks or surreptitiously charging admission to their invited concert guests.

Following in the footsteps of other Petersburg performers—namely, a number of the city's top rave-club deejays who had formed their own trade union and gone on strike a month earlier—the striking blues musicians decided to organize themselves as the Association of Blues Musicians (ABM).[27] The principal goal of this effort was to found a new blues club—which they expectantly dubbed the "Real Blues Club"—that would be a haven for bluesmen, a place where they would always be welcome and treated with the respect they felt themselves denied at the Jimi Hendrix Blues Club. In order to accomplish this, the bands decided to pool their small resources, secure legal registration, and recruit some sponsors. However, neither the sponsors nor premises for a new club materialized and within a couple of months Belinov, who had been the prime mover behind both the strike and the ABM, had returned with his band to the Jimi Hendrix Blues Club to play their regular twice-weekly dates. His decision dealt a severe blow to the collective action, but the other groups continued their now-futile strike as a matter of principle and have persevered with the ABM project.

At this writing, the ABM has an application pending for official registration, a process that, under Russian procedures and conditions, can consume years.[28] ABM's composition has changed—Ines and Blues Time and, of course, BBB have dropped out, while Underground Sunburn and Contraband have joined—yet its principal aim of founding its own blues club remains intact. Toward that end, official registration would provide the organization with a tax-exempt status while allowing it to earn the money needed to start the club by engaging in various commercial activities, such as running lotteries, selling products, and staging concerts and festivals. Although still unregistered, the ABM has been active in this last respect, serving as the base on which the *Del'ta Nevy* Blues Festival was organized in June 2001. Although financial troubles required that the initial plan for a three-day event hosting groups from both Russia and abroad had to be pared down to a single day with only Russian performers, the festival brought together some ten bands from around the country who performed to an enthusiastic crowd in the stately surroundings of the city's Iusupovskii Gardens. From the standpoint of gathering together the city's blues community, this event represented a step level improvement over the experience of the previous year, when two small festivals—each named for Robert Johnson—were held on the same day in different quarters of the city, the organizers of each apparently unaware of the activities of their counterparts.

For our purposes, however, the remarkable thing about the ABM project lies in what it suggests about the St. Petersburg blues community as a bearer of the city's ethos, one rooted in the values and mores of the old aristocracy and the cultural intelligentsia.[29] Petersburgers evince a manifest pride in their city, not least for its status as the chief repository of cultural values in Russia. This civic identity informs their norms of interpersonal relations which award tremendous status to those engaged in cultural pursuits, whether *belles lettres*, painting, sculpture, or music. Petersburg bluesmen appropriate these cultural identities and, as scions of the creative intelligentsia, tend to denigrate the idea of commercial success as some unwelcome intrusion into the aesthetic sphere. Indeed, they often speak with contempt about commercial operations, associating such practices with Moscow, their putatively inferior rival in cultural matters, by employing the derisive expression "Moscow show business." It would seem that social identities forged in the city's cultural context account for the particular style and stance—austerity and dignity—displayed by its bluesmen. For many of them it would be far preferable to go without a job than to perform in an establishment that did not afford them the respect to which they feel entitled.

In this regard, there would seem to be a difference of degree between Petersburg bluesmen and their Moscow counterparts, and the invidious distinctions introduced by the former need not be accepted in order to acknowledge it. Moscow blues musicians do not appear as one-sidedly mercenary as Petersburgers sometimes suggest. They, too, walk in the ways of intelligentsia culture, understanding their roles as fraught with struggle and suffering for their art. And they, too, have experienced their share of hardships and humiliations at the hands of club owners and managers. Consider, for instance, an episode witnessed by Aleksandr Tsar'kov in a Moscow club:

> in which someone who was dancing collided with the microphone on stage, knocking it into the mouth of the female singer. There was blood all over the place. She was knocked down and one of her teeth was knocked out. Not only did the singer not get compensation from the club's manager, but she was docked in pay because she didn't complete her entire performance.[30]

Such scenes would be imaginable in St. Petersburg as well; but so too would be a retaliatory job action, something that Moscow musicians have never mounted.

The Petersburg ethos is also reflected in performance. Again, no hard and fast lines should be drawn here between that city and Moscow. However, as a matter of degree we can observe in St. Petersburg a certain tendency to valorize the refined, the intimate, the exclusive—in short, to embrace the venerable norms of the old aristocracy and the cultural intelligentsia. As a newcomer to the city, Valerii Belinov observed this atmosphere while performing at an art club on the Griboedov Canal.

> It was almost ideal. Petersburg is famous for its chamber music concerts and that was what was happening at this club. There was a kind of intimacy that occurs in close surroundings like that. In Soviet times, the tradition of chamber music was continued with what we used to call "apartment concerts." These were underground. Soviet times are over, but that feeling and tradition have been carried on. Of course, people know this and they love it. And, so, here we were in the thick of Petersburg tradition. . . . Everyone who saw the concert was just delighted; they made a big fuss about it and some gave me presents. And then the concert was continued on the next day, and the day after that. It went on for nine days in a row.[31]

From the perspective of a native Petersburger, Kolia Gruzdev offered a somewhat different characterization, comparing his city with Moscow.

> This city [St. Petersburg] is very, very snobbish. People think of themselves as well-educated, as very intelligent, and are in some ways very selfish. That is a Petersburg characteristic, but it's not all bad. Here people are looking for real things and you have got to be real to play music here. To be understood. This relates to all kinds of things, not just to playing blues. . . . In Moscow, people enjoy clubs and enjoy listening to music like we do. But it's different. We don't have that much money. So, when you play music, it's like [enacting] the social order. But in Moscow you have to feed the standards. They have certain ideas about how it should be and everybody should fit these standards. Here, I do things for myself; I play what I want to play and how I want to play it. And that's what people need, I think.[32]

Blues in the Provinces

We conclude this chapter with a survey of the blues in Russia's provinces. Here, we are working with fragments of knowledge, a condition resulting from the country's vastness and the isolation that still attends its many far-flung population centers. For instance, the group Ragtime, which had been performing blues in the south Volga region of Kabardino-Balkariia since the early 1990s, only came to our attention during the course of this study. In short, we make no claim that our survey is comprehensive. There may be other bands out there about which we simply have no information. We begin with a band on which we have already had occasion to comment, Novosibirsk's Novaia assotsiatsiia bliuza (New Blues Association).

Novaia assotsiatsiia bliuza, or NAB, appears to have been Siberia's first blues band. It was formed by Mikhail Mishuris and Evgenii Solomin, two young residents of Novosibirsk who had been practicing on harp and guitar, rehearsing songs heard on some Chicago blues anthologies that Solomin had brought back from a Finnish Exhibition in town some years earlier. Mishuris had been trying to break in as a singer with some local rock bands, but without much success. As he tells it:

> They would laugh at me because I sang in English and because I wasn't a good musician. I wasn't a good singer. I didn't know scales and licks, I just started to scream, to put in some emotion. I just started to sing the way that I could. It wasn't very good, but there was a lot of emotion [in it] and that gave it a blues feeling. I don't know why, but some people believed in me and wanted to play with me. Maybe because I was full of energy at that time, and because I was a real optimist. I found some musicians who wanted to play in the style of [John Mayall's] Bluesbreakers, and they believed in my energy. And so did a friend of my father who gave us a few thousand dollars to buy instruments and equipment.[33]

As a blues ensemble complete with a horn section, the band first played at a rock festival in Tomsk in 1994. They were well received, but sat idle thereafter for some six months. When jobs finally became available, they were usually at small rock festivals held in provincial towns—or, in one instance, a large state dairy farm—where NAB was listened to more politely than enthusiastically by village girls and country *babushki* more enamored with rock groups covering songs familiar to them than with the relatively strange sounds of the blues. The band also played some rough joints, such as a bar in the run-down mining town of Novokuznetsk where the only drink offered by the house was vodka—by the bottle. In 1996, however, a small jazz club opened in Novosibirsk. Its management accepted Mishuris's argument that blues is a form of jazz and began booking NAB for a couple of dates per month.

As in Moscow and St. Petersburg, clubs have been the key factor in supporting a blues scene in the provinces. In Novosibirsk, the implications of that proposition became immediately apparent. NAB found regular, if infrequent, work at the club which led to the acquisition of a resourceful teenage manager who found them jobs in restaurants as well. Moreover, many of the club's patrons were journalists who provided the group with direct access to the local mass media. In addition to press coverage, television treated every performance of Novosibirsk's first blues band as news. Concert clips were regularly broadcast; a film crew traveled some one hundred miles out of town to provide a live feed from the festival at the state dairy farm; and the band performed in studio for live broadcasts on a few occasions. In one respect, these were reminiscent of the program "Simply Blues" that was airing in Moscow about the same time, in which performance alternated with interviews of the band members and commentary on the sources of the music and its various styles. However, the Novosibirsk station that was broadcasting NAB's studio performances was then having difficulties paying its power bills, a situation that contributed a certain Siberian shading to the visage of the band on screen: musicians clothed in outdoor winter wardrobe, emitting small clouds of frosty breath.

In 1996, NAB rechristened itself Blues Passengers and moved to Moscow. Blues in Novosibirsk revived about a year later when that band had dissolved and most of its members returned home to found Boogie Bottles. This five-piece combo appears to be the leading blues group in Novosibirsk at present, but now that more music clubs have opened in the city, other bands have been forming that may offer them some competition. Boogie Bottles has retained the British blues style of its forerunner, thus making its music more accessible to provincial audiences more accustomed to rock than to blues. They have enjoyed some success playing locally and in nearby regions, as well as performing at the Moscow Blues Festival in 2001.

Moving from Siberia to European Russia, in Rostov-on-Don blues music got a relatively early start in the postcommunist period, thanks to the efforts of Iakob Peterson, a forty-year-old blues aficionado who led the three-piece combo, Helicopter Blues Band, a group that stayed together just long enough to give other young musicians in town a taste of the music performed live. After it dissolved in the early '90s, Peterson's efforts were directed toward bringing blues to the attention of these musicians and assisting their efforts to master it. His greatest success was with a group named The Pride, a four-piece band that had been covering the songs of the Beatles and the Rolling Stones before adding a couple of saxophones in 1994 and switching to a blues and rhythm-and-blues repertoire. This ensemble provided solid musical backing for the grainy voice of Mikhail Pashko whose renditions of blues and soul songs in the fashion of John Fogarty became a hit with local audiences. The familiar combination of limited opportunities to perform and low wages for performances themselves meant that the band's members were required to hold regular day jobs to support themselves. Nonetheless they acquired a sizeable, steady following in Rostov, playing regularly at the club Leila. As their guitarist Vadim Ivashchenko recalled:

> We had our own following in town. These people would regularly come out to our concerts and sometimes even photograph us while we were performing on stage. That was very nice. After a while, they got to know our songs. We used to do a song called "Down by the River" and, on one occasion, all of the electricity in the club went out just as we had begun to play it. So the audience took it up and they sang the whole song for us. That was really great.[34]

The Pride played occasionally on local television and radio and managed a couple of road performances in Taganrog and Krasnodar. After some seven years, differences in the members' musical tastes along with a sense of professional stagnation caused the group to split up. That left the recently formed Professor Blues and His Blues Band as the only blues group playing in Rostov. However, their musical direction has been changing from the country blues of Son House and Robert Johnson to Irish folk music.

Northward on the map, we can locate a group called Café Blues in Smolensk and the Blackmailers Blues Band in Vladimir. The former—a five-piece combo featuring a female vocalist on keyboards—took its current form in 1999. Their sound is light and sophisticated, in the cocktail-blues vein of, say, Charles Brown. The latter group, as their name might suggest, cuts quite a different figure: four young men, whose clothing and stage demeanor connote lives spent on the wrong side of the law, playing blues with controlled power and steady drive. Blackmailers Blues Band is led by guitarist Aleksei Baryshev whose raspy vocals alternate with the clear and impassioned singing of keyboardist Egor Maiorov. The group formed in 1995 after the accumulated accretion of blues material had displaced rock and folk songs from Baryshev's repertoire. The band's set lists have also been influenced by a young woman vocalist from the United States, Liza Vladeck, who was working at Vladimir's America House, promoting economic reform in the region and (fittingly) sponsoring the extension of cultural ties between the United States and Russia. Vladeck has occasionally appeared with the group as its headliner.

Thanks in considerable measure to the group's energetic manager, Aleksei Makarov, Blackmailers Blues Band has become an established presence on Vladimir's cultural landscape. On Friday evenings, the group plays to sold-out crowds at the city's House of Culture; the local press, supplied with information from Makarov, keeps readers informed of the band's activities; local radio stations conduct frequent interviews with Baryshev and local television sometimes films the band's performances. Makarov has also been effective with out-of-town bookings, arranging for reciprocal lodging swaps with bands from Nizhnyi Novgorod, Arzamas, St. Petersburg, and Moscow that enable Blackmailers to tour on a low budget and out-of-town blues bands to perform in Vladimir. The popularity of Blackmailers in Vladimir has created a receptive climate for the music, leading a number of local rock musicians to take it up as well. To date, the group's most important professional outing has been its performance at the Moscow Blues Festival in 2001.[35]

In Russia's more remote recesses, blues bands can be found in the cities of Arzamas and Nal'chik. The former's isolation derives from the fact that it had been a center of the USSR's military-industrial complex and, thus, a closed city in Soviet times. A rock 'n' roll group calling itself J.A.M. formed there in 1988. After many changes in personnel and musical styles, the band jelled in 1995 as a four-piece unit and settled on blues. Anatolii Morozov—the group's vocalist, guitarist, composer, and chief ideologist—had picked up the blues from foreign recordings. But in the closed city, access to this music was minimal and his repertoire was accordingly very limited. Serendipitously, he came across an old book, minus its cover, of blues lyrics in an Arzamas bookshop. Although no one seems to know how such a book found its way into the closed city, it filled the hole in Morozov's blues repertoire, but in a somewhat unusual way. That is, Morozov had no idea how the songs in the book actually sounded; he only had the lyrics. Relying on the limited range of blues numbers that he had heard on recordings, he set about combining their melodies with the words in the book. The results were rather uniformly unwonted. For instance, the band can be heard playing Jimmy Reed's slow-rolling "Shame, Shame, Shame" as a driving blues with an entirely new melody. On Howlin' Wolf's "Killin' Floor," traces of the original melody have remained, but the arrangement has retarded Wolf's up-tempo rendition, turning the song into a slow shuffle.[36] The musicianship, however, is quite respectable and benefits enormously from the full sounds of keyboardist Evgenii Lepikhin's Hammond B-3 organ. Some of the band's material consists of original compositions that ring with an authenticity rarely encountered among blues songs written by Russians.[37]

The commercial prospects for bluesmen in Arzamas have been limited, to say the least. J.A.M. plays the occasional club or restaurant date in town, supplementing its performance schedule with a number of engagements at Moscow's top clubs: the Arbat Blues Club, B. B. King Blues Club, Forte

Club, and Armadillo. The band has also performed in Nizhnyi Novgorod, Vladimir, and St. Petersburg, and opened for the British funk-and-punk group Fun-Da-Mental, in Moscow during their 1999 tour. In 2000, the group celebrated its fifth anniversary with a blues gala held in Arzamas's main concert hall where they were joined by Blues Hammer Band, Black-mailers Blues Band, and a few groups from surrounding provinces. At this writing, J.A.M. has been busy recording its first professionally produced album.

Nal'chik, a city in the north Caucasus province of Kabardino-Balkariia, is home to a four-piece, blues-rock combo called Ragtime. The group's members—all of whom are ethnic Kabardintsy or Balkartsy—selected this name for literary rather than musical reasons. Along the lines of a pattern familiar in the late-Soviet period, the band was formed by classmates in 1990 as a three-piece, hard-rock combo. In the following year, when they added keyboards, E. L. Doctorow's *Ragtime* was published in the USSR in Russian translation. This novel inspired the group to undertake a musical journey toward recovering the forms that underlay the music that they had been playing, a journey in the direction of simplicity that led them to the blues. Having scored some successes in local rock competitions with their developing blues sound, Ragtime was selected in 1996 by a leading show business firm in Russia, BIZ Enterprises, as one of the ten groups yielded by its talent search of Russia's provinces. Accordingly, they were brought to Moscow to produce a music video, but were forced to leave the city before this could be accomplished. They had no money for lodging and somehow BIZ Enterprises had not included that expense in their budget. Having missed their first chance to break into the big time, Ragtime returned to Nal'chik undeterred. Although performance dates there have been exceptionally few and far between—especially because the band's location is too remote geographically for them to hook up with the provincial circuit orchestrated by Makarov in Vladimir—the group has continued to rehearse in the evening while relying on regular day jobs to support themselves. In 1999, they managed to pool enough money to cut a CD in a cheap local studio, securing its lowest rate by recording at the least preferred times of day.[38]

Ragtime's vocalist, Arsen Shomakhov, sings in a throaty voice in the style of blue-eyed soul. His guitar phrasings, however, have been lifted from the likes of Stevie Ray Vaughn, thus producing a novel and effective contrast between voice and instrument. Because Vaughn's music has been relatively easy to obtain in far-off Nal'chik, the band's repertoire has been heavily laced with his songs. However, to the extent that the group has been able to get a hold of other blues recordings—in particular, those of Albert King—they have broadened the range of their material and have improved their sound by incorporating more guitar bends, strategic silences, and overall blues feel. The band has also composed a few songs—in English—but these tend to stray off in the direction of Russian soft rock. Their bread-and-butter blues numbers, on the other hand, are rendered in danceable, up-tempo fashion. In 2001, Ragtime finally broke out of its geographic isolation, delivering a performance at St. Petersburg's Del'ta Nevy festival that ignited the audience with its driving rhythms and tasteful guitar work.

More than any other band reviewed in this section, Ragtime exemplifies the difficulties besetting any group of musicians in Russia's provinces who had gotten it into their heads that they wanted to play blues. To one degree or another, however, the problems issuing from Ragtime's geographic isolation would also be reflected in the histories of the other bands surveyed here. That list of difficulties would begin with access to recorded blues music from which to fashion a repertoire. Inasmuch as available recordings—say, those by the Rolling Stones, Led Zeppelin, or Stevie Ray Vaughn—have usually come from the blues-rock genre, set lists and styles of performance tend to be quite standardized and limited. As a consequence, we find provincial groups at the end of the nineties were playing much the same music that Moscow's blues bands started out with at the beginning of the decade.

In addition to the scarcity of musical material, provincial bands confront a general deficit of information about blues music. Not only are they often completely unaware of the legendary performers of the past, they might equally have no idea about who in their own country is playing blues today. For instance, Mishuris—a veritable bloodhound when it comes to tracking down information about blues music—has confessed that when he brought his group to the capital in 1997, he "didn't know that there was a blues boom in Moscow [thinking that] the only blues groups there were Liga bliuza and Crossroadz."[39] If musicians in Moscow and St. Petersburg complain about their lack of opportunity to hear Western bluesmen perform live and thus to learn from them directly, that lament would go double or triple for their counterparts in the provinces who rarely get the chance even to hear other Russian bands covering Western covers of blues originals. Naturally, this shortage of stimulation does little to develop their musicianship, enhance their style, or expand their range. However, although this may represent the most stultifying aspect of their geographic isolation, it is not necessarily the most dispiriting: viz., the dearth of opportunities to perform before an audience. That problem is double-sided. On one hand, without the chance to perform publicly, incentive goes missing for many musicians. The music itself may be enjoyable to play, but sticking to the discipline of a rehearsal schedule requires something more, namely, the prospect of turning private rehearsals into public performances. It is only in communion with listeners that a player can feel fortified by an audience's response to his music, soak up the emotional energy that they emit, and channel it back to them in heightened performances. On a good night, a musician might enter "the zone," a sought after and highly prized state of altered consciousness enabling him to play beyond his ordinary capacities. An audience is generally required for that moment to occur. On the other hand, the shortage of venues translates directly into a shortage of pay. Even when fortunate enough to secure a club booking, the members of a provincial blues band are likely to be taking home remuneration on the order of five or ten dollars apiece. Consequently, effectively all of them are required to support themselves and their families with regular jobs outside of their calling as musicians. As Rostov's Ivashchenko remarked, "blues exists [here] solely on the basis of enthusiasm—that is, people work somewhere in the daytime and play blues in the evenings, mainly rehearsing but sometimes, if they are lucky, playing in a club."[40] The remarkable thing, then, about blues in Russia's provinces concerns not the particular style or quality of the music performed but the simple fact that these individuals have somehow found this music, have adopted it as their own, and have kept on playing it.

CHAPTER SIX

Identity and Community

Attention turns in this and the following chapter toward an investigation of the issues broached in chapter 1: principally, the meanings that the music holds for those Russians who have built a community around it and the significance that they invest in it. Accordingly, this chapter reviews the structure and dynamics of identity construction and community formation, adjusting the analytic focus in order to bring into view relevant aspects of the community as a whole. In this respect, it would be apposite to note that Russia's blues community shares some key characteristics with other subcultures that have taken root in the country during the late and postcommunist periods. Like many of these subcultures—punks, bikers, Rastafarians, rockabillies, and others—the imported idiom has been more or less consciously constructed from cultural materials reaching the country in the form of printed material, films, television, radio, recordings, the reports of those who have traveled abroad, and the presence of knowledgeable foreigners whose actions and advice enter the subcultural mix. Membership in the blues community, as is the case with other subcultures of this type, would thus admit to a large measure of personal choice. In conjunction with their conscious construction, chosen membership in these subcultures would indicate the presence of a sizeable cognitive component, suggesting an active inclination among adherents to pursue valorized, but unconventional, social practices that provide the basis for alternative communities.[1]

The growth of subcultures represents one effort to forge community amid the social debris littering the country's postcommunist landscape. In the face of the hardships, turbulence, and uncertainty that have followed the USSR's collapse, the bulk of the population has effectively withdrawn from civic life, preferring the solace and security offered by those informal networks of mutual aid that had constituted communism's vibrant underside.[2] The growth of subcultures appears congruent with that pattern, particularly with respect to their provision of relatively safe harbors for adherents—alternative worlds in which new forms of social interaction can be experienced. And inasmuch as their members are engaged in collective activity, subcultural life enables them to locate their individual identities in the circle of familiar others. Perhaps especially for subcultures based on an imported musical idiom, companionship can provide the epoxy for joining the familiar with the new.[3] In that context, as John Blacking has pointed out, the very sound of the music announces a social situation, cueing individuals to their respective roles, recalling feelings, reinforcing community values.[4] Of course, it is in live performance—in which two-way communication transpires between musicians and their audience, and where the social function of art is directly experienced in the company of others—that music's power to engender community is most evident.[5] During interviews and conversations, Russian bluesmen have mentioned this aspect of the performance situation, often describing it with the term drawn from the old (*sistema*) underground: *tusovka*, an informal gathering or stroll about involving much amiable meeting and greeting. As guitarist Vadim Ivashchenko, commenting on a particularly good outing for his band, put it, "suddenly life begins to flow and roll around. Various people had come to our concert from different [social] locations, you might say, but once there, with the music going, they are all pulled in and a kind of *tusovka* takes place."[6]

As a distinct subculture, Russia's blues community would also constitute a site on which claims to status and recognition can be redeemed. For our purposes, it is unimportant whether such claims have been frustrated by the prevailing order—say, the denial of placement in institutions of higher education or the foreclosing of career prospects—or whether individuals themselves have eschewed involvement in it. The relevant factor, here, would be that subcultural life contains its own status distinctions wherein individuals can locate themselves and experience social recognition. However, in direct correspondence to their conscious construction, subcultural norms on which distinction and recognition are based often become matters of dispute.[7] Deviations from prescribed behaviors can always elicit censure, just as extant practices and norms always invite reinterpretation on the basis of information drawn from the very sources on which they are purportedly based. This condition would be especially symptomatic of those subcultures such as the blues community, which base themselves on an imported idiom. Relying on limited information from abroad, their project always represents a work in progress, subject to the arrival of new information and the (re)interpretations that it might provoke.

An examination of Russia's blues community necessarily pays particular attention to the principal concerns attending the maintenance of community boundaries: What is real blues? Who plays it? These questions pertain to the community's overarching norm, authenticity, and to the dimensions in which it is manifest—faithfulness to the (interpreted) standards of the genre, sincerity, simplicity, style, language, and the construction of others. The discussion begins, however, a little closer to the ground by reviewing the community's core mode of organization: small groups of performers whose dense social relations exhibit certain characteristics associated with the Soviet *kollektiv* (collective). These units lend a certain monadic character to the country's blues community and provide the basis for conflicts within it that we have occasion to discuss later in this chapter and in chapter 7. They also occupy a pivotal position with respect to maintaining community norms and standards.

Organizing Social Relations

Michel Foucault's "genealogies," along with Pierre Bourdieu's "habitus," are especially useful concepts for analyzing the construction of the blues community's fundamental units, blues bands. Foucault's "genealogies" links social adaptation to a process in which elements of the past are recombined in new ways that enable a reconstruction of selves and the creation of new communities.[8] The past, in this understanding, represents a larder of cultural norms and practices from which social actors draw the ingredients for novel institutional recipes. Bourdieu's "habitus"—something akin to the phenomenological notion of lifeworld, but more focused on the practices of individuals and the not necessarily conscious strategies that they follow—can be represented as a kind of operationalization of the process by which the old gives birth to the new. As he defines it, habitus refers to "systems of durable, transposable *dispositions* . . . [that include] principles of the generation and structuring of practices and representations which can be objectively 'regulated' and 'regular' without in any way being the product of obedience to rules." Moreover, he continues, practices generated within a particular habitus are "objectively adapted to their goals without presupposing a conscious aiming at ends . . . [they are] collectively orchestrated without being the product of the orchestrating action of a conductor . . . [and always tend] to reproduce the objective structures of which they are the product."[9] If Foucault's concept connotes the notion that individuals adapt in particular ways to new circumstances because they share a common institutional past, then Bourdieu's idea reminds us that this past remains active in given lifeworlds or habiti, secreted there in layers of background understandings and unconscious knowledge that structures actors' perceptions, plans, and practices, admitting in some possibilities while screening out others in patterns of collective self-enforcement. The discussion in chapter 4 of

Moscow nightclubs—which focused on the ways in which Russian cultural practices and authority relations conditioned the adoption of this innovation—might serve as an illustration of the influence of habitus. An examination of Russian blues bands themselves brings it into sharper relief.

Utilizing Foucault's method, Oleg Kharkhordin has analyzed the USSR's modal institution—the *kollektiv*—showing how this form of social organization with its attendant set of practices had been confected from elements of earlier religious traditions and installed throughout society by the Communist Party. The purpose had been to nurture people in a new morality that joined individual achievement to the welfare of the immediate institutional group and thence to the larger society by promoting direct face-to-face accountability of the individual to those in his or her *kollektiv*. Although these attempts in the official sphere proved largely futile and often disastrous, many of the features of the workplace *kollektiv* were later reproduced within circles of friendship where, in uncoerced fashion, they became instrumental in shaping both interpersonal relations and the structures of individual personalities.[10]

Today, it is often the case that a Russian bluesman will speak of his group as *nash kollektiv* [our collective]. There appears to be more involved here than an unreflective naming using holdovers from the Soviet era. Rather, by transposing elements of their habitus onto a novel situation requiring organization and action—that is, to play blues under commercial circumstances while keeping both body and soul together—Russian bluesmen have appropriated and adapted certain aspects of the Soviet *kollektiv* to their new purposes. Accordingly, blues bands are usually organized as something more than functionally specific units that perform blues music. Instead, they are regarded as creative communities that involve whole individuals in pursuit of a common purpose. Although outwardly disavowing association with the communist past, Sergei Voronov describes his band in precisely these terms.

> I don't like the word *kollektiv*. It reminds me of the Komsomol [Communist Union of Youth] in Soviet times. So we call our band a group. We are a kind of family. . . . In these ten years [since we've been together] I have realized that it is better that I lead the band because I am more involved in this music. . . . But when I don't know what to do, I just say it. In this way, everyone—different musicians with different experience and skills—brings something to the group. That's why I am not playing with other groups anymore. The main thing in my family is Crossroadz.[11]

In even greater detail, some of the members of St. Petersburg's Big Blues Revival commented on their experience of forming a musical *kollektiv*.

Sasha Rozhdestvenskii: You do have in this group the idea of an organic unity. I play pure blues and another member prefers bluegrass and another likes funk, and so forth. As a result, the internal makeup of this *kollektiv* is complex, and therefore it has life, especially as long as our individual directions are interesting for others. . . . We are already in our second year and no one has left, no one else has joined. We came to the realization that it has to be just this way. We can't be seven or five, we must be six. In part, this is due to the fact that there are certain niches already occupied in this town with respect to blues. . . . So, when we came along we realized that we had to do something different. Sergei [Starodubtsev's] mandolin is part of that effort to establish our own sound. More than once, comrades have come up to me and asked, "What kind of blues is this? With a mandolin?" Well, that's just it. This is our blues band. It has a mandolin.

Sergei Starodubtsev: Our group is a *kollektiv* in the full sense. I am not a blues musician, I play country. But I play in a blues band because of the people in it and the blend of sounds that we get. . . . We have just come back from the road. Our purpose was to make money. But there is a distinction here between the *kollektiv* that we have and some *popsa* band. For the *popsa* band, the money is the only thing. For our *kollektiv*, there are other, more human aspects.

Sasha Suvorov: But it's more than that. We argue. We argue over the music. One person tells another, "You shouldn't play it that way, I'll show you how to do it." And musicians don't always like to hear that. We sometimes verbally abuse one another. But our relationships are such that it never matters, at least for very long.[12]

This notion of unity-in-diversity was underscored by Boris Bulkin, who likened it to the ditty, "'Swan, crab, and pike' which stands for having various vectors: the pike stays in the river while the swan flies into the sky and the crab moves onto the land. Stainless Blues Band will remind you of that very thing. We've had a lot of deep discussions about one another's strong and weak points and we are prepared to put up with our shortcomings. It's almost like a family."[13] Using a slightly different metaphor, Vadim Ivashchenko, makes a similar point about blues bands that he has known: "Making blues into a living thing in Russia, a country with an absolutely different culture, is no easy matter. These people are united by something that is, to a certain degree, strange or foreign. So, they construct for themselves a small world in which to live. You don't know what changes life will bring, so you continue to exist in this small world, letting in only the things that you need."[14]

But conscious attempts to institute the *kollektiv* form have not always resulted in smooth sailing. As Valerii Belinov recalled:

As the leader of our *kollektiv*, BBB [Belinov Blues Band], I knew very well that there had to be a balance of opinions in it and that I must represent that balance. . . . A *kollektiv* is a mutually free and harmonious joining of creative forces. . . . Under Soviet conditions music was still very regimented and the leader counted for everything. . . . So, given this context, despite my own plans for our musical *kollektiv*, the members really didn't respond. They would give no accounting of themselves. They practiced total irresponsibility. . . . We decided that I would have to enforce discipline—you know, fine them for being drunk, or for an absence from rehearsal. We all agreed on this, but you can see what this meant for our plans to have a real musical *kollektiv*. . . . Moreover, it was one thing to agree in principle, and another to accept a fine for your lack of discipline. And with the inevitable change of personnel, that is where the Belinov Blues Band has been for the last three years: struggling along, with me holding it together, along with the inevitable number of conflicts and resentments that go with that arrangement.[15]

These remarks recorded during interviews warrant the inference that Russia's blues community consists, first and foremost, of tightly knit groups of performers organized along the lines of the *kollektiv*. Social relations within these groups tend to be characterized by high degrees of solidarity, affect, and continuity, amounting to "families" or "little worlds" in the words of our respondents. Whether this is a specifically "Russian" pattern would be a question that cannot be decided here. However, pieces of available information indicate that this hypothesis cannot be ruled out. For instance, Thomas Cushman's study of rock bands in Leningrad/St. Petersburg recorded the same pattern of thick, durable social relations within performing groups that are now evident in the country's blues community.[16] Moreover, this "Russian" pattern appears to contrast sharply with the way in which blues bands have been organized in other places, where considerably more emphasis in group composition has been placed on securing the most proficient players and enhancing thereby both the artistic and commercial aspirations of performers. For example, in the British blues community of the 1960s and 1970s—which produced the very variety of this music that Russians later were to emulate—one encounters a very fluid situation in which a collection of between fifty and one hundred players would morph into various ensembles whose personnel varied from job to job. Bands stayed together when the proceeds were high, but not because their members were enmeshed in a set of thick personal relations.[17] Equally, in Britain's semiprofessional music communities in which the importance of sociability would far outweigh commercial considerations, studies have disclosed a certain level of affect and bonding among band members that, although noticeable, would still seem to pale in comparison to what one encounters in the Russian case.[18]

The Norm of Authenticity

Simon Frith has drawn particular attention to the manner in which social identities are mediated through music. "Identities" in this context admit to a pronounced ideal element, referring to preferred or imagined visions of selves rather than to some objective classification. "What makes music special in this familiar cultural process," he argues, "is that musical identity is both fantastic—idealizing not just oneself but also the social world one inhabits—and real: it is enacted in activity. . . . [Thus] musical pleasure is not derived from fantasy . . . but is experienced directly: music gives us a real experience of what the ideal could be." The quality of authenticity captures this dialectical exchange between identity, the idealized social self, and the particular music in which imaginary forms of social interaction have been encoded. It arises out of the story that the music "is heard to tell, the narrative of musical interaction in which the listeners place themselves."[19]

This notion of authenticity underlies the discussion of the subject in chapter 1, which drew attention to the ethos of Western rock music—stressing the values of sincerity, directness, and so forth—that had traveled with the music when it was imported into the Soviet Union in the 1960s and 1970s. For present purposes, I call this authenticity *in* the music, recognizing full well that this designation refers to that which is heard rather than to some objective quality of the music per se. For the blues community, this side of authenticity concerns the expression of deep-seated emotions. It involves the way in which the music touches something in performers and audiences, something that they identify as integral to their being.

The other side of authenticity—the authenticity *of* the music—represents a judgment about the degree to which a given performance meets the standards of a particular genre. For blues, it begins with the question: Is this song, or a given rendition of it, actually blues, *real* blues? Inasmuch as the music—still a relatively exotic import in today's Russia—defines the boundaries of this particular community, it is commonly subject to close inspection and strict policing. Moreover, this aspect of authenticity enters directly into the community's social structure, according to which recognition and status are conferred. Those acknowledged to perform real blues, or to know it when they hear it, not only tend to play leading roles in the border police but, in so doing, accumulate "subcultural capital" that designates their positions in the community's status hierarchy.[20]

Beginning with the first aspect of the matter—authenticity *in* the music—a number of comments made by Russia's bluesmen and fans during interviews or in casual conversations can be cited. One comes from an acquaintance struck up in a blues club with a man named Oleg, who works as scenery director for St. Petersburg's Children's Puppet Theater. His remarks on the soulfulness of the music tap categories seminal to Russians' self-understanding: soul and music's role in evoking it.[21]

> Some music is played with the head, some with the heart and soul. Blues is like that, it comes from the soul. It's like our bards, such as [Vladimir] Vysotskii. It's not the same, of course, but a parallel tradition. Russians like that kind of music. When I first heard blues, I thought that this is my life that is being expressed.[22]

Aleksei Kalachev reported on the phone calls and letters that he receives regarding his radio broadcasts.

> Unexpectedly, I will hear from people who have never listened to the blues before, maybe someone sitting in prison in Siberia or someone out in Kamchatka (I just got a letter from there yesterday). A person who might be fifty years old tells me, "Good lord, all my life I thought that there was something that I lacked and then I heard your show. I was immediately paralyzed by the first note." I don't want to exaggerate, but I think that this happens because blues is a great music. Blues is about something authentic.[23]

For many, a personal investment in blues accents the value of authenticity. A young Moscow fan states that she likes "to watch the faces of the players [which often are contorted while playing]. It's part of the music, it shows that they do it from their hearts. Some musicians try to perform, while these guys don't care how they look and what other people think. They just play and that's the most important thing for them."[24] A Petersburg devotee engages that same point, explaining that he appreciates "blues mainly because of the way that they over-perform. It's more than improvisation. In blues, the player goes beyond himself. He achieves something that lies in the moment, not in his ordinary being or consciousness."[25] Similarly, a Petersburg journalist had this to say on the matter:

> Blues is not fashionable but durable. You should learn about it if you are serious about music rather than about following ephemeral fads. Blues is not commercial. Bluesmen are not rich and do not strive for a comfortable life, for "the European standard." For them, it is all about the music. They don't even care where they play, over a warm street grate or in Carnegie Hall. Only the blues matters.[26]

Along these lines, bluesman Mikhail Sokolov, mentioned that his

> interest is in serving [*sluzhenie,* service in the religious sense of serving the
> deity], serving a particular form, a particular genre. That's what I do. So, if
> tomorrow they stopped paying to hear blues music, then I would have no
> pay at all. But I would continue to work without pay.[27]

The second side of authenticity—authenticity *of* the music—would
concern the maintenance of community boundaries as well as one's standing within them. It can therefore become a far more fractious issue. Nikolai Arutiunov, echoed comments frequently made during interviews by
drawing the line against what many Russian bluesmen often refer to as
"fake" or "false" blues. "There is such a concept as 'Russian blues,'" he remarked:

> There are even groups that consider themselves to be Russian bluesmen.
> But we, bluesmen, do not consider those Russian bluesmen to be real blues-
> men. Because these groups like Chizh & Co. are simply Russian rock with
> a few elements of blues thrown in. They don't have the blues mood [*nas-
> troienie*], the "feeling" [in English]. So, Chizh is a good group, but not blues.
> They just play more blues in their sound than do other groups. We don't
> consider them as one of our own.[28]

As an artist oriented toward the more traditional sound of Delta and
early Chicago blues, Mikhail Sokolov confessed his chagrin at the lack of
understanding that greeted his first performances of this music. "We
thought right away," he explained, "that the public would not understand
this music. Well, we were right. When we started to play some songs, no
one was at all involved. . . . Even blues musicians who were there said,
"Hey, I thought that you were supposed to be playing blues. What is this
stuff?"[29] Other performers pointed less to the actual content of the music
than to the setting in which it is performed and, more important, to the
purpose for which it is played. Vovka Kozhekin, complained that "what
we have been experiencing is a great profanation of this style of music on
the commercial market just to make money."[30] Similarly Vitalii Andreev
objected to the fact that "there's a group in this town. A blues band? Now
they are playing in casinos as a kind of background music, like the woman
in the Hotel Astoria who plays the harp in the lobby. I think that this is a
discreditation, not only of musicians, but of the music that they play."[31]
In the view of Giia Dzagnidze the issues of authenticity *of* and *in* the
blues are directly joined. "Speaking from direct experience," he maintains:

if a person is not expressing his soul in his music, if he is just playing music technically well, we can say that this is not bad. But at the same time, it is not good. This is really the core of blues music, too. Blues is not just playing "Hoochie Coochie Man." Rather, blues expresses what you have survived. Blues is recalling what you have survived.[32]

Along similar lines, Mikhail Sokolov recounted an episode in which he was unexpectedly telephoned by a guitarist with whom he had played many years ago.

This guy had moved out of Moscow and then one day in the early 1990s I got a call from him saying, "Petrovich, they say that blues is now in vogue. So the boys and I have decided to play some blues. Tell me what kinds of places are available to play there. We'll practice up and we're on our way." Well, I just went limp from this conversation. These guys think that blues is real simple. Three chords. By tomorrow we'll have a whole show ready. I was just aghast at this and I asked him not to call again. He didn't understand that he had insulted me, that he had offended me so much.[33]

Sokolov's reference to his interlocutor's assumption "that blues is real simple" indexes a pivotal concept in the self-understanding of the blues community, one that distances it from outsiders. Whereas the uninitiated might regard simplicity as an indication that blues can be easily mastered, Russian bluesmen insist that just the opposite is the case. Among the many comments made during interviews, three might be cited as representative of a general consensus on this issue.

Aleksei Baryshev: Rock is largely based on a pentatonic scale and includes a lot of blues phrases, and so more and more I became oriented to playing blues. Quickly, I began to discover that blues is outwardly a very simple music, but that appearance conceals a great complexity within it. It is very difficult to reproduce the full sense of blues, in particular the emotional element that it contains.[34]

Sergei Mironov: I can say that my first reaction [to blues] was that this is very simple, primitive music, especially after the kind of jazz-rock that I had come to listen to a lot. At first, it was kind of boring [to play]. Then, after I had begun to play with Hands [Kolia Gruzdev], I began to understand that this was absolutely not simple music at all. Very unsimple. And, secondly, I began to understand that this is a very deep music and that managing to play this music would be a real trip.[35]

Sasha Suvorov: Blues music is very intelligent. When you think about the number of emotions and the amount of information and, for that matter, the amount of music that is packed into a very simple blues form, it's incredible. It's like a shot in billiards making about two hundred banks [off the cushion]. It's a simple form, but look how many possibilities are available to the player.[36]

Within the blues community, then, the valence of simplicity is reversed. What outsiders regard as undemanding music that need not be taken seriously is reframed on the basis of an esoteric knowledge that valorizes the very elements that others dismiss. Initiates take an obvious pride in themselves for having unlocked this secret. The music seems simple to those who do not understand it. For those who do, however, this shared knowledge supplies one of the bonds of community, distinguishing its members from others who might have access to the same information but who are unable to understand and appreciate it.

Style

Authenticity, socially displayed, raises the question of style. As a social concept, style has elicited conflicting assessments. Some theorists, such as Dick Hebdige, regard subcultural style (mediated through music, dress, and argot) as "a gesture of defiance or contempt" toward the hegemony of capitalist social relations and their attendant ideology. Style functions to disrupt the taken-for-granted world with its ready-made structures in which those relations and ideology dictate the choices confronting the individual. Style draws a circle around subjects in a community liberated by virtue of their lived opposition to the surrounding hegemony of the prevailing order. It thus buttresses individual identity and dignity.[37] However, other theorists, sensitive to the repressive side of commodity consumption, might challenge that thesis. Jean Baudrillard, for instance, would argue that these same elements of style—music, dress, and argot—can be understood as signs that determine the "obligatory registration of individuals on the scale of status, through the mediation of their group and as a function of their relations with other groups." Moreover, he continues, "this scale is properly the social order, since the acceptance of this hierarchy of differential signs and their interiorization by the individual of signs in general (i.e., of the norms, values, and social imperatives that signs are) constitute the fundamental, decisive form of social control—more so even than acquiescence to ideological norms."[38] Because style represents a symbolic opposition to capitalist social relations, it would be determined by those relations themselves. Rather than abolishing the commodity form, style would faithfully reproduce it as its putative other. Consequently, it can enter and replenish capitalism's market place of signs, whether in the form of mass-marketed gangsta rap, the down-at-the-heel look in the fashion industry, or corporate executives slapping high fives on the occasion of concluding a business deal.

Arguments advanced by either side in this debate can claim some purchase with respect to blues music and culture in postcommunist Russia. There, the idea of blues, and images related thereto, have been pressed into service by the advertising industry. Incongruously, the word has appeared prominently in such things as magazine advertisements hawking a new line of office furniture. Images—such as the stud-like figure in leather jacket, blowing blues on his harp as he thumbs a ride—have been featured in TV ad campaigns imploring Russians to use contraceptives. Indeed, as noted previously, American movies such as *The Blues Brothers* or *From Dusk Till Dawn* have provided images of blues style that have served as access points to blues music for many Russians. In particular, the impact of the film *Crossroads*—which combines a sense of freewheeling adventure with a young aesthete's encounter with blues culture and a music that he eventually masters through fierce determination—often surfaced during interviews.[39]

On the other hand, a cursory perusal of a blues performance in Russia would likely indicate the absence of any outward markers of style, such as clothing or speech. In the overwhelming majority of cases, blues bands are completely indistinguishable from other collections of (male) persons by virtue of their dress or hair length. Likewise, no particular dialect seems to set members of the blues community apart from others in society. These proclivities stand in marked contrast to, for example, Russia's rockabilly subculture in which more or less uniform manifestations of style—clothing, hairdos, motorcycles, and so forth—are prominently displayed.

Some of the more commercially successful bluesmen count this as a debit. Nikolai Arutiunov, for instance, contrasts rockabilly, heavy metal, and reggae with blues "for which no such style is visible. And that," he continues,

> is for us a minus because young people are first interested by what is visible, they are attracted by what can be seen. . . . Through these external aspects they are able to pursue and find something deeper, and I've always campaigned for that kind of thing among bluesmen. . . . But we don't develop any particular style and I think that this is a big shortcoming. . . . We must be interesting people, we must look good. Take, for instance, Stevie Ray Vaughn. He would be a good example for everyone to follow.[40]

His colleague, Mikhail Sokolov, would agree, arguing that:

> I could work without my hat. I'm not embarrassed by my balding head.
> But inasmuch as I've already created this kind of image with my hat, I work
> with it on even when it is very hot and I have to carry a towel to mop up
> the sweat. That is because people can't really sort out the blues for them-
> selves. Usually, they are more involved with the show. That is, a person will
> say, "Look how this guy plays! He wears this black hat and he's got a big
> beard and he plays harmonica." So, it's all the elements together that pro-
> vide this show that seems to be the most attractive thing for most peo-
> ple. . . . If I were able to juggle while I played harmonica, then I would do
> that.[41]

But these appear to be minority views. Most bluesmen consider their
style a reflection of that very sense of individuality that is celebrated in
blues music. Aleksei Agranovskii, for instance, regards outward manifestations of style as indicative of an absence of content.

> When you see these guys come out on stage with the dark glasses and big
> hats, I am already thinking that this is going to be boring. I don't have in
> mind here, say, John Lee Hooker—to me, he is very interesting. But these
> people I'm talking about, are they expressing themselves or something
> else? And if it's not themselves, then it's going to be boring. They are just
> beating something with a sausage. It's actually funny.[42]

Likewise, Kolia Gruzdev sees in these accoutrements a subversion of the
idiom itself.

> Some people need to be bluesmen. They need to wear hats. It comes from
> a couple of movies: *The Blues Brothers,* which is fake, sure, and *Crossroads,*
> which is closer [to the matter] but too romantic. . . . But sometimes people
> try to be like that. I tried to be like that for awhile, but it's not the goal it-
> self. . . . I love the way they [American bluesmen] look and what they do,
> but we are just different people, and it doesn't have any influence on the
> music. . . . Your style and your music are all the same. [Blues] style means
> to be yourself.[43]

In part, this controversy over style and its trappings reflects different
emphases present in the blues community: one, to promote the music by
putting on an eye-catching show; the other, to express in outward appearance that same individuality that is encoded in blues music. Inasmuch
as the value placed on authenticity can impede efforts to popularize the

music, the issue of style reflects a normative divide within the community itself. This divide can be conceptualized by positing two species of capital that performers seek to accumulate: commercial and (sub)cultural.[44] Some follow a strategy of distinguishing themselves by accumulating the former—both money and a public following—while others tack toward the latter by performing blues in a way that coincides with their notion of the individuality that constitutes part of the music's appeal. Furthermore, this distinction owes something to place. The outward features of style seem to be best represented among certain Moscow bluesmen whose levels of commercial success—albeit modest—put them in a league far removed from that of their impecunious counterparts elsewhere in the country. Access to commercial capital thus distinguishes the Moscow blues scene from others and represents a palpable division in Russia's blues community that is examined in chapter 7. Here, however, I would underline the fact that although a certain discord attends the question of style, the music associated with it also seems to bridge, or at least temper, this division in the community. In the words of Nikolai Arutiunov, himself an advocate for the use of visible markers:

> We have different subgroups in our society, different musical societies. We have, let's say, heavy metal or grunge. You will meet someone like that and ask what kind of music he likes and that person will tell you, "I like grunge" or "I like metal." And the reply is something along the lines of, "Well, you're a fine person but you're not my brother. I like to listen to blues." And you meet another person and you say, "What music do you listen to?" And he might say, "The Rolling Stones, John Mayall, Leadbelly, Otis Spann." You think right away, "You're my brother."[45]

Language

Adherence to musical canon has meant that blues in Russia, with very few exceptions, is sung in English. This preference for a foreign language over the native one probably has something to do with preserving the features of a valorized Western import, thus contributing to the cultural capital of local performers and consumers of the music. It may also have resulted from the prehistory of blues in Russia when the music was a little-differentiated appendage of rock 'n' roll. Following a pattern recorded in a number of non-English-speaking countries, imported rock eventually became a domesticated idiom in the USSR once local bands ceased mimicking the English-language sounds that they heard on recordings and began performing in the vernacular. Subsequently, in order to distinguish blues from Russian rock, English has served as a prominent sonic marker. This tendency was reinforced by communism's collapse and with it, the devaluation of protest songs, making the words themselves less central to the music's appeal.[46] But, perhaps most important, the issue of language is inherently bound up with questions related to the authenticity *of* the music: whether or not the music sounds genuine in a given language. This would be the prevailing view within the blues community, underscoring its preference for English.

In this respect, two aspects of vocalizing have been mentioned by Russian bluesmen as central to their preference for English. The first is related to their commitment to a faithful reproduction of the music, a concern especially important to the first generation of performers who discovered blues before it had become at all popular. For instance, while functioning in the capacity of emcee for the weekly program, "Simply Blues," Mikhail Sokolov answered a telephone caller's question on the matter of language use by remarking that the reason for singing in English is "to preserve tradition. That is the main reason, to copy the foreign tradition and to master it. When we have mastered the English, then we shall create the Russian."

The second factor concerns the relative unsuitability of Russian—due largely to its grammatical complexity and the plethora of polysyllabic words—to the standard blues verse.[47] As Petersburg bass player and vocalist Sergei Semenov put it, "We have to perform in English because the melodic structures correspond to the English language. . . . If you were singing in Russian, then the language would correspond more to Russian folk sounds and the timbre of the music would be changed."[48] Emphasizing rhythm rather than melody, Sasha Suvorov has argued that "if you sing blues in Russian, it comes across very strange. . . . The words and the dynamics of the phrasing are totally different in Russian and English. The rhythms of the languages are different."[49] Aleksei Agranovskii would concur. "If you perform blues in Russian," he has remarked, "then it is already another genre with entirely different associations. . . . The real feeling of blues is when you are able to sing this music in English with a black accent or intonation."[50]

Does it matter for the listener that the music is performed in English? To a great extent it does. The compactness of blues lyrics—especially the element of double-voicing in which signification is registered and negated in a single act—would be largely lost on an audience with little or no command of the language. The verbal plane of blues expression is thus only partially available, at best, to the great majority of listeners.[51] But Russians, as they are apt to do in many endeavors, find ways of compensating. As a young St. Petersburg guitarist, Volodia Rusinov, remarked, "Russians are used to listening to music in unintelligible foreign languages. With blues, it's just the same."[52] Oleg, our scenery director from St. Petersburg, speaks little English, but enough, he says, to catch the gist of most songs.[53] Iaroslav Sukhov feels that "in blues the music itself does the talking and that is completely sufficient," while Sergei Starodubtsev dismisses the import of the language issue, contending that "people are making music before they can talk."[54] From the other end of the microphone, Petersburg blues singer Inessa Kataeva has sought to turn the language barrier to her advantage.

> Just to survive this life and its problems, well, it comes out in the music that I sing. I really enjoy improvising, and it has always been difficult to do that in a foreign language. However, in blues I can vocalize around the melody and, even though it's in English, I don't feel uncomfortable about that. . . . So, I try to work those problems into my singing and to discuss them musically. . . . [Sometimes] I'm worried that I'm not singing the words correctly, because I don't understand many of the texts that I sing. And there are times when I forget the words entirely. So what do I do then? Well, I just keep going and hope that I get lucky. And sometimes it turns out better. They tell me afterwards: "That was great the way you sang that song." But it was only because I was improvising completely.[55]

As noted earlier, there have been some attempts at rendering blues in Russian. Sometimes the results have been good, such as the episode at the Moscow Blues Festival in 2001 where Kozhekin and Zhuk won over an initially hostile audience with their talking-blues. Other attempts in the recording studio have produced mixed results: some successful, others, less so.[56] The trick seems to involve recasting English-language texts into sonorously comparable Russian ones. In this respect Nikolai Arutiunov describes a painstaking, laborious process that for a long while had produced only "*kasha*" (porridge).[57] "I try to write blues in Russian," he explained:

> that actually has a kind of English-language feel to it. It is very difficult to work Russian words into a blues text. They are quite a bit longer than English ones. I use the help of various poets. They don't understand blues rhythm or the blues sense, but they help me because I am not really equipped to be a composer myself. It is very complicated work to get this sound so that the music itself is a bit like English.[58]

In his "Ty spoesh' 'Hoochie Coochie Man,'" Arutiunov uses this technique in the first verse of the song, then switches to English after the first line of the second verse.[59]

Pomniu kak-to davno	I remember somehow long ago
Mne prisnilsia chudesnyi son	I had a marvelous dream
Budto vetrom sud'by,	As if by the wind of fate
Ia v Chikago byl zanesen	I was carried off to Chicago
I budto vstretilsia mne Madi Uoters,	And it was as if I met Muddy Waters
V tot den' kogda on zapisal svoi	On the day when he recorded
"Rolling Ston"	his "Rolling Stone"
On skazal mne togda	He said to me then

Listen son, why don't you try to play the blues?
Yes, you got no black skin
And you ain't from Chicago or St. Louis
But everybody's got their trouble
Don't worry boy, choose to sing the blues
Sing the blues, boy!

Along with the tongue-in-cheek playfulness of the lyrics, here, the Russian-language segment of these verses is notable for its compact phrasing based mainly on one- and two-syllable words (the longest ones—"*prisnilsia,*" "*chudesnyi,*" and so on—contain three syllables, no more than "remember" or "Chicago"). As such, the meter of the Russian lines meshes with that of the English ones that follow, making the song's shift from one language to the other almost imperceptible from a prosodic point of view.

Valerii Belinov has also collaborated with a poet in order to write blues lyrics in Russian. However, their efforts have not aimed to produce original lyrics per se, but to translate songs into Russian in such a way that the proper rhythm and meter are retained. This often has involved rewriting the lyrics, inserting new tropes and images that evoke a comparable mood and feeling even while they tell a quite different story. The resulting sound is unmistakably blues, yet its unusual timbre startles an ear expecting to hear an English-language lyric but encountering a fluid Russian one. Belinov has followed this approach in recording his 2000 CD, cutting it in two versions: one in English, the other, with the same (but modified) songs, in Russian. However, the finished product—perhaps reflecting his longstanding doubts about performing "real blues" in Russian—includes only the English-language versions.[60]

Preachin' the Blues

The importance that Russian bluesmen attach to their music's authenticity, their commitment to preserve and enhance it, along with their corresponding disdain for commercially oriented activities, are factors that tend to cast them in the role of aristocrats. Considering the sources of the music that they play, their generally disheveled appearance while performing it, as well as the modest—or, for many, poverty-stricken—character of their material conditions, this would appear to be a very improbable observation. However, the sense of it consists in the position that bluesmen have carved out for themselves within Russian society, appropriating from their habitus many of the norms and practices associated with the Russian intelligentsia—bearers of aristocratic values—and refitting them to the contours of their community. As such, bluesmen see themselves as engaged in a struggle for the pure and the good; they lay claim to enlightenment about an immensely valuable cultural form that is unintelligible to most people; they distinguish themselves from others by mastering the esoterica of the genre, defending its integrity behind a language barrier; and they think of their own activity as a form of service to, and sacrifice for, others. In the following chapter, I develop this characterization further. This chapter concludes with an examination of proselytizing practices apparent in the community, noting how these appear to have far more to do with enacting an ethos linked to elements of Russia's aristocratic and intelligentsia traditions than with actually bringing this music of theirs to others in the society.

A longstanding tendency within the Russian intelligentsia—one not unrelated to buttressing the group's social position as the bearers, interpreters, and creators of cultural values—has been to regard the surrounding society as in one way or another degenerate, fallen, morally threatened and, thus, in need of enlightenment and salvation.[61] Reinforcing this tendency would be the cultural proclivity to perceive the larger society in simplified terms, reducing it to the more proximate and familiar pattern of familial relations. This reduction is not uncommon in the modern world in which people have little if any knowledge about the forces actually driving their societies, yet are required on all manner of occasion to state their opinions about such things. By viewing the unknown through the prism of the familiar, the family, they are able to state opinions, indeed, to formulate worldviews.[62] This pattern appears to be specially pronounced in Russia.[63] As Aleksandr Arinin has pointed out, the nation-as-family metaphor in the social consciousness derives much of its influence on thought and perception from the very fact that it is so deeply ingrained in everyday thinking that it has become naturalized and escapes critical attention.[64] As with others of their number in the intelligentsia both past and present, many Russian bluesmen evince a responsibility toward the family/nation, seeing it as their charge to perfect this music that so inspires them and to bring it to their unenlightened brothers and sisters.[65]

There seems to be a common opinion, in this respect, that were blues music featured more on radio and television, then its popularity would expand geometrically. As Mikhail Sokolov remarks, "Unfortunately, 90 percent of the people in Russia just take what they have been given on television and radio and no more. They don't even think about the possibility that there are more interesting musical directions to be explored."[66] Vladimir Berezin likewise believes that the issue is one of exposure:

Unfortunately, no one propagandizes the blues in this country. You won't see anything about the blues on television. And the common masses are left out of this music because it is not being popularized or propagandized. If you put Stevie Ray Vaughn's clips [music videos] on TV, then the people [narod] would react to this very positively.[67]

Along these lines, a number of bluesmen regard it as their obligation "to open people's eyes," in the words of Aleksandr Dolgov.[68] "There is no question here," observes Vitalii Andreev, "that the audience must be brought up, nurtured."[69] Often, this obligation is expressed in very personal terms. Vovka Kozhekin reported that:

I see myself with this task, namely, to do my best to acquaint the country with this part of world culture, the blues, and perhaps also to try to create something of the blues on Russian soil. Above all, for me this is an attempt to raise the general cultural level of the country. And personally, because of the way that culture has lagged so much in this country, it makes it simply hard to live [here]. I want people to know and to love what I know and love.[70]

The dramaturgy of a typical blues concert in Russia is apt to contain a didactic moment in this respect. Sometimes it is confined to the introduction of the song about to be played, identifying (not always correctly) in somber and serious tones the individual who wrote it. Because the audience is unlikely to place the name of, say, Willie Dixon or Lowell Fulson, the transfer of information that occurs in these episodes actually seems to involve a subtextual statement to the effect that: "This is serious music; we know about it; you should listen to it and learn about it too." At other times, the audience is treated to brief lectures "to instruct them about the blues that they're hearing."[71] As noted in chapter 4, this format has been consistently employed for television and radio broadcasts of blues music.

The impulse to proselytize that informs the identity of most bluesmen is also associated with the music's capacity to invert social hierarchies by including in performance the representation of socially marginalized elements.[72] Thus, on one hand, a musical form stemming from "low" culture has been imported into the country and received by members of the intelligentsia who reverse the valence of its status markers, transforming it into an object to be appreciated by discerning and sophisticated people. On the other, those who do not participate in the consumption of this music are themselves included in it as an absence, as that great potential audience who would appreciate the blues if only they had been informed ("enlightened") about it. This approach is made all the more seductive because of traces of "low" culture that remain in the music, despite its status inversion. As an especially earthy music, blues evokes a sense of the rough-and-tumble world surrounding those educated, young middle-class males who constitute its principal constituency.[73] To many members of the blues community, the question seems elementary: Wouldn't ordinary people also enjoy this music that speaks so much about their lives?

A related element in this proselytizing posture would involve opposition to the reigning mass-music genre: *popsa*. During interviews, members of the blues community offered explanations for the popular success of this music, but most explanations seem to be variations on the theme of improper nurturing. Here, it would be worth recalling Alla Gladkikh's comments, referenced in chapter 5, about the guilt that she and her associates bear for failing "to advance the musical upbringing" of their rock club's young patrons, providing them with *popsa* instead. Mikhail Sokolov has directed the blame at television and radio.

> The horrible thing here is the means of mass communications. . . . We have good artists from the old, pre-perestroika period, but now they can't find a spot on television. Instead, anybody's girlfriend—if he had enough to pay for a music video and could make the right payments [bribes]—can make a video that would soon be on our television . . . And tomorrow, she's a star! So, this kind of crap information acts on our people and I can sense how we lost a lot of our audience because of the influence of this crap information.[74]

Similarly, Vovka Kozhekin assigned culpability to some former officials of the Communist Party who built new careers for themselves in the music industry.

> In Russia, the situation is completely unique. The kind of music that you hear on television and radio does not correspond to people's actual taste. It is artificially thrust on us and has a horrible quality . . . like a certain Italian *popsa* music, such as disco, but a whole lot worse. . . . This *popsa* came about because some young Communist functionaries decided after 1991 to

involve themselves in show business. They chose this type of music because it doesn't require any mastery whatsoever. The words practically don't matter; everything about the rhythm and melody are completely standardized. It is precisely for this reason that if we are going to move our country musically to the standards of Europe and America, then we have to take a strong social position against our own system of show business. . . . I guess you might say that any musical attempt is simultaneously a struggle against *popsa*.[75]

The proselytizing posture among bluesmen adds another dimension to their social identities. Recapitulating old arguments about a fallen society in need of enlightenment and salvation, bluesmen construct themselves as those engaged in a struggle against the forces of crass commercialism that have degraded mass culture, as those whose mission it is to bring "real music"—blues—to people victimized by sinister forces in control of the airwaves. These notions, in turn, reframe relations between the blues community and the surrounding society. Rather than a self-enclosed subculture, they portray the community as open to those as yet uninformed about the music but expected to embrace it once they have been exposed to it properly. The Russian blues identity is thus linked to a conception of community whose potential for growth tomorrow informs the significance of its practices today.

On the basis of the information presented thus far, something of an ideal type can be formulated which captures the broad outlines of the blues community, its identity construct and the norms and practices integral to it. This ideal type contains a number of elements present in the larger culture that members of the community have refashioned and combined in new ways to produce a distinct social identity. The influence of the *kollektiv* inherited from the Soviet era, is evident in this respect. Bands are more than blues-playing musical units; they are understood to be creative communities based on strong, affective ties in which whole individuals realize their artistic potential by joining forces in a common enterprise. That enterprise is layered with the ethos of the old aristocracy, incubated throughout most of the past century by the intelligentsia. Accordingly, bluesmen shun the commercial and disparage the gaudy. They pursue refined things: appreciating and performing genuine blues music. They adopt an unintelligible foreign language in order to preserve its authenticity. They take pleasure in unlocking the music's secrets, in fathoming the richness masked by its outwardly simple form. Moreover, their endeavors to master and to replicate the blues idiom faithfully commit them to the service of others toward whom they express a responsibility to spread enlightenment. In this last respect, noblesse oblige intersects with a certain democratic impulse encoded in the music itself. Blues is about the everyday life of everyman, his troubles, desires, setbacks, and triumphs. Bluesmen thus see it as their duty to share the particular treasure that they have discovered with those for whom it has obviously been intended.

This sketch of the Russian blues identity is provisional and incomplete. Thus far, only a positive characterization has been attempted, simply a laying out of those norms and practices exhibited by the community as the identity markers that define its boundaries. These are taken up again in the following chapter, focusing there on the inconsistencies and contradictions that obtain among them to disclose the ways in which community norms pull against one another, thereby involving community members in a politics in which patterns of both conflict and cooperation are amply represented.

CHAPTER SEVEN

Politics

Politics is a concept as contentious as the phenomena that it references. There are reminders of this fact in the quotidian questions that permeate our public discussions: Who is "playing politics"? Who is operating out of "political motives"? Moreover, the restricted concept of politics that informs conventional parlance—something related to government, political parties, public policy, elections, and so forth—can itself be comprehended as political: it constructs a discursive universe into which only some, and not necessarily the most important, political phenomena are admitted.[1] Along these conventional lines, Russia's blues community would be bereft of politics. The only instance of such activity—the blues musicians' strike in St. Petersburg and the subsequent organization of the Association of Blues Musicians there—would be the exception showing the rule. In correspondence with blues traditions and with the messages encoded in the music, Russia's bluesmen stand aside from politics as it is conventionally understood and practiced. Nonetheless, many of them reported on aspects of their roles that evince a political content and it is these that I examine by using a more robust concept of the political, one that focuses on that side of human activity in which individuals act in concert to forge collective identities, to alter or sustain their conditions of life, to struggle for the achievement of common objectives, and, in the course of all of these endeavors, to negotiate shared meanings and values. This chapter employs such a conception in order to retrieve and reknit various threads running through the discussion thus far, reconsidering them from the perspective of politics.

Conscious construction of, and chosen membership in, a subculture such as Russia's blues community would make political concerns particularly salient. "Political," in this instance, would refer to fundamental issues of community building: Who is in and who is not? What norms define community boundaries and how are these negotiated and established? How is access to the means of performance distributed and who occupies positions that make these determinations? What is more, the blues community represents for its members an imagined alternative to the existing social order. In this respect, there would be no reason to suppose that a musical expression of an alternative way of life would be less important, effective, and influential than a verbal one expressed in manifestos, programs, or public speeches in promoting the process of social learning and adaptation. Indeed, it would be altogether uncertain in cases such as the 1960s youth movement in the United States whether the movement's politics informed the music associated with it or whether its politics were an extension of that music, acting on, as well as out, the values of peace, justice, truth, and so forth that it professed. As Timothy Rice has pointed out with respect to musical subcultures in general:

> Musicians make differences in musical style partly to make aesthetically satisfying music, but what makes music aesthetically satisfying has partly to do with what the music means, that is, with the world it references. Musicians and audiences choose sides and select one kind of music over another for the same reasons. The question of what kinds of music are the most aesthetically satisfying and deeply meaningful is linked to the possibility that music can act as both a critique of the existing world and as an imaginary construction of a new and perhaps better world.[2]

Viewed from this perspective, three political aspects of Russia's blues community can be readily distinguished and will organize the discussion in this chapter.[3] Moving by degrees of relative abstraction from the concrete, we begin with the most mundane of the three: a struggle over the means of performance that involves bands in patterns of conflict and cooperation. The thread of discussion to be retrieved in this respect would concern their mode of organization—that is, along the lines of the Soviet *kollektiv*—that tightly integrates individual members into their respective groups while simultaneously shaping the relations among bands in ways that generate divisions and conflicts within the community. The second thread involves normative contests within the community, expressed most directly by the inconsistencies that obtain between the desideratum of authenticity and the impulse to proselytize. The final one is a politics of culture. This, by far, is the most difficult of the three to circumscribe. It concerns the production of meaning and, as such, the production of the blues community itself. The examination of this process returns us to the principal issue addressed in the first chapter: Why blues?

Competition and Conflict

The organization of bands along the lines of the Soviet-era *kollektiv* furnishes the interior of the blues community with small, outwardly identical groups, most of which are based on strong, affective ties. In direct correspondence to their ability to integrate members into cooperative activities yielding distinguishable identities and interests, *kollektivi* had been characterized in communist times as a form of "group egoism."[4] Under postcommunist conditions in which bluesmen compete in a commercial milieu for access to the means of performance, certain aspects of that "egoism" still hold true. They would be most visible in the relations that exist between blues bands in Moscow and those in the remainder of the country.

At present, about a dozen clubs in Moscow continue to feature blues music, each relying on an "artistic director" to assist in, if not entirely manage, bookings. Often these artistic directors are themselves bluesmen, usually the leaders of their respective bands. Consequently, the organization of blues performances around the city has generally transpired through informal, reticulated relations in which reciprocity obtains: You book us in your club and I'll book you in mine. Naturally, this pattern has made for a certain bonding among Moscow groups represented in the network as well as for a certain resentment among outsiders who sometimes speak of this arrangement as consisting of "clans," "a little mafia," or a "holding company."[5] These terms register their indignation toward Moscow counterparts unwilling, in their view, to share access to the means of performance.

The tendency among many Moscow bluesmen—especially inasmuch as they are ensconced at the geographical center of Russia's blues community—is to ignore developments on the periphery. This was apparent during a number of interviews in which Muscovites claimed no knowledge of one or another blues band or musician performing in other cities. A Petersburger complained that when "I go to Moscow to play a concert, I call around all over town telling other musicians about it. Do you think that they would come to listen to me? None of them, or maybe one. They think that they are the great musicians of Moscow who do not have time for someone from Petersburg."[6]

To some extent, the social distance between Moscow bluesmen and others in Russia reflects an economic one. Financial rewards are many times greater for those fortunate enough to play blues in Moscow. According to the view from St. Petersburg:

In Moscow, there is so much money. And here it is just the opposite, we play concerts for laughable sums. Yesterday we played a concert for ten dollars apiece. That's enough [the total receipts] maybe to buy a harmonica. As a matter of fact, we blew out a harmonica yesterday, so we will have to use that money to buy a new one.[7]

And from that of the provinces:

There is this expression: "Moscow is the state of the state." They are only concerned with themselves [there] and they don't pay much attention to the provinces. For instance, there is a lot going on in Vladimir that people in Moscow just don't know about. Because Moscow groups are established and have set rates of pay, when I write a Moscow band to come to Vladimir for a concert they say: "What kind of money?" And when I tell them, they say that they can only play for five times that much. When it comes to blues bands in other regions . . . their problems are just like ours. We all speak the same language. They don't share the Moscow mentality which seems to revolve around money.[8]

These views outwardly concern the matter of privilege. They express the notion that Moscow bluesmen enjoy special access to the means of performance that they are reluctant to share with others. But as factual as such claims appear, they also might mask another factor, the influence of the *kollektiv* form of social organization.

The countermovement to the centripetal pull of the *kollektiv* would be the varying shades of otherness falling on those outside it. When the Moscow/provinces distinction is under discussion, Moscow assumes the part of the other, and non-Moscow groups become "like us." However, an examination of the relations among blues bands in a given city would show that equivalent distinctions often obtain among them. These are usually reflected as relative indifference. Some established performers in St. Petersburg, for example, mentioned in interviews that they had no knowledge of certain young bluesmen who had been playing around town for years. Just as I found myself during interviews in Moscow informing bluesmen of the names and talents of certain Petersburg performers unknown to them, so on another occasion in St. Petersburg I fell into the role of informant, describing various top players and bands in Moscow about whom my interlocutors were equally unaware. The matter of indifference toward others involved with the same pursuit would be highlighted by the episode mentioned in chapter 5 involving St. Petersburg's two simultaneous blues festival with identical names.

Moreover, indifference can easily shade into exclusion. This consideration calls to mind the way in which certain Moscow artists have relied on notions of authenticity to defend community boundaries, drawing the line against "fake" blues bands and discouraging or denying them bookings in clubs. It may be that their aesthetic judgments to some extent have been influenced by their positions in the city's network of established performers. In St. Petersburg, the outsider status of The Way seems to represent just such a case. Owing its inception to none of the four major patrons of the music in that city—Edik Tsekhanovskii, Vladimir Golovanov, Nikita Vostretsov, and Valerii Belinov—the group has had a difficult time winning the acceptance of the local community of blues musicians. On one hand, invitations have not been extended to them to perform at festivals, and the group evinced no solidarity with other bands striking against the Jimi Hendrix Blues Club in 1999 and afterwards. On the other, a negative attitude toward them has developed in blues circles, indicated by Vitalii Andreev's oblique reference to the group—quoted in chapter 6—as discrediting both themselves and blues music generally by performing in unsuitable establishments. It would appear that the bonds established within blues bands and reticulated through the community can have the effect of turning competition into conflict, framing difference as a strong category that can authorize exclusion.

Normative Divisions

The second aspect of politics in the blues community concerns the inconsistencies that stem from its normative structure. Two orientations discussed thus far come into play here: 1) blues is regarded as a form of high art that must be authentically rendered in performance; and 2) blues is understood to address the issues confronting everyman and, therefore, has a large potential audience in Russia to whom this music must be brought. I have referred to the orientations deriving from these injunctions as strategies according to which performers seek to accumulate, respectively, either cultural or commercial capital. However, these differing strategic orientations take on added significance when placed in the specific context of the blues idiom as an identity construct. As Clyde Woods has suggested, blues from its inception has represented a "counternarrative of the American dream" and has subsequently become an international idiom, traveling on the underside of the process of globalization that has brought features of American commercial culture to societies around the world.[9] Blues is tied to that culture as its inveterate other, voicing the laments and complaints of those who have been crushed by it, disdaining submission to it. Its adoption by Russians seems to be quite consistent with this characterization. For instance Boris Bulkin remarks that:

There is a great deal that I don't like about American culture. You see the kinds of films that they show on television, all the fights and so forth—I don't like that at all. I think that our films are a lot better. It's horrible when American culture begins to crowd out our culture, to replace our culture. Films are one good example of that. I can't even watch American films, except for a few, such as *Crossroads*. But blues is an altogether different thing. . . . This is a real wonder of American culture. With blues, it is what the people [*narod*], the American people, itself has devised to express its life.[10]

Aleksei Agranovskii speaks of the evolving consciousness of his peers, singling out the blues as one of the few things that remains from their earlier attraction to all things American.

Under communism, jeans were not clothing, they were your philosophy. In those days, a record [from the West] would be an object of worship. And then a period of freedom came and our outlook on America changed radically. However, with blues there is still that bridge to America. . . . So now in this period Russia has lost its honor vis-à-vis America and we are in an inferior position and we resent that. But it is really good that some things still exist that bring us together.[11]

In the Russian context, then, adoption of the blues idiom would place one in a community distinguished from others in two important ways. On one hand, blues is valorized as a Western import setting those in the community invidiously apart from uncomprehending others. But on the other, this particular import has nothing in common with the vulgar materialism and indiscriminate consumption of Western cultural products practiced by the country's nouveaux riches as their way of being modern. Blues is thus marked as both a Western cultural form and, simultaneously, as the bad conscience of actually existing Westernization. Consequently, any diminution of the music's authenticity for the sake of its popularity would pose a threat to identity, undermining, as it were, the force of the counternarrative and risking association with the hegemonic form of Western commercialism: pop.

An episode that occurred during a performance of Russia's then most popular blues band, Blues Cousins, in Moscow's Alabama Club in summer of 2001 would bring this issue into sharp relief. I sat at a stage-side table with two prominent members of the country's blues community who recounted the efforts of the group's leader, Levan Lomidze, to develop an act that drew the audience into the performance and thus increased the music's availability to those unfamiliar with it. They praised him extensively for this and argued that he was showing the way forward for all Russian bluesmen. Blues Cousins were playing a room filled with some two hundred people, the great majority of whom appeared to be "middle class." When the music commenced, an unspoken question seemed to hang over our conversation: In which middle class are these individuals participating tonight? Is it the one informed by genuine (blues) culture or the other one based on the consumption of commercial products (pop)? As the performance progressed, the audience exhibited its greatest enthusiasm when Lomidze played the two Beatles songs added to the set list as crowd-pleasers. My companions, sitting impassively throughout the show, became somewhat irritated each time that the more popish sounds reached their ears, occasionally grousing that "this is turning into a rock concert" and "we are back ten years" as far as the authenticity of the music was concerned. Their remarks seemed to indicate disappointment with the entire tenor of the evening, and chagrin at the fact that the middle class in that particular room did not respond in preferred ways to the performance, just as the performers were apparently remiss in catering to what was, indeed, popular. The reactions of my companions were not lost on Lomidze himself. As if smarting from the silent censure of their gaze, he spoke to me after the performance with a note of consternation in his voice: "Do you know how difficult it is to be playing and to see people in the audience glaring at you like that? You should know how hard it is to play the blues here in Moscow with that kind of audience." This episode and others like it that I have witnessed reflect the push and pull of musical authenticity and commercial success. Such cases, of course, are not uncommon for musicians anywhere who perform within the context of market relations that drive a wedge between artistic expression and popularity, and thus confront individual performers with choices between their art and the demands of the commercial world. What appears to be distinctive about members of Russia's blues community in this respect would be the relative novelty—and, consequently, the raw, unpalatability—of the choice itself. Unaccustomed to the idea of selling their cultural products, bluesmen tend to resist the notion of commercial compromise, as many of the negative comments about "money" and "show business" already recorded in this study would suggest. However, a second consideration seems to obtain here as well. That is, individual choices are often apprehended by others as having a direct impact on the community's common store of cultural capital. This notion would be captured in my interlocutor's disdainful remark that "we are back ten years," and explain the tacit censure that he and my other companion visited on Lomidze's band. As such, this episode and others demonstrate the importance attached by community members to the maintenance of collective norms and practices that they regard as essential to the cultural struggle in which they are engaged.

Politics of Culture

The final aspect of politics in the blues community concerns a related issue: the struggle for culture. In this respect, culture can be regarded in a broad sense as "the signifying system through which necessarily (though among other means) a social order is communicated, reproduced, experienced, and explored."[12] As Murray Edelman has argued, cultural products provide society with a finite number of vantages from which the political world is apprehended, assessed, and, indeed, constructed.[13] Culture is therefore political in the deepest sense. Its "meanings are constitutive of processes that, implicitly or explicitly, seek to redefine social power."[14] Members of Russia's blues community experience their activities as a struggle along those lines, as many of their remarks would indicate. The coherence of their community itself hinges on the meanings derived from the music on which it is based. How does this fundamental process, this engendering of community, occur?

Community Formation

At bottom, the formation of a musical community depends on some shared conception among its members regarding what their music communicates. Paradoxically, however, these shared conceptions can neither be fully revealed nor directly known. Inasmuch as revealing or knowing in this context would amount to lexicalizing the music, translating a musical message into a linguistic one, something—indeed, something of critical importance—would be lost in the process. As John Blacking has put it, "musical discourse is essentially nonverbal . . . and to analyze nonverbal languages with verbal language runs the risk of destroying the evidence."[15] Consequently, our subject, here, requires a change of tack away from the conventional approach that has been relied on thus far—namely, saying things about music, appending adjectives to sound—and toward a consideration of music making per se as a signifying practice with its own particularities and possibilities.

Roland Barthes's reflections on nonverbal media are particularly useful in this respect. Barthes distinguishes three levels of meaning present in films and photographs: "communication" (the transfer of information), "signification" (the framing of the information's relevance, import, connotations, and so forth) and a "third meaning" which cannot be named but can be perceived and grasped intuitively. This third meaning involves the production of a signifier that has no corresponding signified, a something that not only refers to nothing but contains no specifiable meaning itself, yet is present in the image, contributing a kind of mood, perhaps provoking association with other signifiers and their signifieds, available to perception as a layer of meaning that is suspended somewhere between the image itself and its description. As an ethereal presence in the image, the third meaning seems to appear and to disappear just as quickly. Its presence, in Barthes's words, "maintains a state of perpetual erethism, desire not finding issue in that spasm of the signified which normally brings the subject voluptuously back into the peace of nominations."[16] This characterization of a third meaning—a signifier without a signified—in photographic images would seem equally to pertain to the sound of a musical phrase.

Although he did not make the connection explicitly, Barthes has employed a comparable approach to music in formulating his influential concept, "the grain of the voice."[17] This term refers to that something that is heard in vocal or instrumental music over and above the words or notes themselves. Its signifying ceases the moment that one drags it down to the level of connotation by loading it up with adjectives: "Her voice sounds so . . . earthy/troubled/joyous." As noted previously, blues is a highly textured sound replete with this "grain." In its propulsive rhythm, distorted notes, screams, and wails, it conveys any number of third meanings available for association with other signifiers present in social consciousness.[18] These associations, triggered by the indefinable third meaning, enable listeners themselves to construct meanings, to speak about what they hear in the music and what it means to them; in short, to dissolve the third meaning into a lexicalized chain of signs. These two distinct moments in musical signification—sonic and verbalized—would be apparent in the differing modes of apprehension displayed during performance: on stage, musicians smiling and nodding as they wind their way through some improvised passage, unified by the purely musical communication transpiring among them; at a side table, a music reviewer translating the sounds into language for a column in tomorrow's newspaper.

In writing that column, our reviewer would be tapping into socially available associations. He might compare the band's sound to that of other groups, appending the appropriate adjectives; he might identify particular features of their sound in this same way ("The plaintive phrasing of the guitar work provides a startling counterpoint to the relentless drive of the rhythm section."); and he might draw on metaphoric associations to describe their music ("The howling harmonica delivered a pulsating current of pure power."). In the process, the reviewer would be making manifest some of the meanings available in the music, there to be heard, interpreted, and articulated. These meanings, of course, do not stand outside of culture any more than music does. They are immanent to both.[19]

However, encoded in music, the meanings appear in an ambiguous fashion. Charles Keil describes this aspect of musical meaning as "participatory discrepancies," the disjunction that often obtains between the musical moment in which performers have found a groove and play within it as a single unit, and a reflective moment that follows in which they discover that they have radically different perspectives on what they were just doing.[20] Music's participatory discrepancies thus broaden its scope of involvement. Listeners, of course, must be sufficiently enculturated in order to "hear" the music and, thus, become involved with it. Yet they need not hear it in the same way or hear the same things in it in order to appreciate it collectively. The act of listening to the same music together suspends the differences that might exist among them with respect to its meaning. Thus, collective involvement rather than explicitly shared interpretations creates musical community. Particularly in the context of live performances—where music is simultaneously produced and consumed, and where dancing, call-and-response, and other forms of participation blur the lines separating performers and their audience—individual interpretations are enclosed in the common experience of a collective practice.[21]

Overtly, blues does not address itself to common experiences in a way that would thematize them as political, at least in the conventional understanding of the term. There are exceptions to this rule—songs such as Leadbelly's "Bourgeois Blues" or John Brim's "Tough Times" would be counterexamples—but they are very few and far between. As a music sung almost invariably in the first person singular, blues seems to lack that component essential to the production of political discourse: "we." Moreover, references to general conditions, all the more a critique of them, are quite sparse. But it would be a mistake to conclude on the basis of these observations that blues music lacks a politics. Its very source in a repressed and exploited community stigmatized by the hegemonic culture of white America represents one powerful set of associations.[22] As mentioned previously, those associations are not absent from the consciousness of Russian performers who refer to the feeling of "becoming Negroes" in communism's aftermath or "blackening" as a result of their efforts to master this musical idiom.[23] In addition, as demonstrated by Brian Ward's study of the role played by rhythm and blues in shaping African American consciousness during the U.S. civil rights struggles of the 1950s and 1960s, popular music without an explicit political content can nonetheless tap into broad-based expectations and aspirations, thus engendering a community aware of its common dispositions.[24] Many Russian bluesmen are quite sensitive to these considerations, as the remarks of one would suggest:

> Blues is the most apolitical music one can think of. . . . The political moment is excluded, at least on the surface of things. Blues is individual. A blues-man never says "we"; he sings about himself. But, on the other hand, it is the most political music imaginable inasmuch as blues always sings about freedom. Even if the song doesn't use the word "freedom," the implica-tions, the context is always about achieving some liberation from condi-tions that surround the person. Therefore, in any society the bluesman is a kind of dissident. I think that in America in the 1960s, people like The Band, Canned Heat, Paul Butterfield, or the Blues Project were not overtly polit-ically oriented but at the same time were participants in a broad social movement that concerned itself with freedom. I think that much the same thing is true here today.[25]

Vitalii Andreev responded to my question about blues as a social move-ment in Russia in comparable terms.

> *Vitalii Andreev:* Well, if rock 'n' roll is a music of protest, then blues is about freedom.
> *Interviewer:* Do you mean that it's the demand for freedom or the use of freedom?
> *Andreev:* No, it's the feeling of freedom. It's the feeling that you are free.[26]

As did Kolia Gruzdev:

> [Blues] is some type of inner freedom. I think that when black people play blues, they feel the same way. Like Lightnin' Hopkins, who spent his life in small pubs and bars in Texas and didn't want to play to huge audiences. He was free to do this. He was a bluesman. Whether he was sitting on the street one day and playing and then playing in some club, it was all the same. He was the same. There was no conflict inside of him. He was con-gruent.[27]

Much like his counterpart anywhere, in singing about himself the Rus-sian bluesman is simultaneously serving as a vicarious voice for unseen others who lack the means of self-expression. Whether these others actu-ally appreciate this benefaction is an issue that is beside the point here. For present purposes, it is sufficient to note the congruity that obtains between the bluesman's role and the traditional norms and practices of the country's intelligentsia which has historically seen itself as the voice of a silent and long-suffering people. Russian bluesmen continue that tradition and, as Arutiunov's remarks about the bluesman qua dissident would suggest, in at least some cases they do so self-consciously. However, the medium that they employ dispenses with the sermonizing for which the intelligentsia has been renowned and tends to disguise the function itself by confining expression ostensibly to the first person singular. Moreover, communication is channeled through the artifice of blues aesthetics which creates the effect of experiencing performance as a kind of reality. This effect—that the performer is not merely performing, but actually conveying his own feelings—stems from the music's saturation with a direct, emotive content which works to suppress the perception of artifice itself, and to conjure the impression that one is listening to the unadorned truth. This aspect of blues represents the kernel of what I have called "authenticity *in* the music," a quality central to Russians' appreciation of the idiom. The spell cast by the music's emotional authenticity invites listeners to identify with the bluesman's personal statements. It is on that basis that the bluesman is able to speak *to* and *for* others.[28] Muddy Waters once referred to this communitarian aspect of blues performance by noting that when a person "gets to realize that others have the same kind of trouble—or even worse—he understands that life isn't just pickin' on him alone."[29]

To whom and for whom do Russia's bluesmen speak? When I raised this question with some of them during interviews, pointing out that rather than society's downtrodden, their audiences primarily consist of young, middle-class professionals, they smiled at my lack of comprehension. Aleksei Agranovskii told me that:

This middle class that you are talking about always feels that they are sitting under a bomb, waiting for it to fall. This is a young capitalism and it has no stability to it. Second, we have the experience of just yesterday, slavery. So there is no way that you can consider this middle class to be a bourgeois middle class. Moreover, this is a middle class in constant intercourse with bandits and with the police. Maybe I am exaggerating this. Maybe these same people won't tell you about these parts of their lives. Maybe they will just say that they like the music. But I think that this is the actual case. I see it among students because we play for them a lot.[30]

Kolia Gruzdev put it this way:

Even if you are a rich man here, you have most of the same problems that other people do. The difference is that you're not hungry. You might be listening under different circumstances, but you have the same problems, the same troubles. Because in Russia it is not actually that easy to be wealthy. Because [referencing the rash of contract killings that still plague the country] you get killed.[31]

It may be that this pivotal capacity of blues—singing in the first person singular while employing the performer's artifice of emotional involvement that stimulates the identification of others—is particularly relevant to the creation of community in contemporary Russia. As has been noted, the disappointments and dislocations following communism's collapse have led individuals to withdraw from the public sphere and to focus their attentions and energies on survival strategies, hinged on cooperation with kin, friends, and acquaintances organized in informal networks. As Vladimir Kostiushev and his collaborators have shown in their study of the related phenomena of contemporary Russian subcultures, identities are not constructed on the basis of ideology, program, or formal organization—even among ostensibly political groups—but instead entail a display of surface markers such as symbols, rituals, jargon, and dress serving to distinguish members from others. Rather than a commitment to programmatic objectives, sociability seems to be the primary incentive for participation in subcultural life.[32] It may even be that the population evinces a certain caution, if not fear, with respect to mobilization for larger purposes. Having experienced the catastrophes attending the communist revolution and then those of the anticommunist one that followed, they appear to have grown distrustful of would-be mass movements and their eschatological ends. As a result, the category "we" tends to be excluded from practical consciousness.[33]

The blues community's form of organization reflects much of that pattern. However, the music on which it is based allows for a certain transcendence of it as well. Rather than recoiling from an inhospitable world, the blues ethos insists on standing one's ground. Although things may be bad and unlikely to change, "that's all right." Those participating in this music thus register their membership in a "we," an imagined blues community that spans continents and a century or more.

Subversion and Resistance

The sound of blues is itself subversive. The music's signature tonality—especially the distortion and dissonance effected by its texture and drive—disrupts the familiar and undercuts the sense of order inherent in standard European melodic structures. Adding to this effect, the music's overlay of rhythmic patterns on top of the basic beat engenders "the feeling . . . of . . . trying to break out of the constraining, divisive meter" that structures the song itself.[34] As suggested by the Russian slang term *ugar* [loosely: "rush"] that respondents have often used during interviews and conversations, the sound and propulsion of the music is experienced as an undoing of constraints. Vocal techniques can further enhance the music's subversive impact. Whether stretching meaning beyond the words employed or communicating through nonverbal shrieks and moans, blues can index extramusical memories and aspirations. Numerous quotations scattered throughout this book attest to the way in which Russian bluesmen appreciate these features of the music.

Blues in Russia is subversive in other ways as well. The transformation of a "low" cultural form into a "high" one would appear to be transgressive on its face.[35] As previously outlined, this transgression for those in the country's blues community is twofold: their subculture is not based on a domestic cultural product, but on a foreign, Western one; at the same time, this particular cultural product carries its own reproachful valence vis-à-vis standard manifestations of Westernization. Moreover, because the social origins of blues are imprinted in the music itself, performing it inverts the social hierarchy by presenting the world from the perspective of the marginalized and oppressed. In consonance with this social inversion, the capacity of blues to undercut conventional musical constraints has meant for Russian performers, as it has for white players everywhere, that "to step out in the guise of the blues is to step out of line."[36]

The line in question, here, is racial as well as musical. Crossing it may not have been much on the minds of Russia's first generation of bluesmen who cut their teeth on the music performed by British artists, but as they and others delved deeper into the roots of blues, a vicarious identification with African Americans has been fostered, as made clear by many interviewee's comments. That identification contrasts sharply with the invidious racial distinctions that one encounters in Russia today. In this context, blues represents a subversion of a racialized social consciousness, but a subversion that is indirect, operating through the medium of a distant other: black bluesmen in the United States, and the ensuing spool of associations to their audiences, conditions of life and so forth that supply imaginary links to Russians. By playing blues, Russians are neither staging a direct assault on racism in general nor explicitly criticizing the racism present in their own society. Rather, they are contributing to social learning by undermining racial categories in subtler and perhaps more effective ways simply by inviting listeners to participate in this music and thus to share in its associations.

Obviously, the problem of racism among Russians concerns their relations with a proximate other, people of color in their own society. Seventy-four years of communism—which outlawed openly racist expressions and installed an explicitly antiracist code for all forms of public speech—did not succeed in erasing racial antagonism from the social landscape, in part because the Soviet state often tacitly incorporated racist categories into its policies as if they were self-evident matters of fact, thereby reinforcing and naturalizing racist practices.[37] When that state collapsed, the threshold for overt expressions of racism came down as well, as illustrated dramatically by the periodic pogroms visited on people of color in those public markets where they peddle their wares, or routinely by city police singling out and shaking down dark-skinned individuals in public places. Moreover, in quotidian terms, race seems a central marker on the social maps drawn by many individuals, for whom "dark" or "black" references the inferior, the unworthy, and the dangerous. By contrast, "white"—that is, the speaker and his preferred reference group—would be commensurably valorized.

Some observers have remarked on the rationale that appears to underlie this racist orientation among Russians, seeing it as an attempt to position the self against uncomprehended but apparently threatening forces connected to the new and mysterious commercial economy and its criminal contingents, as well as an effort to signal through their whiteness an affiliation with some imagined transnational community composed of developed and cultured people.[38] Yet this positioning can be ambivalent: dark-skinned people who are proximate may be marked negatively whereas those who are remote, such as African Americans, can assume the form of blank slates on which individuals are free to inscribe their own aspirations and fantasies.[39] The identification evinced by Russia's bluesmen with blacks in the United States would seem to follow that second pattern, imagining an idealized other who can be enlisted for the construction of personal and collective identities.[40] However, the fact remains that bluesmen are performers who actively express those identities in performance. In the act of playing blues, they therefore disturb the black/white dichotomy central to racial stereotyping, stripping the concept "black" of its negativity and joining it to a positive assertion of "us." This subversive moment is therefore a subtle one, dispensing with didacticism or any overt statements on the value of racial equality and so forth. Rather, the reverence shown the music itself both communicates and instantiates the idea of racial harmony as a matter of fact.

Resistance is a second face that blues music turns toward the hegemonic culture of the larger society. It sometimes appears as imaginary excursions to another place and time, as exemplified by the episode recounted in chapter 4 in which a jump-blues performance served as the occasion to reenact dances and sartorial modes associated with the United States in the 1940s. Even if the "nostalgia" in this instance had been borrowed from another culture—or, perhaps, especially because it has—it nonetheless serves to position individuals outside of their everyday milieu, representing some ground on which to stand that is experienced as an alternative free of society's constraints.[41] The same would appear to hold for the music, itself, which indexes another place and time sonorously delivered to the here and now. That capacity to transform the present would be additionally apparent in improvisation that comprises such an important feature of blues. By stressing spontaneous, cooperative, and creative activity, improvisation forms a resistive counterpart to the standardization of social relations in commodity-based cultures as reflected in the repetitive nature of most contemporary popular music. The Russian bluesman's hot solo thus appears as the community's ultimate weapon in the struggle against *popsa*. Improvised passages reconstruct musical codes for performers and listeners alike, amounting to forms of dialogue around the issue of musical problem-solving that may suggest in their turn more open-ended and negotiated forms of human relationships.[42]

As is the case with a message of freedom that Russians find encoded in blues, resistance appears in subtle forms: palpable, but difficult to pinpoint or to circumscribe. A number of comments recorded during interviews and already cited in this book reflect a personal resonance with this intangible element of resistance: Sergei Mitrokhin's reference to "experiencing terrible things but at the same time surviving them, and knowing that you are able to survive them"; Aleksandr Bratetskii's appreciation for the "primordial energy" that he detects in the music; Iaroslav Sukhov's feeling that "in blues you remain yourself"; and Giia Dzagnidze's point that "blues is recalling what you have survived." Enduring and surviving are qualities that Russia's bluesmen associate with resistance rather than with retreat. In their music they have found a particular stance in that regard, one positioning them against both the remnants of the unexpunged past and the troubling conditions surrounding the still unfolding present.

Notes

CHAPTER ONE. WHY BLUES?

1. The contents of this paragraph derive from a number of conversations with bluesmen, club managers, and observers, the most important of which were with: Levan Lomidze (Moscow, 25 July 1999), Mikail Sokolov (Moscow, 23 July 1999), Michael Osley (Moscow, 21 October 1998), and Vladimir Padunov (by telephone, 4 August 1998).

2. Boris Kagarlitsky, *Russia Under Yeltsin and Putin* (London: Pluto, 2002), p. 200.

3. *Vechernaia Moskva*, 17 November 1998.

4. National news program *Vremia*, Russian Public Television, 21 June 1999.

5. Paul Gilroy (*"There Ain't No Black in the Union Jack": The Cultural Politics of Race and Nation* [Chicago: University of Chicago Press, 1987], p. 187) has called attention to the problems attending the use of such terms as "subculture" with respect to identifying social groups distinguished by certain discourses and practices that center on music. However, his recommendation to substitute the term "movement" does little to overcome the same lack of clarity present in the marker that he has rejected. Although "movement" may capture the notion of overt resistance to a dominant culture that is mediated musically—as it would for hippies and punks—it is much less certain that this term would convey an accurate representation of other social groups organized around a musical idiom (such as bluegrass or, for that matter, blues). The term "community" does not admit to that problem. Moreover, its very ambivalence—suggesting, on one hand, affective relations within a tightly knit group and, on the other, a collection of persons bound together simply by common practices, norms, and interests (say, the journalistic or scholarly communities)—sits well with the circumstances under consideration here. The Russian blues community is constituted both by strong, affective, face-to-face relations at microlevel and, with respect to the country as a whole, by a common sense of identity that individuals share with (imagined) others who perform and listen to this music. Moreover, the term "blues community" has been used to designate a comparable collection of individuals in Britain by Theodore Gracyk in his *I Wanna Be Me: Rock Music and the Politics of Identity* (Philadelphia: Temple University Press, 2001), p. 108. Blues Community was also used as a name by a St. Petersburg blues band in the late 1990s.

6. Francis Davis, *The History of the Blues* (New York: Hyperion, 1995), p. 23–47; Robert Palmer, *Deep Blues* (New York: Viking, 1981), pp. 17–18; LeRoi Jones (Amiri Buraka), *Blues People: Negro Music in White America* (Westport, Conn.: Greenwood Press, 1963), pp. 62–65.

7. William Barlow, *"Looking Up at Down": The Emergence of Blues Culture* (Philadelphia: Temple University Press, 1989), p. 8; Ray Pratt, *Rhythm and Resistance: Explorations in the Political Uses of Popular Music* (New York: Praeger, 1990), pp. 79, 87–88; Angela Davis, *Blues Legacies and Black Feminism* (New York: Pantheon, 1998), pp. 4–5, 45–46, 67–72.

8. Peter Kolchin, *Unfree Labor: American Slavery and Russian Serfdom* (Cambridge, Mass.: Belknap Press, 1987), esp. pp. 2–41.

9. Marshall Poe, *"A People Born to Slavery": Russia in Early Modern European Ethnography, 1476–1748* (Ithaca: Cornell University Press, 2000), esp. pp. 196–226; Robert Tucker, *The Soviet Political Mind: Studies in Stalinism and Post-Stalin Change* (New York: Praeger, 1963), esp. pp. 83–89.

10. Michael Urban, "Conceptualizing Political Power in the USSR: Patterns of Binding and Bonding," *Studies in Comparative Communism* 18 (Winter, 1985), pp. 207–26.

11. Katherine Verdery, *What Was Socialism, and What Comes Next?* (Princeton: Princeton University Press, 1996), pp. 222–23.

12. Kolchin, *Unfree Labor*, pp. 229–36; Dale Peterson, *Up from Bondage: The Literatures of Russian and African American Soul* (Durham, N.C.: Duke University Press, 2000).

13. Aleksei Agranovskii, interview by author, Moscow, 23 August 2001.

14. Vitalii Andreev, interview by author, St. Petersburg, 13 July 1999.

15. Iaroslav Sukhov, interview by author, St. Petersburg, 17 July 1999.

16. See Eliot Borenstein, "Public Offerings: MMM and the Marketing of Melodrama," and idem, "Suspending Disbelief: Cults and Postmodernism in Post-Soviet Russia," both in *Consuming Russia: Popular Culture, Sex and Society since Gorbachev*, ed. A. Barker (Durham, N.C.: Duke University Press, 1999), pp. 49–75 and pp. 437–62, respectively.

17. Oleg Pachenkov, "Nekotorye aspekty deiatel'nosti sovremennykh rossiiskikh 'selitelei,'" (St. Petersburg's Center for Independent Social Research, 1998), p. 1.

18. Aleksandr Tsar'kov, the former director of Moscow's Arbat Blues Club, noted that his establishment regularly employed English in its advertisements in order to discourage the "wrong" clientele from attending, interview by author, Moscow, 16 August 2001.

19. Adam Gussow, *Seems Like Murder Here: Southern Violence and the Blues Tradition* (Chicago: University of Chicago Press, 2002), esp. pp. 23, 83.

20. Mikhail Mishuris, interview by author, Moscow, 13 August 2001.

21. Aleksei Kalachev, interview by author, Moscow, 24 August 2001.

22. Kolia Gruzdev, interview by author, St. Petersburg, 15 July 1999.

23. Valerii Belinov, interview by author, St. Petersburg, 21 July 1999.

24. Palmer, *Deep Blues*, pp. 134–35; Mike Rowe, *Chicago Blues: The City and the Music* (New York: Da Capo Press, 1975), pp. 26–39; Lee Hildebrand, "Oakland

Blues, Part I: Essay," in *California Soul: Music of African Americans in the West*, ed. J. C. Dje Dje and E. S. Meadows (Berkeley: University of California Press, 1998), pp. 104–12.

25. Inter alia, Paul Oliver, "Savannah Syncopators" in *Yonder Come the Blues: The Evolution of a Genre*, Paul Oliver et al. (Cambridge: Cambridge University Press, 2001), esp. pp. 21–73.

26. Paul Oliver, *The Story of the Blues* (2nd ed.; Boston: Northeastern University Press, 1997), pp. 11–15; Giles Oakley, *The Devil's Music: A History of the Blues* (2nd ed.; New York: Da Capo Press, 1997), pp. 21–40.

27. Susan McClary, *Conventional Wisdom: The Content of Musical Form* (Berkeley: University of California Press, 2000), p. 33. Comparable characterizations can be found in: Mary Ellison, *Extensions of the Blues* (London: John Calder, 1989), pp. 52–54; Tony Mitchell, *Popular Music and Local Identity: Rock, Pop and Rap in Europe and Oceania* (London: Leicester University Press, 1996), p. 8.

28. For a dissection of the twelve-bar blues form revealing the complexity of tensions produced by the vocal and musical accompaniment which propels a given song in disparate directions bound together by the pattern itself, see McClary, *Conventional Wisdom*, pp. 38–42.

29. Richard Leppert, "Desire, Power and the Sonoric Landscape: Early Modernism and the Politics of Musical Privacy," in *The Place of Music*, ed. A. Leyshon, D. Matless, and G. Revill (New York: Guilford Press, 1998), pp. 305.

30. Jacques Attali, *Noise: The Political Economy of Music* (Minneapolis: University of Minnesota Press, 1985), pp. 4–30, esp. p. 29.

31. Charles Keil and Steven Feld, *Music Grooves* (Chicago: University of Chicago Press, 1994), p. 55.

32. The first two of these terms appear in ibid. The third is used by Palmer, *Deep Blues*, pp. 29–30.

33. Keil and Feld, *Music Grooves*, pp. 59–67, 97–98.

34. Aleksandr Bratetskii, interview by author, Moscow, 29 August 2001.

35. Nikolai Arutiunov, interview by author, Moscow, 25 July 1999.

36. Keil and Feld, *Music Grooves*, p. 98; Charles Keil, *Urban Blues* (Chicago: University of Chicago Press, 1966), pp. 53, 125, 130; Barlow, "*Looking Up at Down*," pp. 3–4.

37. Ellison, *Extensions of the Blues*, p. 52.

38. Sasha Suvorov, interview by author, St. Petersburg, 5 July 2000.

39. Edik Tsekhanovskii, interview by author, St. Petersburg, 14 July 2000.

40. Aleksei Baryshev, interview by author, St. Petersburg, 8 July 2000.

41. Giia Dzagnidze, interview by author, Moscow, 18 June 2000.

42. Keil, *Urban Blues*, pp. 51–53.

43. Keil and Feld, *Music Grooves*, pp. 204–5.

44. Mikhail Sokolov, interview by author, Moscow, 23 July 1999.

45. Palmer, *Deep Blues*, pp. 18–19.

46. Paul Garon, *Blues and the Poetic Spirit* (2nd ed.; San Francisco: City Lights, 1996), p. 10.

47. Barry Shank, *Dissonant Identities: The Rock 'n' Roll Scene in Austin Texas* (Hanover, N.H.: University Press of New England, 1994), p. 99.

48. Quoted in *Good Times*, 13 May 1999, p. 16.

49. Volodia Rusinov, interview by author, St. Petersburg, 28 June 2000.

50. Paul Gilroy, *There Ain't No Black in the Union Jack*, p. 155; Garon, *Blues and the Poetic Spirit*, pp. 54–55.

51. Keil, *Urban Blues*, pp. 118–22; Barlow, *"Looking Up at Down,"* pp. 4–5.

52. Compare, for example, Walter Benjamin's treatment of these terms in the work cited in the following note with that of Sigmund Freud in his *General Psychological Theory: Papers in Metapsychology* (New York: Collier, 1963), pp. 164–79.

53. Walter Benjamin, *The Origin of German Tragic Drama* (London: Verso, 1977), pp. 119–57, esp. p. 157.

54. Sergei Mitrokhin, conversation with author, Santa Cruz, Ca., 6 January 1999.

55. Vitalii Andreev, interview by author, St. Petersburg, 13 July 1999.

56. Ivan Kovalev, interview by author, St. Petersburg, 31 July 1999.

57. On the issue of cultural transmission and receptivity with respect to musical forms in particular, see Mark Slobin, *Subcultural Sounds* (Hanover, Conn.: Wesleyan University Press, 1993), pp. 68, 76–78.

58. Quoted in Clyde Woods, *Development Arrested: The Blues and Plantation Power in the Mississippi Delta* (London: Verso, 1998), p. 25.

59. Robert Rothstein, "Popular Song in the NEP Era," in *Russia in the Era of NEP*, ed. S. Fitzpatrick, A Rabinowitch, and R. Stites (Bloomington: Indiana University Press, 1991), pp. 268–94; idem, "How It Was Sung in Odessa: At the Intersection of Russia and Yiddish Folk Culture," *Slavic Review* 60 (Winter, 2001), pp. 781–801.

60. Aleksandr Dolgov, interview by author, St. Petersburg, 26 June 2000.

61. Aleksei Agranovskii, interview by author, Moscow, 23 August 2001.

62. Aleksei Kalachev, interview by author, Moscow, 24 August 2001.

63. The term "effect of meaning" has been coined by A. J. Greimas in his *Structural Semantics* (Lincoln, Neb.: University of Nebraska Press, 1982).

64. Nancy Ries, *Russian Talk: Culture and Conversation during Perestroika* (Ithaca: Cornell University Press, 1997).

65. Dale Pesman, *Russia and Soul: An Exploration* (Ithaca: Cornell University Press, 2000)

66. Sergei Mironov, interview by author, St. Petersburg, 13 July 1999.

67. Vitalii Andreev, interview by author, St. Petersburg, 13 July 1999.

68. Kolia Grudzev, interview by author, St. Petersburg, 15 July 1999.

69. Dale Peterson, *Up from Bondage*, p. 70.

70. Iaroslav Sukhov, interview by author, St. Petersburg, 17 July 1999.

71. Nikolai Arutiunov, interview by author, Moscow, 25 July 1999.

72. Svetlana Boym, *Common Places* (Cambridge: Harvard University Press, 1994), pp. 1, 275–78, 289.

73. Garon, *Blues and the Poetic Spirit*, pp. 194–97.

74. Henry Louis Gates, Jr., *Figures in Black: Signs and the "Radical" Self* (New York: Oxford University Press, 1987), p. 240, quoted in Peterson, *Up from Bondage*, p 191. See also pp. 108–24, 186–99.

75. Garon, *Blues and the Poetic Spirit*, pp. 144–49.

76. Greil Marcus, *Mystery Train: Images of America in Rock 'n' Roll Music* (3rd ed.; New York: Plume, 1990), pp. 22–29.

77. Katerina Clark, *Petersburg: Crucible of Cultural Revolution* (Cambridge: Harvard University Press, 1995), pp. 40–57;
Neil Carrick, *Daniil Kharms: Theologian of the Absurd* (Birmingham: Dept. of Russian Language and Literature, University of Birmingham, 1998).

78. Vania Zhuk. Interview by author, St. Petersburg, 29 June 2000.

79. Studies outlining this process in various contexts include: James L. Watson, ed., *Golden Arches East: McDonald's in East Asia* (Stanford: Stanford University Press, 1997); Mark Slobin, ed., *Retuning Culture: Musical Changes in Central and Eastern Europe* (Durham, N.C.: Duke University Press, 1996); Gregory Lee, "The 'East is Red' Goes Pop: Commodification, Hybridity and Nationalism in Chinese Popular Song and its Televisual Performance," *Popular Music* 14 (January, 1995), pp. 95–110; Robert Hanke, "Yo Quiero Mi MTV! Making Music Television for Latin America," in *Mapping the Beat, ed.* T. Swiss, J. Sloop, and A. Herman (Malden, Mass.: Blackwell, 1998), pp. 219–45.

80. S. Frederick Starr, *Red and Hot: The Fate of Jazz in the Soviet Union* (New York: Oxford University Press, 1983), pp. 43–79; Timothy Rice, "The Dialectic of Economics and Aesthetics in Bulgarian Music," in *Retuning Culture,* ed. Slobin, pp. 179–99.

81. D. Palumbo-Lice and H. U. Gumbrecht, "Introduction" to their *Streams of Cultural Capital* (Stanford: Stanford University Press, 1997), pp. 8–13; Irmela Schneider, "Wide Worlds in Confined Quarters: American Movies on German Television," in ibid., pp. 129–53; Eric Zolov, *Refried Elvis: The Rise of the Mexican Counterculture* (Berkeley: University of California Press, 1999), pp. 17–34.

82. Andrew Lass, "Portable Worlds: On the Limits of Replication in Czech and Slovak Republics," in *Uncertain Transitions: Ethnographies of Change in the Postsocialist World,* ed. M. Burawoy and K. Verdery (New York: Rowman and Littlefield, 1999), pp. 273–300.

83. Varying treatments of the effects of the global music industry can be found in: Georgia Born, "Afterword: Music Policy, Aesthetic and Social Difference," in *Rock and Popular Music: Politics, Policies, Institutions,* ed. T. Bennet et al. (London: Routledge, 1993), pp. 266–92; Roy Shuker, *Understanding Popular Music* (London: Routledge, 1994), pp. 33–37; Tony Mitchell, *Popular Music and Local Identity,* pp. 49–52; John Lovering, "The Global Music Industry: Contradictions in the Commodification of the Sublime," in *The Place of Music,* ed. Leyshon, Matless, and Revill, pp. 31–56.

84. Valerii Belinov, interview by author, St. Petersburg, 7 August 1999.

85. Mikhail Sokolov, interview by author, Moscow, 23 July 1999.

86. Sergei Voronov, interview by author, Moscow, 18 July 2000.

87. Ruth Finnegan, *The Hidden Musicians: Music-Making in an English Town* (Cambridge: Cambridge University Press, 1989). David Coplan, *In Township Tonight! South Africa's Black City Music and Theatre* (London: Longman, 1985).

88. Clark, *Petersburg: Crucible of Cultural Revolution,* p. 294.

89. Palmer, *Deep Blues,* p. 17. For instance, two bands of this type—Moscow's Blues Hammer Band and St. Petersburg's Big Blues Revival—play regularly in

their respective cities' most elegant blues venues: Forte Club in Moscow and JFC in St. Petersburg.

90. Levan Lomidze, interview by author, Moscow, 25 July 1999.

91. Aleksei Kalachev, "Prikliucheniia bliuza," *Nezavisimaia gazeta* 2 June 1997, p. 8; Nikolai Arutiunov, interview by author, 25 July 1999.

92. James Salem, *The Late Great Johnny Ace and the Transition from R&B to Rock 'n' Roll* (Urbana: University of Illinois Press, 1999), pp. 103–4, 172.

93. Paul Oliver, "Introduction (to Part Two)," in *Black Music in Britain*, ed. P. Oliver (Milton Keynes: Open University Press, 1990), pp. 80–82.

94. On the derivation of rock from blues, see in particular Allan Moore, *The Primary Text: Developing a Musicology of Rock* (Philadelphia: Open University Press, 1993), esp. pp. 66–73.

95. This thesis on the ideology of rock has been extensively developed by Simon Frith. See his: "The Magic That Can Set You Free: The Ideology of Folk and the Myth of the Rock Community," in *Popular Music 1*, ed. R. Middleton and D. Horn (Cambridge: Cambridge University Press, 1981), pp. 159–68; *Sound Effects: Youth, Leisure, and the Politics of Rock 'n' Roll* (New York: Pantheon, 1981), pp. 27–36, 70–72; and *Performing Rites: On the Value of Popular Music* (Cambridge: Harvard University Press, 1996), pp. 40–41. See also Keir Keightley, "Reconsidering Rock," in *The Cambridge Companion to Pop and Rock*, ed. S. Frith, W. Straw, and J. Street (Cambridge: Cambridge University Press, 2001), pp. 109–42.

96. Thomas Cushman, *Notes from Underground: Rock Music Counterculture in Russia* (Albany: State University of New York Press, 1995), pp. 34–194.

97. On a history of rock 'n' roll in the USSR, see: Artemy Troitsky, *Back in the USSR: A True Story of Rock in Russia* (London: Omnibus, 1987); Timothy Ryback, *Rock Around the Bloc: A History of Rock Music in Eastern Europe and the Soviet Union* (Oxford: Oxford University Press, 1990); Sabrina Petra Ramet, ed., *Rocking the State: Rock Music and Politics in Eastern Europe and Russia* (Boulder: Westview, 1994); Thomas Cushman, *Notes from Underground*.

98. Sabrina Petra Ramet, Sergei Zamascikov, and Robert Bird, "The Soviet Rock Scene," in *Rocking the State*, ed. Ramet, p. 181.

99. Mitchell, *Popular Music and Local Identity*, p. 95; Julia Friedman and Adam Weiner, "Between a Rock and a Hard Place: Holy Rus' and Its Alternatives in Russian Rock Music," in *Consuming Russia*, ed. Barker, pp. 110–37.

100. Anna Szemere, *Up from the Underground: The Culture of Rock Music in Postsocialist Hungary* (University Park: Pennsylvania State University Press, 2001), p. 7. Sabrina Petra Ramet, "Rock: The Music of Revolution (and Political Community)," in *Rocking the State*, ed. Ramet, p. 3.

101. Alexei Yurchak, "Gagarin and the Rave Kids: Transforming Power, Identity and Aesthetics in Post-Soviet Nightlife," in *Consuming Russia*, ed. Barker, p. 91.

102. Bob Brunning, *Blues: The British Connection* (New York: Blandford Press, 1986), p. 9.

103. McClary, *Conventional Wisdom*, pp. 43–45, 52–58.

104. Aleksei Baryshev, interview by author, St. Petersburg, 8 July 2000.

105. Vladimir Berezin, interview by author, St. Petersburg, 31 July 1999.

CHAPTER TWO. FIRST ENCOUNTERS

1. S. Frederick Starr, *Red and Hot: The Fate of Jazz in the Soviet Union* (New York: Oxford University Press, 1983), p. 70.

2. G. Schuller, *Early Jazz* (Oxford: Oxford University Press, 1968), p. 44, quoted in Phil Virden and Trevor Wishart, "Some Observations on the Social Stratification of Twentieth-Century Music," in *Whose Music? A Sociology of Musical Languages*, ed. J. Shepherd et al. (London: Latimer, 1977), p. 166.

3. Starr, *Red and Hot*, pp. 237–43. Artem Troitsky, *Back in the U.S.S.R.: A True Story of Rock in Russia* (London: Omnibus, 1987), pp. 2–6. On the *stiliagi* in general—including their latter-day descendents—see Hilary Pilkington, *Russia's Youth and Its Culture: A Nation's Constructors and Constructed* (London: Routledge, 1994).

4. Troitsky, *Back in the U.S.S.R.*, pp. 6–9; Timothy Ryback, *Rock Around the Bloc: A History of Rock Music in Eastern Europe and the Soviet Union* (New York: Oxford University Press, 1990), p. 30.

5. Richard Stites, *Russian Popular Culture* (Cambridge: Cambridge University Press, 1992), p. 132.

6. Valerii Belinov, interview by author, St. Petersburg, 19 July 1999.

7. Nikolai Arutiunov, interview by author, Moscow, 25 July 1999.

8. Vladimir Berezin, interview by author, St. Petersburg, 31 July 1999.

9. Aleksei Kalachev, interview by author, Moscow, 24 August 2001.

10. Aleksei Belov, interview by author, Moscow, 22 August 2001.

11. Ryback, *Rock Around the Bloc*, pp. 32–33.

12. Aleksei Belov, interview by author, Moscow, 22 August 2001.

13. *Udachnoe priobretenie: Live '74* (Moscow: Solyd Records, 2000).

14. Aleksei Belov, interview by author, Moscow, 22 August 2001.

15. One such individual was Iurii Naumov, a Siberian singer and guitarist whose lyrical compositions earned him a following in *sistema* before he immigrated to the United States in 1990. Although he has been billed as a Russian blues artist his work is far more in the folk-rock mode. Accordingly, his subsequent visits to Russia in the 1990s attracted effectively no attention in the country's blues community. For these reasons he is not treated in this study. An analysis of the texts of some of Naumov's compositions can be found in Julia Friedman and Adam Weiner, "Between a Rock and a Hard Place: Holy Rus' and Its Alternatives in Russian Rock Music," in *Consuming Russia: Popular Culture, Sex and Society since Gorbachev*, ed. Adele Barker (Durham, N.C.: Duke University Press, 1999), pp. 121–25.

16. Svetlana Boym, *The Future of Nostalgia* (New York: Basic Books, 2001), pp. 150–56. See also Pilkington, *Russia's Youth and Its Culture*, p. 236.

17. Aleksei Kuz'min, conversation with author, Moscow, 12 August 2001.

18. Aleksei Agranovskii, interview by author, Moscow, 23 August 2001.

19. Edik Tsekhanovskii, interview by author, St. Petersburg, 14 July 2000.

20. Vitalii Andreev, interview by author, St. Petersburg, 13 July 1999.

21. Valerii Belinov, interview by author, St. Petersburg, 11 July 1999.

22. Boris Bulkin, interview by author, Moscow, 28 August 2001.

23. Nikolai Arutiunov, interview by author, Moscow, 25 July 1999.

24. Aleksei Belov, interview by author, Moscow, 22 August 2001.

25. Aleksei Agranovskii, interview by author, Moscow, 23 August 2001.

26. Giia Dzagnidze, interview by author, Moscow, 18 June 2000.

27. Aleksei Kalachev, interview by author, Moscow, 24 August 2001.

28. Aleksei Belov, interview by author, Moscow, 22 August 2001, and Nikolai Arutiunov, interview by author, Moscow, 25 July 1999.

29. Giia Dzagnidze, interview by author, Moscow, 18 June 2000.

30. Aleksandr Tsar'kov, interview by author, Moscow, 16 August 2001.

31. Aleksei Belov, interview by author, Moscow, 22 August 2001.

32. The information in this paragraph comes from Nikolai Arutiunov, interview by author, Moscow, 25 July 1999, and Sergei Voronov, interview by author, Moscow, 18 July 2000.

33. Aleksandr Tsar'kov, interview by author, Moscow, 16 August 2001.

34. Mikhail Sokolov, interview by author, Moscow, 23 July 1999.

35. One of the songs performed at that concert, "Nineteenth Nervous Breakdown," has been included on Liga bliuza's CD, *Neuzheli proshlo 15 let?* (Moscow: RDM, 1995).

36. Liga bliuza, *Da zdravstvuet ritm end bliuz!* (Moscow: SNC, 1991). This album's first side contains five blues-rock numbers in Russian that were written by members of the band; the second side consists of six blues and rhythm-and-blues standards such as "Hoochie Coochie Man," Walkin' the Dog," and "True Fine Mamma."

37. Information for the previous two paragraphs comes from Nikolai Arutiunov, interview by author, Moscow, 25 July 1999, and Sergei Voronov, interview by author, Moscow, 18 July 2000.

38. Vania Zhuk, interview by author, St. Petersburg, 29 June 2000.

39. Sasha Suvorov, interview by author, St. Petersburg, 5 July 2000.

40. Edik Tsekhanovskii, interview by author, St. Petersburg, 14 July 2000.

41. Mikhail Mishuris, interview by author, Moscow, 13 August 2001.

42. Aleksei Kalachev, interview by author, Moscow, 24 August 2001.

43. Volodia Rusinov, interview by author, St. Petersburg, 28 June 2000.

44. *Bol'shaia Sovetskaia Entsiklopediia* (Moscow: Bol'shaia Sovetskaia entsiklopediia, 1950), Vol. 5, p. 321.

CHAPTER THREE. MOSCOW BLUES: MUSICIANS AND THEIR MUSIC

1. On the political and social movements of the late 1980s, see Michael Urban *The Rebirth of Politics in Russia* (Cambridge: Cambridge University Press, 1997), pp. 103–6.

2. The double LP was entitled "Bliuz v Rossii" (Moscow: Evita, 1992) while the CD by the same name was issued by Moscow Evita Records in 1992 and reissued by the Moscow firm Lad' in 1994.

3. A. Evdokimov, "Bliuz v Rossii," *Kuranty,* 12 December 1992.

4. Mikhail Sokolov, interview by author, Moscow, 23 July 1999.

5. Sergei Voronov, interview by author, Moscow, 18 July 2000.

6. For instance, the band's CD—*Salado* (Moscow: Music X, 1999)—features twelve songs composed by Voronov and others in the group, some of which have a blues-rock feel while others are outside of the genre entirely.

7. Boris Bulkin, interview by author, Moscow, 28 August 2001.

8. Chernyi khelb i Doktor Agranovskii, *Tik* (Moscow: Dr. Agranovsky, 2001).

9. Denis Mazhukov, son of a popular Soviet composer, Aleksei Mazhukov, took his own musical direction early in life, embracing with great seriousness and determination the piano style of Jerry Lee Lewis.

10. The collapse of the old Soviet promotional network affected all bands in the 1990s. A private agency did secure a Siberian tour for Liga bliuza in 1993 that was highly successful, but no follow-up occurred to this one-time effort, despite the fact that a market seemed to exist.

11. This band's name—on first inspection, a rather odd one for a group of school-aged lads—derived from a popular form of address in youth slang of the period: "starik" ("old man"). The slang term itself came from Ernest Hemingway's novel, *The Old Man and the Sea*, a favorite among Russian youth. Fittingly, it was another American, John Anderson, who influenced the group's sound after joining it in 1992.

12. Boris Bulkin, interview by author, Moscow, 28 August 2001.

13. Mikhail Sokolov (Petrovich), interview by author, Moscow, 23 July 1999.

14. Boris Bulkin, interview by author, Moscow, 28 August 2001.

15. Mikhail Sokolov, interview by author, Moscow, 23 July 1999.

16. Aleksandr Tsar'kov, interview by author, Moscow, 16 August 2001.

17. Some of the information on Blues Cousins in this and the following three paragraphs comes from conversations with Levan Lomidze, conversations with author, Moscow, 25 July 1999 and 29 August 2001.

18. Blues Cousins, *Dozhd'* (no copyright, 1999).

19. Levan Lomidze and Blues Cousins, *Hoochie Coochie Man* (Moscow: Landy Star Music, 2001).

20. *Blues Cousins* (Paris: JP Poutka, 1996).

21. *Blues Festival 2000* (Paris: Saken, 2001).

22. Aleksandr Bratetskii, interview by author, Moscow, 29 August 2001.

23. Their homemade CD, *The Best of Blues Rhythm Section* (no copyright, 1998) contains twenty-two songs, only two of which fall outside the Chicago genre. The recording, itself, was made with the intention of capturing the authentic sound of the material that they were performing. Consequently, the band scouted out some ancient amplifiers (mostly of Czech manufacture) and, on a few numbers, added the effect of a stylus scraping on old worn-out records. The mushiness of the sound thereby produced did not benefit the vocals, but the harmonica's tone is nicely wrapped in raspy full-throated vibrato. Although the product of these recording techniques sounds as much amateurish as it does authentic, the band should be congratulated for experimentation.

24. This song appears on the anthology *Ia ne uvizhu Missisipi: Rossiiskii bliuz v 90–kh* (Moscow: Salon AV, 1999).

25. This song has been featured on John Sanchillo's homemade CD, *Bright Lights, Big City* (no copyright, 2000).

26. Dmitrii Krasivov, conversation with author, Moscow, 18 August 2001.

27. The initial name for the group was supplied by its sponsor, Music Hammer. When the sponsor dropped them, the name was altered accordingly.

28. Mikhail Sokolov, interview by author, Moscow, 23 July 1999.

29. Their CD—Green Square, *Sing, Sing, Sing* . . . (no copyright, 2000)—includes material by Cole Porter, Benny Goodman, Duke Ellington, and Irving Berlin.

30. This paragraph is based largely on the author's interview with Giia Dzagnidze, Moscow, 18 June 2000.

31. The information in this paragraph comes from Mikhail Mishuris, interview by author, 13 August 2001.

32. Mikhail Mishuris, *Zdravstvui moriak!* (Moscow: Moroz Records, 2000).

33. Mikhail Mishuris, interview by author, Moscow, 13 August 2001.

34. Vadim Ivashchenko, interview by author, Moscow, 19 August 2001.

35. The information in this and the following paragraph was provided by Vovka Kozhekin, interview by author, Moscow, 16 June 2000.

36. They can be heard performing their composition "Ia nenavizhu devochek" ("I Hate Girls") on *Ia ne uvishu Missisipi: Rossiiskii bliuz v 90–kh.*

37. Fedor Chistiakov, *Baian, Harp & Blues* (Moscow: BH&B, 2000).

CHAPTER FOUR. MOSCOW BLUES: SITES AND SOUNDS

1. There were, of course, a few exceptions in which bands were able to perform their preferred material to appreciative fans. Aleksei Belov, interview by author, Moscow, 22 August 2001.

2. Mike Osley, interview by author, Moscow, 17 October 1998.

3. Aleksandr Tsar'kov, interview by author, Moscow, 16 August 2001.

4. The club's prices actually stimulated a reaction in hippie circles that led to the formation of an alternative blues scene with free street music as discussed in chapter 3. Vovka Kozhekin, interview by author, Moscow, 16 June 2000.

5. Mike Osley, interview by author, Moscow, 17 October 1998. Osley's evaluation was confirmed at the time by bartender Kostia Andriukin.

6. Aleksei Kalachev, interview by author, Moscow, 24 August 2001.

7. This condition also affected many patrons of the Arbat Blues Club. Having shot their spending money on admission and a few beers, they would be stranded in the city center after the night's performances, waiting for public transportation to return at 5 a.m. Obviously these two- or three-hour waits were more easily accomplished in summer than in winter.

8. Aleksei Kalachev, interview by author, Moscow, 24 August 2001.

9. Nikolai Kalandareshvili, interview by author, Moscow, 22 August 2001.

10. This episode appears to constitute an instance in a larger pattern of nostalgia based on borrowed memories that prevails in much of contemporary youth culture in Russia. As Svetlana Boym has observed in this respect, "Young

Russians restore the dreams of someone else's youth, mimic the fantasies of others." See her *The Future of Nostalgia* (New York: Basic Books, 2001), p. 69.

11. It is interesting to note that a parallel tradition, that of the *stiliagi* who appeared in Russia in the 1950s, has been eclipsed by the appropriation of Western nostalgia. The third generation of *stiliagi* whom Hilary Pilkington studied in the early 1990s has already evolved into a variety of *Russian* retro, its members thus distinguishing themselves from those adopting Western styles and, in this case, Western nostalgia. Pilkington's analysis of latter-day *stiliagi* appears in her *Russia's Youth and its Culture: A Nation's Constructors and Constructed* (London: Routledge, 1994), esp., pp. 220–48.

12. The episode in question took place on 30 August 2001. It might be added that on Sundays, Kantri bar regularly puts on special programs for children—complete with music, clowns, and so forth—while the sex club and bordello continue to function on the floor above and the parade of young women in and out goes on as usual. (I am grateful to Aleksei Kuz'min for information on the club's Sunday program.)

13. In 1999, Evdokimov's peripatetic program found a temporary home at Militseiskaia vol'na (Police Band), a new station owned and operated by the Moscow police force. As musical director for the station, Evdokimov punctuated its propaedeutic programming with six hours of blues from midnight on Saturdays until 6 a.m.

14. The information in this paragraph was supplied by Aleksei Kalachev, interview by author, Moscow, 24 August 2001.

15. While watching tapes of these broadcasts with me in the summer of 1999, a young Nadia Chilcote remarked: "This is not my point of view. They look at blues like something in history."

16. Aleksei Kalachev, "Blue Note," *Music Box* 2 (1997), p. 80.

17. Vladimir Kuznetsov, "Ot Khukera do Khendriksa," *Sankt-Peterburgskie novosti* (30 December 1995); Gleb Tarabutin, "Neznakomyi dzhazz," *Rockfuzz* 22 (June, 1995), p. 8; Andrei Bol'shakov, "Moia professiia—vokalist bliuz-benda," *Music Box* 1 (1997), pp. 5–12; and the interview with Aleksei Belov that appeared in *Music Box* 2 (1997).

18. Inter alia, Andrei Evdokimov, "Buddy Guy," *Music Box*, 1 (1998), pp. 10–19; idem, "O shchastlivchik," ibid., 3 (1999), pp. 86–87; Nikolai Meinert, "Dzhon Meiell, kotoryi vsiu zhizn' znal, chto delaet," ibid, 1 (1998), pp. 6–8; Artem Lipatov, "Piter Grin, izgoniaiushchii demonov," *Fuzz* (December, 1997), p. 36–38, 47.

19. Vladimir Elbaev and Andrei Evdokimov, "Bliuz rodom iz Del'ty," *Audio Magazin*, 3 (1999), pp. 127–29.

20. This was especially evident at a Crossroadz concert staged in St. Petersburg's Spartak hall on 23 June 2000. There, a large table with hundreds of blues tapes and CDs had been set up in the foyer; but none of the items on sale was recorded by a Russian band. Asked about this—especially in view of the fact that the country's most popular blues band, which had already issued four CDs, was performing that night—the attendant replied simply, and with a laugh, that no one would be interested in buying them.

21. For example, Liga bliuza's LP, *Da zdravstvuet ritm end bliuz!* (Moscow: SNC, 1991).

22. Udachnoe priobretenie, owing to the special nature of the event, agreed to a compromise figure: four hundred dollars. Most other groups received between two hundred and 250 dollars, from which out-of-town groups had to recoup their traveling expenses. A few of the less senior groups received only about fifty dollars for their performances, and Evergreens—all of whose members earn reasonably good salaries in their various professional careers—played gratis. Evdokimov and Kozhekin ended up splitting between themselves the fifty dollars that remained after the musicians had been paid and Tochka had recouped its two thousand dollar advance from ticket receipts.

23. That list would include Udachnoe priobretenie, Blues Cousins, Blues Hammer Band, Stainless Blues Band, and Serebrianyi rubl'.

24. From St. Petersburg were Big Blues Revival, The Way, and *Kliuch* (Key); from the provinces, Aleksei Baryshev and the Blackmailers from Vladimir, J.A.M. from Nizhnyi Novgorod, and Boogie Bottles from Novosibirsk; and from Moscow, Mishuris and His Swinging Orchestra, Chernyi khleb i Doktor Agranovskii, Modern Blues Band, Kozhekin and Zhuk, Green Square, and Evergreens.

25. Writing in Russia's most popular daily, *Moskovskii komsomolets,* 27 April 2001, Margarita Pushkina singled out Big Blues Revival for "their very special style, some hippiness, and wonderful sense of humor, performing Deep Purple's overdone 'Smoke on the Water' in a country style and sounding amazingly free."

CHAPTER FIVE. ST. PETERSBURG AND THE PROVINCES

1. Solomon Volkov, *St. Petersburg: A Cultural History* (New York: Free Press Paperbacks, 1995), p. 532.

2. Thomas Cushman, *Notes from Underground: Rock Music and Counterculture in Russia* (Albany: State University of New York Press, 1995), pp. 103–4.

3. Alla Gladkikh, interview by author, St. Petersburg, 16 July 2000.

4. Cushman, *Notes from Underground,* pp. 231–36.

5. Zoopark, *Belaia polosa* (St. Petersburg: Eriotrek, 1996); Maik (Mike Naumenko), *Zhizn' v Zooparke* (Moscow: Otdelenie VYKHOD, 1997). Guitarist Dmitrii Dibrov, having picked up a National guitar, has collaborated with slide guitarist Aleksandr Novoselov in recording a blues album consisting of Naumenko's songs: *Rom and Pepsi-Cola* (Moscow: Real Records, 2002). Their project is discussed in Aleksei Kirshevskii, "Starinnye liudi moi batiuska," *Nezavisimaia gazeta,* 21 November 2001, p. 9.

6. Edik Tsekhanovskii, interview by author, St. Petersburg, 14 July 2000.

7. Vitalii Andreev, interview by author, St. Petersburg, 13 July 1999.

8. Alla Gladkikh, interview by author, St. Petersburg, 16 July 2000.

9. An example would be Golovanov's "Tikhii bliuz" ("Soft blues") that Kliuch performs on the anthology, *Blues.ru 2001* (Moscow: Itchy & Scratchy, 2001)

10. Vitalii Andreev, interview by author, St. Petersburg, 13 July 1999.

11. This song appears on the CD, King B and BBB, *Let the Big Dog Eat* (Moscow: Landy Star Music, 2000).

12. Valerii Belinov, interview by author, St. Petersburg, 11 July 1999.

13. Both are electrified instruments. The savitar is a five-string, guitar-shaped invention that combines features of the cello and viola. Fretless, it can be plucked or played with a bow. It emits an exotic sound with heavy overtones of the Far East. The pizicator is also guitar-shaped and carries a strong resonance that one might associate with Indian music.

14. Valerii Belinov, interview by author, St. Petersburg, 7 August 1999.

15. Inter alia, Irina Psadchaia "Tema gitarista Belinova," *7em' piatnits* 15 (14 December 1996), pp. 18–20; I. Reshchikova, "Bliuz rodilsia v Peterburge," *Kuznetskii rabochyi,* 26 April 1997; Vladimir Kuznetsov, "Vospominaniia o bliuze, kotorogo ne bylo," *Sankt-Peterburgskie vedomosti,* February 1996.

16. Belinov Blues Band, *Just like I Play* (St. Petersburg: no copyright, 1995).

17. Valerii Belinov, interview by author, St. Petersburg, 7 August 1999.

18. This paragraph is based on interviews by author with Kolia Gruzdev, St. Petersburg, 15 July 1999, and 8 July 2000.

19. Inessa Kataeva, interview by author, St. Petersburg, 4 August 1999.

20. Kataeva's predicament has stemmed primarily from the fact that she is a single parent without official residence registration in St. Petersburg and therefore is not entitled to any state subsidies for her child. Until he left to join relatives in Khabarovsk in 2001, the two shared a one-room communal flat on the top floor of a tumbledown building in central St. Petersburg, subsisting on a minimal diet purchased with the proceeds derived primarily from returning empty bottles for the deposit and selling newspapers on the street.

21. The information on Big Blues Revival was supplied by its members during interviews by the author: Vitalii Andreev, 13 July 1999, and 5 July 2000; Sergei Mironov, 13 July 1999; Aleksandr Rozhdestvenskii and Sergei Starodubtsev, 12 July 2000; Aleksandr Suvorov and Evgenii Bobrov, 5 July 2000.

22. This obsession with the pure sound of the strings has led to the introduction of a stricture that all players scrub their hands thoroughly before rehearsing or playing a concert.

23. Big Blues Revival, *Blues in Use* (St. Petersburg: Sintez, 2001).

24. Sergei Nekrasov, interview by author, St. Petersburg, 28 April 2003.

25. Sergei Semenov, Sergei Kuznetsov, and Vladimir Berezin, interview by author, St. Petersburg, 31 July 1999.

26. Anna Badkhen, "Bluesmen Band Together to Fight for Their Rights," *St. Petersburg Times,* 17 August 1999, p. 16.

27. Ibid.

28. *Ustav Sankt-Peterburgskoi obshchestvennoi organizatsii "Assotsiatsiia bliuzovykh muzikantov"* (proekt, no date).

29. See Volkov, *St. Petersburg: A Cultural History;* Katerina Clark, *St. Petersburg: Crucible of Cultural Revolution* (Cambridge, Mass.: Harvard University Press, 1995).

30. Aleksandr Tsar'kov, interview by author, Moscow, 16 August 2001.

31. Valerii Belinov, interview by author, St. Petersburg, 7 August 1999.

32. Kolia Gruzdev, interview by author, St. Petersburg, 15 July 1999.

33. The information in this and the following paragraph comes from Mikhail Mishuris, interview by author, Moscow, 13 August 2001, and from videotapes in Mishuris's personal archive.

34. Vadim Ivashchenko, who also provided the information on Rostov in this section, interview by author, Moscow, 19 August 2001.

35. Information on the Blackmailers Blues Band was supplied by Aleksei Baryshev and Aleksei Makarov, interviews by author, St. Petersburg, 8 July 2000.

36. These and other of the group's uniquely arranged songs are heard on J.A.M., *Blues Hits* (no copyright, songs recorded 1995–98).

37. An example would be the group's "Mouse Trap" that appears on the anthology, *Ia ne uvizhu Missisipi: Rossiiskii bliuz 90–kh* (Moscow: Salon AV, 1999).

38. Ragtime, *Out of the Blues* (Nal'chik: no copyright, 1999).

39. Mikhail Mishuris, interview by author, Moscow, 13 August 2001.

40. Vadim Ivashchenko, interview by author, Moscow, 19 August 2001.

CHAPTER SIX. IDENTITY AND COMMUNITY

1. This consideration touches on the character of new social movements, theorized in particular by Alberto Melucci in his *Challenging Codes: Collective Action in the Information Age* (Cambridge; Cambridge University Press, 1996). See also Ron Eyerman and Andrew Jamison, *Social Movements: A Cognitive Approach* (University Park: Pennsylvania State University Press, 1991); idem, *Music and Social Movements: Mobilizing Traditions in the Twentieth Century* (Cambridge: Cambridge University Press, 1998); and Manuel Castells, *The Power of Identity* (Oxford: Blackwell, 1997).

2. Marc Howard, *Demobilized Societies: Understanding the Weakness of Civil Society in Post-Communist Europe* (Cambridge: Cambridge University Press, 2003); Victoria Bonnell and George Breslauer, eds., *Russia in the New Century: Stability or Disorder* (Boulder: Westview, 2001); James Alexander, *Political Culture in Post-Communist Russia: Formlessness and Recreation in a Traumatic Transition* (New York: St. Martin's, 2000); Victor Sergeyev, *The Wild East: Crime and Lawlessness in Post-Communist Russia* (Armonk, N.Y.: M. E. Sharpe, 1998).

3. Simon Frith, *Performing Rites: On the Value of Popular Music* (Cambridge, Mass.: Harvard University Press, 1996), pp. 205–6, 270–75.

4. John Blacking, *Music, Culture & Experience: Selected Papers of John Blacking,* ed. R. Byron (Chicago: University of Chicago Press, 1995), pp. 39–40.

5. Inter alia, Susan McClary, *Conventional Wisdom: The Content of Musical Form* (Berkeley: University of California Press, 2000), pp. 23–25; Simon Frith, *Sound Effects: Youth, Leisure and the Politics of Rock 'n' Roll* (New York: Pantheon, 1981), p. 88; Sara Cohen, *Rock Culture in Liverpool: Popular Music in the Making* (Oxford: Clarendon Press, 1991), pp. 39–40.

6. Vadim Ivashchenko, interview by author, Moscow, 19 August 2001.

7. For the postcommunist period, this aspect has been treated in empirical de-

tail in the essays in V. V. Kostiushev, ed., *Molodezhnye dvizheniia i subkul'tury Sankt-Peterburga* (St. Petersburg: Norma, 1999). Comparable analyses for the late-Soviet period can be found in D. V. Ol'shanskii, *Neformaly: gruppovoi portret v inter'ere* (Moscow: Pedagogika, 1990) and in M. V. Maliutin, "Neformaly v perestroike: opyt i perspektivy," Iu.N. Afanas'ev, ed., *Inogo ne dano* (Moscow: Progess, 1988), pp. 210–27.

8. Michel Foucault, *The History of Sexuality,* vol. 1 (New York: Random House, 1978); idem, *Power/Knowledge,* ed. C. Gordon (New York: Pantheon, 1980).

9. Pierre Bourdieu, *Outline of a Theory of Practice* (Cambridge: Cambridge University Press, 1977), pp. 72–73.

10. Oleg Kharkhordin, *The Collective and the Individual in Russia* (Berkeley: University of California Press, 1999). On the continued existence and importance of the *kollektiv* in Russia after communism, see also: Sarah Ashwin, *Russian Workers: The Anatomy of Patience* (New York: St. Martin's, 1999); Risto Alapuro and Markuu Lonkila, "Networks, Identity and (In)Action: A comparison between Russian and Finnish teachers," *European Societies,* vol. 2, no. 1 (2000), pp. 65–90; Caroline Humphrey, *The Unmaking of Soviet Life: Everyday Economies after Socialism* (Ithaca: Cornell University Press, 2002), pp. 10–14, 27, 166.

11. Sergei Voronov, interview by author, Moscow, 18 July 2000.

12. The conversation with Sasha Rozhdestvenskii, Sergei Starodubtsev, and Sasha Suvorov was recorded by the author in St. Petersburg on 12 July 2000.

13. Boris Bulkin, interview by author, Moscow, 28 August 2001.

14. Vadim Ivashchenko, interview by author, Moscow, 19 August 2001.

15. Valerii Belinov, interview by author, St. Petersburg, 7 August 1999.

16. Thomas Cushman, *Notes from Underground: Rock Music and Culture in Russia* (Albany: State University of New York Press, 1995).

17. Bob Brunning, *Blues: The British Connection* (New York: Blandford Press, 1986), pp. 12–67.

18. Sarah Cohen, *Rock Culture in Liverpool,* pp. 21–46; Ruth Finnegan, *The Hidden Musicians: Music-Making in an English Town* (Cambridge: Cambridge University Press, 1989).

19. Frith, *Performing Rites,* pp. 274–75.

20. The notion of "subcultural capital" has been developed by Sarah Thornton in her *Club Cultures: Music, Media and Subcultural Capital* (Cambridge: Polity Press, 1995), esp. p. 105.

21. Dale Pesmen, *Russia and Soul: An Exploration* (Ithaca: Cornell University Press, 2000), esp., pp. 80–94.

22. Oleg, scenery director, conversation with author, St. Petersburg, 30 July 1999.

23. Aleksei Kalachev, interview by author, Moscow, 24 August 2001.

24. Nadia Chilcote, interview by author, Moscow, 26 July 1999.

25. Kirill Bykov, conversation with author, St. Petersburg, 10 August 1999.

26. Vladimir Kuznetsov, "Vospominaniia o bliuze, kotorogo ne bylo," *Sankt-Peterburgskie novosti,* 6 July 1997.

27. Mikhail Sokolov, interview by author, Moscow, 23 July 1999.

28. Nikolai Arutiunov, interview by author, Moscow, 25 July 1999.

29. Mikhail Sokolov, interview by author, Moscow, 23 July 1999.

30. Vovka Kozhekin, interview by author, Moscow, 16 June 2000.

31. Vitalii Andreev, interview by author, St. Petersburg, 5 July 2000.

32. Giia Dzagnidze, interview by author, Moscow, 18 June 2000.

33. Mikhail Sokolov, interview by author, Moscow, 23 July 1999.

34. Aleksei Baryshev, interview by author, St. Petersburg, 8 July 2000.

35. Sergei Mironov, interview by author, St. Petersburg, 13 July 1999.

36. Sasha Suvorov, interview by author, St. Petersburg, 5 July 2000.

37. Dick Hebdige, *Subculture: The Meaning of Style* (London: Methuen, 1979), pp. 3–19, 90–114, esp., p. 3; Charles Keil and Steven Feld, *Music Grooves* (Chicago: University of Chicago Press, 1994), pp. 202–17.

38. Jean Baudrillard, *For a Critique of the Political Economy of the Sign* (St. Louis: Telos Press, 1981), p. 68.

39. Vania Zhuk referred to *Crossroads* as "a milestone for every bluesman in Russia, especially of this [the younger] generation." Interview by author, St. Petersburg, 29 June 2000.

40. Nikolai Arutiunov, interview by author, Moscow, 25 July 1999.

41. Mikhail Sokolov, interview by author, Moscow, 23 July 1999.

42. Aleksei Agranovskii, interview by author, Moscow, 23 August 2001.

43. Kolia Gruzdev, interview by author, St. Petersburg, 15 July 1999.

44. These categories have been developed by Pierre Bourdieu. See his: *Distinction: A Social Critique of the Judgement of Taste* (Cambridge, Mass.: Harvard University Press, 1984); *The Field of Cultural Production,* ed. R. Johnson (New York: Columbia University Press, 1993); and *In Other Words* (Cambridge: Polity Press, 1990).

45. Nikolai Arutiunov, interview by author, Moscow, 25 July 1999.

46. This process of rock's domestication in Austria, Sweden, and Mexico is discussed, respectively, in Edward Larkey, *Pungent Sounds: Constructing Identity with Popular Music in Austria* (New York: Peter Land, 1993); Ron Eyerman and Andrew Jamison, *Music and Social Movements,* pp. 143–55; Eric Zolov, *Refried Elvis: The Rise of Mexican Counterculture* (Berkeley: University of California Press, 1999).

47. Tony Mitchell, *Popular Music and Local Identity: Rock, Pop and Rap in Europe and Oceania* (London: Leicester University Press, 1996), p. 37.

48. Sergei Semenov, interview by author, St. Petersburg, 31 July 1999.

49. Sasha Suvorov, interview by author, St. Petersburg, 5 July 1999.

50. Aleksei Agranovskii, interview by author, Moscow, 23 August 2001.

51. During our interview, Aleksei Agranovskii showed me a rather detailed "blues dictionary" that he has composed, a thick notebook full of English-language tropes and expressions for which he has penned definitions, explanations, and Russian equivalents. Agranovskii promotes "blues literacy" by passing around this dictionary to friends and acquaintances in the blues community.

52. Volodia Rusinov, interview by author, St. Petersburg, 28 June 2000.

53. Oleg, scenery director, conversation with author, St. Petersburg, 30 July 1999.

54. Iaroslav Sukhov, interview by author, St. Petersburg, 17 July 1999; Sergei Starodubtsev, interview by author, St. Petersburg, 12 July 2000.

55. Inessa Kataeva, interview by author, St. Petersburg, 4 August 1999.

56. Among the better efforts of recording blues in Russian would be Dikii med, *Vesel'aia vdova* (Munich and Moscow: Interus International Feelee Records, 1993). A less successful attempt can be heard on Aura, *Russkii bliuz* (Moscow: self-produced, 1994).

57. Nikolai Arutiunov, interviewed by Andrei Bol'shakov, *Music Box* 1 (1997), pp. 6–10.

58. Nikolai Arutiunov, interview by author, Moscow, 25 July 1999.

59. Liga bliuza, "Ty spoesh' 'Hoochie Coochie Man,'" *Ia ne uvizhu Missisipi: Rossiiskii bliuz 90-kh* (Moscow: Salon, AV, 1999).

60. King B and BBB, *Let the Big Dog Eat* (Moscow: Landy Star Music, 2000).

61. Richard Stites, *Russian Popular Culture* (Cambridge: Cambridge University Press, 1992) pp. 6–12; Oleg Kharkordin, *The Collective and The Individual in Russia;* Svetlana Boym, *Common Places* (Cambridge, Mass.: Harvard University Press, 1994), esp., pp. 41–88.

62. Katherine Verdery has described the "nation as family" phenomenon in contemporary Romania in her *What Was Socialism and What Comes Next?* (Princeton: Princeton University Press, 1996), pp. 62–81; esp., p. 64. George Lakoff has produced a comparable and much ramified study of the family metaphor in U.S. politics in his *Moral Politics: What Conservatives Know and Liberals Don't* (Chicago: University of Chicago Press, 1996).

63. Nancy Ries, *Russian Talk: Culture and Conversation during Perestroika* (Ithaca: Cornell University Press, 1997).

64. Aleksandr Arinin, "Partnerskie otnosheniia vlasti i obshchestva," *Nezavisimaia gazeta,* 28 October 1999, p. 3.

65. With respect to music in particular, this inclination to spread enlightenment in the postrevolutionary period was the raison d'etre of journals such as *Muzyka i revoliutsiia* and *Proletarskoi muzykant.* In the 1920s and early 1930s, a mass movement for proletarian music was organized to struggle against the "bourgeois" music associated with the period of the New Economic Policy (the *popsa* of the day) and to bring authentically "proletarian" music to the masses. An outline of the goals, program, and cadre organization of this movement appeared in L. Lebedinskii, "Dvizhenie proletarskoi muzyki dolzhno stat' dvizhenie massovym," *Proletarskoi muzykant* 7 (1930), pp. 5–10. See also Amy Nelson, "The Struggle for Proletarian Music: RAPM and the Cultural Revolution," *Slavic Review* 59 (Spring, 2000), pp. 101–32.

66. Mikhail Sokolov, interview by author, Moscow, 23 July 1999.

67. Vladimir Berezin, interview by author, St. Petersburg, 31 July 1999.

68. Aleksandr Dolgov, interview by author, St. Petersburg, 26 June 2000.

69. Vitalii Andreev, interview by author, St. Petersburg, 13 July 2000.

70. Vovka Kozhekin, interview by author, Moscow, 16 June 2000.

71. Kuznetzov, "Vospominaniia o bliuze kotorogo ne bylo."

72. Barry Shank, *Dissonant Identities: The Rock 'n' Roll Scene in Austin Texas* (Hanover, N.H.: University Press of New England, 1994) p. 34–37.

73. Aleksei Kalachev, "Prikliucheniia bliuza," *Nezavisimaia gazeta,* 2 June 1997, p. 8.

74. Mikhail Sokolov, interview by author, Moscow, 23 July 1999.

75. Vovka Kozhekin, interview by author, Moscow, 16 June 2000.

CHAPTER SEVEN. POLITICS

1. See, for instance, Murray Edelmen, *Constructing the Political Spectacle* (Chicago: University of Chicago Press, 1988).

2. Timothy Rice, "The Dialectic of Economics and Aesthetics in Bulgarian Music," in *Retuning Culture: Musical Changes in Central and Eastern Europe,* ed. M. Slobin (Durham, N.C.: Duke University Press, 1996), p. 190.

3. The second and third aspects of the blues community's politics have been adapted from the categories supplied by William Barlow in his *"Looking Up at Down": The Emergence of Blues Culture* (Philadelphia: Temple University Press, 1989), pp. 325–28.

4. Aleksandr Zinov'ev, *Kommunism kak real'nost'* (Lausanne: Editions L'Age D'Homme, 1981). Both Sarah Ashwin and Oleg Kharkhordin have called attention to the association between this pejorative characterization and what the authorities have labeled the "false collective": that is, an affective group actually animated by the members' common interests but lacking official sanction. Sarah Ashwin, "Redefining the Collective: Russian Mineworkers in Transition," in *Uncertain Transition: Ethnographies of Change in the Postsocialist World,* ed. M. Burawoy and K. Verdery (Lanham, Md.: Rowan and Littlefield, 1999), pp. 245–71; Oleg Kharkhordin, *The Collective and the Individual in Russia* (Berkeley: University of California Press, 1999), esp., pp. 315–28.

5. Aleksei Baryshev, interview by author, St. Petersburg, 8 July 2000; Vovka Kozhekin, interview by author, Moscow, 16 June 2000; Kolia Gruzdev, interview by author, St. Petersburg, 15 July 1999.

6. Valerii Belinov, interview by author, St. Petersburg, 13 April 1998.

7. Vitalii Andreev, interview by author, St. Petersburg, 13 July 1999.

8. Aleksei Makarov, manager of Vladimir's Blackmailers Blues Band, interview by author, St. Petersburg, 8 July 2000.

9. Clyde Woods, *Development Arrested: The Blues and Plantation Power in the Mississippi Delta* (New York: Verso, 1998), p. 167.

10. Boris Bulkin, interview by author, Moscow, 28 August 2001.

11. Aleksei Agranovskii, interview by author, Moscow, 23 August 2001.

12. Raymond Williams, *Culture* (Glasgow: Fontana, 1981), p. 13.

13. Murray Edelman, *From Art to Politics* (Chicago: University of Chicago, 1995). With respect to music in particular, see also Ron Eyerman and Andrew Jamison, *Music and Social Movements: Mobilizing Traditions in the Twentieth Century* (Cambridge: Cambridge University Press, 1998), p. 42; and Anna Szemere,

Up from the Underground: The Culture of Rock Music in Postsocialist Hungary (University Park: Pennsylvania State University Press, 2001), p. 69.

14. Sonia Alvarez, Evelino Dagnino, and Arturo Escaban, "Introduction: The Cultural and the Political in Latin American Social Movements" in their *Culture of Politics, Politics of Culture* (Boulder, Colo.: Westview, 1998), p. 7.

15. John Blacking, *Music, Culture & Experience: Selected Papers of John Blacking*, ed. R. Byron (Chicago: University of Chicago Press, 1995), p. 226. This same point is argued by Simon Frith in his *Performing Rites: On the Value of Popular Music* (Cambridge, Mass.: Harvard University Press, 1996), pp. 146, 263–65.

16. Roland Barthes, *Image-Music-Text* (New York: Hill and Wang, 1977), pp. 52–68, esp., p. 62.

17. Ibid., pp. 179–89.

18. Susan McClary, *Conventional Wisdom: The Content of Musical Form* (Berkeley: University of California Press, 2000), pp. 6–7.

19. John Shepherd, *Music as a Social Text* (Cambridge: Polity Press, 1991), esp. pp. 6–35, 77–88, 214–19; Steven Feld and Aaron Fox, "Music and Language," *Annual Review of Anthropology* 23 (1994), pp. 25–53.

20. Charles Keil, "The Theory of Participatory Discrepancies: A Progress Report," *Ethnomusicology* 39 (Winter, 1995), pp. 1–19.

21. Sara Cohen, *Rock Culture in Liverpool: Popular Music in the Making* (Oxford: Clarendon Press, 1991), pp. 39–40, 94–96.

22. LeRoi Jones (Amiri Baraka), *Blues People: Negro Music in White America* (Westport, Conn.: Greenwood Press, 1963); Giles Oakley, *The Devil's Music: A History of the Blues* (2nd ed.; New York: Da Capo Press, 1997), esp., pp. 7–8; Adam Gussow, *Seems Like Murder Here: Southern Violence and the Blues Tradition* (Chicago: University of Chicago Press, 2002).

23. Vladimir Kuznetsov, "Ot Khukera do Khendriksa," *Sankt-Peterburgskie novosti*, 30 December 1995.

24. Brian Ward, *Just My Soul Responding: Rhythm and Blues, Black Consciousness and Race Relations* (Berkeley: University of California Press, 1998).

25. Nikolai Arutiunov, interview by author, Moscow, 25 July 1999.

26. Vitalii Andreev, interview by author, St. Petersburg, 13 July 1999.

27. Kolia Gruzdev, interview by author, St. Petersburg, 15 July 1999.

28. Albert Murray, *The Hero and the Blues* (New York; Vintage Books, 1995), pp. 83–87.

29. Quoted in Sandra Tooze, *Muddy Waters: The Mojo Man* (Toronto: ECW Press, 1997), p. 116.

30. Aleksei Agranovskii, interview by author, Moscow, 23 August 2001.

31. Kolia Gruzdev, interview by author, St. Petersburg, 15 July 1999.

32. V. V. Kostiushev, ed., *Molodezhnye dvizheniia i subkul'tury Sankt-Peterburga* (St. Petersburg: NORMA, 1999).

33. I am indebted to Aleksei Kuz'min for this idea. Conversation with author, Moscow, 30 August 2001.

34. Shepherd, *Music as Social Text*, p. 131.

35. John Sloop, "The Emperor's New Makeup: Cool Cynicism and Popular Music Criticism," *Popular Music and Society* 23 (Spring, 1999), p. 63.

36. Tony Russell, "Blacks, Whites and Blues" in *Yonder Come the Blues: The Evolution of a Genre,* ed. Paul Oliver et al. (Cambridge: Cambridge University Press, 2001), p. 232.

37. A clear illustration of racist practices operating below the level of official rhetoric can be found in Soviet gender policy in the wake of the so-called "demographic crisis" that surfaced in the 1970s. At that time, population data showed a depressed birth rate among the Slavic and Baltic republics on the one hand, and a robust one in Central Asia and the Caucasus on the other. Within a generation or two, the dark-complected people of the USSR could be expected to outnumber their fair-skinned countrymen. The regime therefore undertook a massive effort in social policy aimed at increasing the birth rate among whites in order to head off the impending—and, from the standpoint of the official antiracist code, thoroughly absurd—imbalance among groups in the population. On this gender policy driven by racial considerations, see: Rebecca Kay, "A Liberation from Emancipation? Changing Discourses on Women's Employment in Soviet and Post-Soviet Russia," *Journal of Communist Studies and Transition Politics* 18 (March, 2002), pp. 51–72, esp., pp. 52–54; Sarah Ashwin, "Introduction," and Olga Issoupova, "From Duty to Pleasure? Motherhood in Soviet and Post-Soviet Russia," in *Gender, State and Society in Soviet and Post-Soviet Russia,* ed. S. Ashwin (London: Routledge, 2000), pp. 1–29 and pp. 30–54, respectively.

38. Alaina Lemon, *Between Two Fires: Gypsy Performance and Romani Memory from Pushkin to Post-Socialism* (Durham, N.C.: Duke University Press, 2000), pp. 62–73; Hilary Pilkington, *Russian's Youth and its Culture: A Nation's Constructors and Constructed* (London: Routledge, 1994), p. 255.

39. Lemon, *Between Two Fires,* pp. 76–77

40. This possibility was suggested by Victor Wolfenstein (personal communication, 10 January 2003) and Mark Slobin (personal communication, 3 September 2002).

41. Frederic Jameson, *The Cultural Turn: Selected Writings on Postmodernism* (London: Verso, 2000), esp., pp. 7–10, 54–62

42. Alan Durant, "Improvisation in the Political Economy of Music," in *Music and the Politics of Culture,* ed. C. Norris (London: Lawrence and Wishart, 1989), pp. 252–81

Index